First World War
and Army of Occupation
War Diary
France, Belgium and Germany

57 DIVISION
171 Infantry Brigade,
Brigade Trench Mortar Battery
12 February 1917 - 22 March 1919

WO95/2983/9

The Naval & Military Press Ltd
www.nmarchive.com
Published in association with The National Archives

Published by

The Naval & Military Press Ltd

Unit 10 Ridgewood Industrial Park,

Uckfield, East Sussex,

TN22 5QE England

Tel: +44 (0) 1825 749494

www.naval-military-press.com

www.nmarchive.com

Contents

Miscellaneous	Appendix "A". Artillery.		
Miscellaneous	Appendix "B"		
Miscellaneous	Appendix "C"		
Miscellaneous	Special Instructions For S.O.S-Night Of 21st/22nd June 1917	20/06/1917	20/06/1917
Miscellaneous	War Diaries	15/08/1917	15/08/1917
Heading	War Diary Vol 6 July 1917 171st Brigade Light Trench Mortar Battery		
War Diary	Armentieres (C.25.c.55.45)	01/07/1917	01/07/1917
War Diary	Armentieres	01/07/1917	31/07/1917
Heading	Appendices To War Diary For July 1917 Volume 6		
Miscellaneous	Appendix 1 War Diary July 1917		
Operation(al) Order(s)	171st Brigade Order No. 18	03/07/1917	03/07/1917
Operation(al) Order(s)	171 Bde Light Trench Mortar Battery Operation Order No. 5	15/07/1917	15/07/1917
Miscellaneous	Special Operation Order 1/1st Bde L.T.M.B.	25/07/1917	25/07/1917
Miscellaneous	Appendix A To Special Operation Orders	25/07/1917	25/07/1917
Miscellaneous	Appendix 2 War Diary July 1917		
Miscellaneous	57th Divisional Daily Bulletin No.18	29/07/1917	29/07/1917
Miscellaneous	57th Divisional Daily Bulletin No.20	30/07/1917	30/07/1917
Miscellaneous	57th Divisional Daily Bulletin No.21	31/07/1917	31/07/1917
Miscellaneous	Report On Gas Shell Bombardment Of Armentieres	29/07/1917	29/07/1917
Heading	War Diary Of 171st Brigade Light Trench Mortar Battery for Month of August 1917 Volume 1		
War Diary	Armentieres (C25.c.55.45)	01/08/1917	03/08/1917
War Diary	Armentieres	03/08/1917	06/08/1917
War Diary	Fleurbaix (H21d.20.70)	06/08/1917	28/08/1917
War Diary	Fleurbaix	29/08/1917	31/08/1917
Heading	War Diary Vol. 8 September 1917		
Miscellaneous	Headquarters 57th Division		
War Diary	Fleurbaix (H.21.d.20.70)	01/09/1917	16/09/1917
War Diary	La Gorgue (L 34a)	16/09/1917	18/09/1917
War Diary	Busnes (P.26.c)	18/09/1917	19/09/1917
War Diary	Lespesses (T.12.c.85.00)	19/09/1917	30/09/1917
Heading	171st Bde Light T.M.B War Diary Vol.9 October 1917		
War Diary	Lespesses (T.12.c.88.05)	01/10/1917	19/10/1917
War Diary	Renescure (4.E.55.85)	19/10/1917	19/10/1917
War Diary	Renescure	20/10/1917	20/10/1917
War Diary	Plumstead Camp (Proven Area No.4)	24/10/1917	24/10/1917
War Diary	Redan Camp (B.22.d.2.8)	26/10/1917	26/10/1917
War Diary	Canal Bank C19c.00.80	27/10/1917	31/10/1917
Miscellaneous	Herewith War Diary For Nov 1917		
Heading	171st Bde. Light T.M.B War Diary Vol.10 November 1917		
War Diary	Canal Bank (C.19.c.00.80)	01/11/1917	02/11/1917
War Diary	Redan Camp (B.22.d.2.8)	04/11/1917	07/11/1917
War Diary	Autingues	09/11/1917	30/11/1917
Heading	171st Bde. Light T.M.B War Diary Vol 11 December 1917		
Miscellaneous	Herewith War Diary For December 1917		
War Diary	Autingues	01/12/1917	08/12/1917
War Diary	Piccadilly Camp 2.1.05.95	09/12/1917	15/12/1917
War Diary	Canal Bank 2.K.20.7.5	16/12/1917	17/12/1917
War Diary	Signal Farm V.21.c.15.05	20/12/1917	23/12/1917
War Diary	Signal Farm	25/12/1917	25/12/1917
War Diary	Marguerite Farm	29/12/1917	29/12/1917

War Diary	Praed Camp F9.a.4.9	30/12/1917	30/12/1917
War Diary	Gode Area	31/12/1917	31/12/1917
Heading	171st Bde Light T.M.B War Diary Vol 12 January 1918		
War Diary	Menegate Camp	01/01/1918	01/01/1918
War Diary	Armentieres (14 Rue Sadi Carnot)	02/01/1918	13/01/1918
War Diary	Geneva Camp	14/01/1918	21/01/1918
War Diary	Armentieres 14 Rue Sadi Carnot	21/01/1918	27/01/1918
War Diary	Geneva Camp A.23.c.1.5	28/01/1918	31/01/1918
Heading	171st Bde Light TMB. War Diary Volume No.13 February 1918		
Miscellaneous	Herewith War Diary For February 1918		
War Diary	Geneva Camp A.23.c.1.5	01/02/1918	02/02/1918
War Diary	Armentieres 14 Rue Sadi Carnot	03/02/1918	05/02/1918
War Diary	130 Boulevarde Faidherbe	05/02/1918	05/02/1918
War Diary	Armentieres 130 Boulevarde Faidnerbe	06/02/1918	14/02/1918
War Diary	Roussel Farm	15/02/1918	15/02/1918
War Diary	Roussel Farm 4.H.24.00	16/02/1918	28/02/1918
Heading	171st Bde Light T.M.B. War Diary Vol 14 March 1918		
Miscellaneous	Herewith War Diary For March 1918		
War Diary	Roussel Farm	01/03/1918	01/03/1918
War Diary	Rely (T.Ld.20.95)	02/03/1918	11/03/1918
War Diary	Roussel Farm	12/03/1918	20/03/1918
War Diary	Sailly (G.22.a.5.3)	21/03/1918	26/03/1918
War Diary	Fleurbaix H.2.a.4.4	27/03/1918	31/03/1918
Heading	57th Division 171st Infantry Brigade 171st Light Trench Mortars April 1918		
Heading	171st Bde L.T.M.B. War Diary Vol 15 April 1918		
War Diary	Fleurbaix	01/04/1918	01/04/1918
War Diary	Estaires	02/04/1918	02/04/1918
War Diary	Doullens	03/04/1918	03/04/1918
War Diary	Ivergny	04/04/1918	04/04/1918
War Diary	Mondicourt	07/04/1918	08/04/1918
War Diary	Beuval	09/04/1918	12/04/1918
War Diary	Grenas	13/04/1918	13/04/1918
War Diary	Authie	14/04/1918	16/04/1918
War Diary	Pas	17/04/1918	30/04/1918
Heading	171st Brigade Light T.M.B. War Diary Vol 16 May 1918		
War Diary	Pas	01/05/1918	06/05/1918
War Diary	Gommecourt	06/05/1918	13/05/1918
War Diary	Bayencourt	14/05/1918	20/05/1918
War Diary	Gommecourt	21/05/1918	31/05/1918
Heading	171st Bde Light T.M.B. War Diary Vol.17 June 1918		
Miscellaneous	Herewith War Diary (Vol.17) For June 1918		
War Diary	Gommecourt	01/06/1918	06/06/1918
War Diary	Bayencourt	07/06/1918	14/06/1918
War Diary	Gommecourt	14/06/1918	30/06/1918
Heading	171st Bde L.T.M.B. War Diary Vol.18 July 1918		
War Diary	Couin	01/07/1918	01/07/1918
War Diary	Louvencourt	02/07/1918	15/07/1918
War Diary	Henu	16/07/1918	28/07/1918
War Diary	Sus-St-Leger	29/07/1918	29/07/1918
War Diary	Arras	30/07/1918	30/07/1918
War Diary	Louez	31/07/1918	31/07/1918
War Diary	Arras (Fampoux Sector)	01/08/1918	08/08/1918
War Diary	Fampoux Sector	08/08/1918	19/08/1918

War Diary	Monchy-Breton	20/08/1918	21/08/1918
War Diary	Givenchy Le Noble	22/08/1918	22/08/1918
War Diary	Ivergny	23/08/1918	25/08/1918
War Diary	Gouy	26/08/1918	26/08/1918
War Diary	Ficheux	27/08/1918	27/08/1918
War Diary	Mercatel	28/08/1918	28/08/1918
War Diary	Heninel	29/08/1918	29/08/1918
War Diary	Hindenburg Line	30/08/1918	31/08/1918
Miscellaneous	Herewith War Diary (Vol20) For September 1918		
War Diary	Hindenburg Line	01/09/1918	07/09/1918
War Diary	V.28.d.0.0	08/09/1918	12/09/1918
War Diary	V.26.d.9.8	13/09/1918	16/09/1918
War Diary	T.30.a	17/09/1918	17/09/1918
War Diary	Barly	18/09/1918	25/09/1918
War Diary	Queant	26/09/1918	27/09/1918
War Diary	Anneux	28/09/1918	29/09/1918
War Diary	F.22.b.9.1	30/09/1918	30/09/1918
Heading	171st Bde Light T.M.B. War Diary Vol.21 October 1918		
Miscellaneous	Herewith War Diary (Vol21) For October		
War Diary	Anneux	01/10/1918	04/10/1918
War Diary	Fontaine-N-D	05/10/1918	10/10/1918
War Diary	D.23.c	12/10/1918	12/10/1918
War Diary	Barlin	13/10/1918	15/10/1918
War Diary	Laventie	15/10/1918	16/10/1918
War Diary	Le Maisnil	17/10/1918	17/10/1918
War Diary	Le Marais	18/10/1918	18/10/1918
War Diary	Hellemmes	19/10/1918	19/10/1918
War Diary	Willems	20/10/1918	20/10/1918
War Diary	Blandain	21/10/1918	21/10/1918
War Diary	Froyennes	22/10/1918	24/10/1918
War Diary	Willems	25/10/1918	30/10/1918
War Diary	Hellemmes	31/10/1918	31/10/1918
Heading	171st Bde Light T.M.B. War Diary Vol.22 November 1918		
Miscellaneous	Herewith War Diary (Vol22) For November 1918		
War Diary	Hellemmes	01/11/1918	30/11/1918
Heading	171st Bde Light T.M.B. War Diary Vol.23 December 1918		
War Diary	Hellemmes	02/12/1918	02/12/1918
War Diary	Carvin	03/12/1918	03/12/1918
War Diary	Arras (4 Rue Lt. Claire)	06/12/1918	16/12/1918
War Diary	Wanquetin	16/12/1918	31/12/1918
Heading	171st Bde L.T.M.B. War Diary Vol 24 January 1919		
War Diary	Dainville	01/01/1919	30/01/1919
Heading	171st Bde L.T.M.B. War Diary Vol.25 February 1919		
Miscellaneous	Herewith War Diary (Vol25) For February 1919		
War Diary	Dainville	01/02/1919	28/02/1919
Heading	171st L.T.M.B. War Diary Vol.26 March 1919		
Miscellaneous	Herewith War Diary (Vol26) To 22/3/19		
War Diary	Dainville	01/03/1919	17/03/1919
War Diary	Maroeil	18/03/1919	22/03/1919

WO95/2983/9

57 DIV

171 INFANTRY BDE

BDE TRENCH MORTAR BATTERY

Feb 1917 – Mar 1919

57TH DIVISION
171ST INFY BDE

TRENCH MORTAR BATTYS

FEB 1917-DEC 1918

Instructions regarding War Diaries and Intelligence Summaries are contained in F. S. Regs., Part II. and the Staff Manual respectively. Title pages will be prepared in manuscript.

WAR DIARY
or
INTELLIGENCE SUMMARY.
(Erase heading not required.)

Sheet 11.

Army Form C. 2118.

Place	Date	Hour	Summary of Events and Information	Remarks and references to Appendices
ARMENTIERES	17/5/17	pm 6.0	Lieut. SMALLPAGE relieved Lieut. BURFIELD in EPINETTE Sector.	
"	"	–	Lieut. EAMES evacuated to 2nd AUSTRALIAN Casualty Clearing Station.	
"	"	–	Our Artillery active throughout the day, firing on CHICKEN RUN (C.17.a) and ruins at C.29.c)	
"	"	pm 9.0	– In response to S.O.S. from north of R. LYS – our batteries were active. Visibility – very poor –	
"	18/5/17	pm 4.0	Presentation of Medals – By ARMY Commander – General Sir Herbert C.O. PLUMER G.C.M.G. K.C.B. A.D.C. Commanding Second Army. at CROIX-du-BAC (G 6.c). No. 24137 Corpl. Bond and No. 266875 Corpl. Kelly attended and were presented with the ribbon of the Military Medal. For details of the circumstances under which these awards were gained see	see APPENDIX 2
"	"	pm 5.30	Sec. Lieut. JARDINE, Batty S.M. AMOS and 16 other ranks left to relieve Lieut. LEONARD and party in HOUPLINES Sector.	
"	"	"	12 other ranks left to relieve party in EPINETTE Sector.	
"	"	6.0	One gun in action EPINETTE Sector. Few rounds fired on to enemy front line (I.17.a) moving sandbagging and earth. Retaliation – 12 pineapples on our front line. Our 18 pounders replied and silenced them.	

Army Form C. 2118.

Instructions regarding War Diaries and Intelligence Summaries are contained in F. S. Regs., Part II. and the Staff Manual respectively. Title pages will be prepared in manuscript.

WAR DIARY
or
INTELLIGENCE SUMMARY.
(*Erase heading not required.*)

Sheet 10.

Place	Date	Hour	Summary of Events and Information	Remarks and references to Appendices
ARMENTIÈRES	15/5/17	pm 6-0	Three guns in action HOUPLINES Sector. Registration with 30 rounds in conjunction with Medium T.M. Battery - on E CENTAUR SWITCH (C.29 a) and CENTAUR TRENCH (C.29.a & c). Results - good - many direct hits into trench and on parapet. Retaliation - Several HE's (5-9"s) on Communication trench (SPAIN AV.)	
✓	✓	pm 6-0	One gun in action EPINETTE Sector - a few rounds fired at M.G. emplacement in INANE AV. (I.5.b). Results - satisfactory. Retaliation - about 15 rifle grenades to left of gun position & also 4 'rum jars' in vicinity of PLANK AV.	
✓	✓	-	Aircraft - enemy aeroplane dropped a blue light over C.23.c. whereupon M.G. fire was opened.	
✓	✓	-	Artillery - noticeable decrease in enemy artillery fire. Visibility - poor.	
✓	✓	-	57th Divisional Order No. 613 of 14/5/17 reads "The Corps Commander has awarded the Military Medal to the undermentioned N.C.O's and men, dated 12/5/17. 171st Bde Light T.M.B. { No 266875 Corpl W.J. Kelly / " 241,337 " G. BOND".	
✓	16/5/17	am 11-0	14 Aeroplane photos of HOUPLINES and EPINETTE Sectors received from Bde HQ with instructions that they be handed over on relief.	
✓	✓	✓	Copy of DEFENCE Scheme - HOUPLINES and EPINETTE Sectors received from Bde HQ	
✓	✓	✓	Artillery - moderately active firing on FRELINGHEIN (C.17.d) and new work at I.5.d. the latter of which was considerably damaged. Visibility - fair.	

2353 Wt. W2544/1454 700,000 5/15 D. D. & L. A.D.S.S./Forms/C. 2118.

Army Form C. 2118.

Instructions regarding War Diaries and Intelligence Summaries are contained in F. S. Regs., Part II. and the Staff Manual respectively. Title pages will be prepared in manuscript.

WAR DIARY
or
INTELLIGENCE SUMMARY.
(*Erase heading not required.*)

Sheet 9.

Place	Date	Hour	Summary of Events and Information	Remarks and references to Appendices
ARMENTIÈRES	14/5/17	10.0 am to 2.15 pm	ARTILLERY – we heavily bombarded the village of FRELINGHEIN (C. 11 central). Enemy retaliation did not affect our sector.	
			In afternoon – enemy shelled HOUPLINES (C 21 d) but not nearly so heavily as recently.	
		pm 5:0	One gun in action EPINETTE Sector. A few rounds were fired on to M.G. emplacement (I.11. b. 5.6 in front of INCARNATE TRENCH). The M.G. which was firing when we commenced soon ceased. Retaliation – limited to 3 rifle grenades.	
		am 7.20 and 7.35 pm	Enemy aeroplanes dropped red lights – no apparent result, but previously this signal has been followed by M.G. fire from the 'planes.	
			Our aircraft – very quiet.	
			Visibility – not too good.	
		pm 7.0	Carrying party took 100 shells from our reserve dump to sector dump (EPINETTE Sector)	
	15/5/17	am 10.30	Lieut. EAMES admitted into hospital suffering from congestion of the liver.	
		pm 4.0	One gun in action (HOUPLINES Sector). Target, enemy front line (C.17.c) Results good – parapet smashed in and sandbagging & earth thrown up. 20 rounds expended. Retaliation – 5" "pineapples" on our front line, causing no damage.	

A5834 Wt. W4973 M687 750,000 8/16 D. D. & L. Ltd. Forms/C.2118/13.

Instructions regarding War Diaries and Intelligence Summaries are contained in F. S. Regs., Part II. and the Staff Manual respectively. Title pages will be prepared in manuscript.

WAR DIARY
or
INTELLIGENCE SUMMARY.
(Erase heading not required.)

Army Form C. 2118.

Sheet 8.

Place	Date	Hour	Summary of Events and Information	Remarks and references to Appendices
ARMENTIÈRES	12/5/17	–	Aircraft – unusual activity throughout the day. At 7.30 am – a Squadron flew over enemy lines, returning in about one hour's time. At 9.15 am – another Squadron, flying South, was fired on by enemy AA. guns. At 10.15 am – Two of our planes encountered and fought 2 enemy machines driving them back. About 7.10 pm – Sounds of firing were heard but owing to the clouds nothing could be seen. Soon afterwards, four enemy planes came into sight heading for their own lines. Our AA. guns brought down an enemy machine which flew over the [illegible] and landed at C.8.d.10.10. One Officer taken prisoner – the other Officer was wounded and died shortly afterwards. Visibility – fairly good.	
	13/5/17	1.0 pm	No. 241337, Corpl G. Bond and 266875, Corpl W. J. Kelly, received mentions from Lt Genl. BROADWOOD, G.O.C. 57th Division for gallant conduct and devotion to duty on occasion of enemy raids on HOUPLINES and EPINETTE Sector on night of 7th/8th May 1917.	
		2.0 pm	Aircraft – Two bombs were dropped on enemy lines silencing [illegible] Machine Gun.	
		–	Artillery – during the day, as long as the light favoured him the enemy shelled various localities in HOUPLINES and ARMENTIÈRES, obviously searching for Battery positions and manufactories.	
		–	Visibility – fairly good.	

A5834 Wt. W4973 M687 750,000 8/16 D. D. & L. Ltd. Forms/C.2118/13.

Army Form C. 2118.

Instructions regarding War Diaries and Intelligence Summaries are contained in F. S. Regs., Part II. and the Staff Manual respectively. Title pages will be prepared in manuscript.

WAR DIARY

~~or~~

~~INTELLIGENCE SUMMARY.~~

~~(Erase heading not required.)~~

Sheet 7.

Place	Date	Hour	Summary of Events and Information	Remarks and references to Appendices
ARMENTIÈRES	11/5/17	pm 1.0	Two guns in action (HOUPLINES Sector) - 40 rounds fired on to new work enemy front line and enemy salient (CENSORS NOSE) (C.23.c). A deal of damage to his trench and parapet, some 10 yards of which was blown in. A few shots fell short, damaging his wire. Retaliation - NIL.	
"	"	9 am to 3-30 pm	Unoccupied area of town on either side of the LILLE - ARMENTIÈRES Railway shelled by enemy hows.	
"	"	pm 12.50	Aircraft - a squadron of ours flew high over enemy lines going East. Earlier in the morning some enemy machines tried to cross our lines, but were driven back by our A.A. guns. Visibility - poor.	
"	"	pm 4.0	Capt BARROW (O.C.) left to proceed to ST. OMER for course with 1st NEW ZEALAND Brigade L.T.M.B.	
"	12/5/17	—	Lieut. J. W. PYBUS assumed Command of Battery, vice Capt. BARROW absent on course.	
"	"	pm 1.0	Authority received from Brigade HQ. to strike off effective strength, all other ranks evacuated out of Divisional Area.	
"	"	6.0	One gun in action EPINETTE Sector on to enemy front line (I.5.c). Results good. Retaliation - NIL.	

2353 Wt. W2544/1454 700,000 5/15 D. D. & L. A.D.S.S./Forms/C. 2118.

Army Form C. 2118.

Instructions regarding War Diaries and Intelligence Summaries are contained in F. S. Regs., Part II. and the Staff Manual respectively. Title pages will be prepared in manuscript.

WAR DIARY
~~or~~
INTELLIGENCE SUMMARY.

~~(Erase heading not required.)~~

Sheet 6.

Place	Date	Hour	Summary of Events and Information	Remarks and references to Appendices
ARMENTIÈRES	10/5/17	am. 10.0	Notification rec'd from 2/6 Kings L'pool Regt. Extract from Pt II orders of 5/5/17 – "No 241414 Pte [illegible] Mason transferred to ENGLAND per hospital ship "[illegible]" 23-3-17.	
"		pm. 5.0	Lieut LEONARD and 17 other ranks left to relieve Lieut JARDINE and 17 other ranks in HOUPLINES Sector	
"		"	Cpl Wiggins & 13 other ranks left to relieve 17 other ranks in EPINETTE Sector.	
"		"	One gun in action EPINETTE Sector, firing on to communication trench (I.5.d) Result – Sandbagging and material blown up. Retaliation – Nil.	
"		–	Aircraft – Several attempts were made by enemy [illegible] to cross our lines but each time our Anti aircraft guns drove them back.	
"		–	Weather – again warm and sunny with fairly good visibility.	
"	10/5/17	pm 6.0	1 other rank wounded in streets of town by piece of anti-aircraft shell, and admitted into Main Dressing Station.	
"	11/5/17	pm 1.0	One gun in action (EPINETTE Sector) firing on to road work in enemy front line (I.11.a) – Results good. Retaliation, 6 "whiz-bangs" on support line behind position from which gun was fired. Our artillery replied to this and enemy fire ceased.	

A5834 Wt. W4973 M687 750,000 8/16 D. D. & L. Ltd. Forms/C.2118/13.

Instructions regarding War Diaries and Intelligence Summaries are contained in F. S. Regs., Part II. and the Staff Manual respectively. Title pages will be prepared in manuscript.

WAR DIARY ~~or~~ ~~INTELLIGENCE SUMMARY.~~

(Erase heading not required.)

Army Form C. 2118.

Sheet 5.

Place	Date	Hour	Summary of Events and Information	Remarks and references to Appendices
ARMENTIÈRES	7.5.17	8.30 pm	One gun in action in EPINETTE Sector in response to SOS signal sent up in connection with enemy raid. Formed a barrage in front of GAP F (I.5.c). Casualties, nil	[illegible]
"	"	11.0 pm	Situation normal again.	
"	"	—	For further report on minor enterprise on night of 7/8th May, see Appendix 1.	
"	8/5/17	1.0 am	Enemy shelled vicinity of billets – officers and mens billets hit by pieces, & houses in vicinity damaged – No casualties	[illegible]
"	9/5/17	4.0 pm	Lieut. BURFIELD relieved Lieut. SMALLPAGE in EPINETTE Sector.	
"	"	7.0	One gun in action – HOUPLINES Sector. 40 rounds fired on to enemy front line and communication trench. Trench badly damaged and parapet blown in. Retaliation – about 12 H.E. shells of very high velocity and some 18" "whizz-bangs" – no casualties. At this shoot, the new ballistite rings were tried for the first time and proved successful, altho' the gun became very hot and [illegible] badly after a few rounds rapid.	[illegible]

A5834 Wt. W4973 M687 750,000 8/16 D. D. & L. Ltd. Forms/C.2118/13.

Instructions regarding War Diaries and Intelligence Summaries are contained in F. S. Regs., Part II. and the Staff Manual respectively. Title pages will be prepared in manuscript.

WAR DIARY
~~or~~
~~INTELLIGENCE SUMMARY.~~
(Erase heading not required.)

Army Form C. 2118.

Sheet 4.

Place	Date	Hour	Summary of Events and Information	Remarks and references to Appendices
ARMENTIÈRES	7/5/17.	–	Enemy artillery very active over both sectors the whole day.	
		pm 7.30	Enemy fired a heavy barrage on front line and communication trenches in left section of HOUPLINES Sector, preparatory to raiding. Raiding party approximately 35 strong, of whom 20 succeeded in entering our lines, about 8.0 pm. These were eventually driven out and sector reported 'all clear' by 9.50 pm. The first few rounds of barrage blocked one of our left defensive gun pits. The other gun was brought into action and a barrage formed in front of our wire – C.17.c. On opening fire this gun was observed by enemy 'plane and soon subjected to a heavy fire from a 5.9" Battery. It was afterwards learnt that our barrage was very effective and probably prevented the enemy from entering our line at that particular part.	
		pm 9.10	Enemy barrage concentrated on to our EPINETTE Sector and 3 parties of the enemy (14 in each) attempted an entry into the SALIENT (I.5.c). The party on the right was unsuccessful, being held up by Lewis Gun fire – the other two gained an entrance and then ensued a struggle between these parties and the surviving members of the Lewis Gun teams, the latter at this time numbering 5 other ranks. A well organised [illegible] attack succeeded in ejecting the enemy by 9.20 pm. [illegible] [illegible] and 4 O.R. left dead in our hands.	

A5834 Wt. W4973 M687 750,000 8/16 D. D. & L. Ltd. Forms/C.2118/13.

Instructions regarding War Diaries and Intelligence Summaries are contained in F. S. Regs., Part II. and the Staff Manual respectively. Title pages will be prepared in manuscript.

WAR DIARY

~~or~~

~~INTELLIGENCE SUMMARY.~~

(Erase heading not required.)

Army Form C. 2118.

Sheet 3.

Place	Date	Hour	Summary of Events and Information	Remarks and references to Appendices
ARMENTIÈRES	6/5/17	am 2-15 to 2-30	Enemy shelled town in vicinity of our billet with 5.9"s. Damage to adjacent property, but no casualties.	
"	"	2-15	In response to S.O.S. signal from front line (EPINETTE Sector) one gun fired on its SOS line (covering the GAPS E & F). Meanwhile enemy shelled the communication trenches (PLANK AV. and WESTRALIA) with great rapidity for about 10 minutes, while a scrap between patrols took place in NO MANS LAND. (Map ref. BOIS GRENIER, TRENCH MAP. 36 N.W.4 1/10000 I.4.b. and I.5.c.)	
"	"	pm 5.0	One gun in action (EPINETTE Sector) on to enemy front line, damaging his trench. No retaliation.	
"	"	6.30	First consignment of Ballistite Rings received from Bde HQ. These rings are used in conjunction with the GREEN Cartridge (120 grains B) as a means of increasing the range of the mortar. NOTE { Using green cartridge + 2 rings increases range from 420 yards (using red cartridge) to 575 yards; [Using green cartridge] + 3 [rings increases range from 420 yards (using red cartridge)] to 740 [yards]	
"	"	—	Weather – warm and sunny with good visibility.	
"	7/5/17	pm 5.30	Instructions received from 3rd Australian Div. HQ. re precautions to be taken from 8.30 pm to midnight, owing to the firing of all guns of the Second Army.	
"	"	pm 7.0	1 Other rank from HOUPLINES trench party sent to Hospital with sprained ankle.	
"	"	8.0	Gas Alarm – 'alert' position ordered.	
"	"	8.20	All parties ordered to cellars and to remain there.	

Instructions regarding War Diaries and Intelligence Summaries are contained in F. S. Regs., Part II. and the Staff Manual respectively. Title pages will be prepared in manuscript.

WAR DIARY ~~or~~ INTELLIGENCE SUMMARY.

(*Erase heading not required.*)

Army Form C. 2118.

Sheet 2.

Place	Date	Hour	Summary of Events and Information	Remarks and references to Appendices
ARMENTIÈRES	3/5/17	–	Weather – again bright sunshine and good visibility. Enemy artillery very active on our trench sectors.	[illegible]
"	4/5/17	pm 4.30	A fire broke out in [illegible] at HOUPLINES (C.21.d) whereupon enemy observation balloon was hoisted over QUESNOY CHURCH and he fired a few rounds of shrapnel over this area.	[illegible]
"	"	pm 11.5	Enemy shelled vicinity of billets, causing no material damage.	
"	"	–	Weather – again sunny and visibility good.	
"	5/5/17	pm 12.30	1 other rank ([illegible]) admitted to 3/2nd West Lancs. Field Amb. suffering from [illegible]	[illegible]
"	"	[illegible] 10	One gun in action (EPINETTE Sector) firing on to enemy front line, damaging his trench – [illegible] sandbagging displaced. Retaliation 2 [illegible] support line, – no damage.	
"	"	[illegible]	Our artillery considerably active, also three "retaliation calls" from EPINETTE Sector answered.	
"	"	pm 7.0	Aircraft activity – ~~[illegible]~~ 6 (?) our machines [illegible] flying low over enemy lines were heavily fired upon by A.A. guns, but [illegible]	
"	"	–	Weather – sunny and again good visibility.	

A5834 Wt. W4973 M687 750,000 8/16 D. D. & L. Ltd. Forms/C.2118/13.

FRANCE
Map Ref. 36 N.W. 1/20000
Edition 6 c.

Instructions regarding War Diaries and Intelligence Summaries are contained in F. S. Regs., Part II. and the Staff Manual respectively. Title pages will be prepared in manuscript.

WAR DIARY
or
INTELLIGENCE SUMMARY.
(Erase heading not required.)

Army Form C. 2118.

Sheet 1.

Place	Date	Hour	Summary of Events and Information	Remarks and references to Appendices
ARMENTIERES (C.25.c.55-45)	1/5/17	am 9.0	Weekly effective strength – Officers 7 Other ranks 80 (including 3 in hosp.)	
			Fighting strength – " 7 " 75	
"	"	noon 12.0	Enemy aeroplane brought down in flames behind our subsidiary line (C.23.a)	
"	"	pm 6.0	Lieut. [illegible] relieved Lieut. EAMES in EPINETTE Sector	
"	"	–	Weather conditions – bright sunshine and good visibility	
"	2/5/17	am 10.0	Lieut BURFIELD and 1 NCO attended demonstration in fitting of extensions to box respirators	
"	"	pm 1.30	No. 306014 Pte Butcher H. reported to 2/8th Bn. King Lpool Regt. prior to proceeding to Transportation Depot, BOULOGNE for Locomotive Driving Work.	
		5.15	17 other ranks left to relieve trench party in EPINETTE Sector.	
"	"	5.30	17 Other ranks left to relieve trench party in HOUPLINES "	
"	"	6.0	2nd Lieut. JARDINE left to relieve Lieut. LEONARD in HOUPLINES "	
"	"	6.0	One gun in action EPINETTE Sector on to enemy's front line – trench [illegible] thrown up in air – Retaliation, nil	
"	"	–	Enemy shelled the town incessantly throughout the day. Direct hit on [illegible] (NOUVEL HOUPLINES) causing several casualties.	
"	"	–	Weather – bright sunshine and good visibility	
"	"	–	Aircraft – considerable activity – numerous patrols being seen along our front.	

A5834 Wt. W4973 M687 750,000 8/16 D. D. & L. Ltd. Forms/C.2118/13.

CONFIDENTIAL.

WAR DIARY

of

171st BRIGADE LIGHT TRENCH MORTAR BATTERY.

from 1st May, 1917 to 31st May, 1917.

Volume 4.

Army Form C. 2118.

Instructions regarding War Diaries and Intelligence Summaries are contained in F. S. Regs., Part II. and the Staff Manual respectively. Title pages will be prepared in manuscript.

WAR DIARY
~~or~~
~~INTELLIGENCE SUMMARY.~~

(*Erase heading not required.*)

Sheet 7.

Place	Date	Hour	Summary of Events and Information	Remarks and references to Appendices
ARMENTIÈRES	30/4/17	–	No 241350 – Sgt Amos, H. promoted Acting Sergt-Major 4-4-17 vice Acting S.M. Hall, died of wounds received in action. ([illegible])	[illegible]
"	"	–	No 241151 – Unpd. Lce/Cpl Wright J.C. promoted acting Sergt. (paid) to fill a vacancy from 4-4-17. ([illegible])	[illegible]
"	"	–	Extract from Pt II Orders No 15 dated 21-4-17 (of 2/6 K(Rifle) Bn Liverpool Regt.) 3. Promotion: 241151. Acting Sgt. Wright J.C. attached 171 Bde L.T.M.B. } Granted substantive rank of Sergeant from 4/4/17.	[illegible]
"	"	–	Base Order No 11 of 7/4/17 (of 2/7 Bn Kings L'pool Regt) received showing that 266214. Pte D. Roberts evacuated to England on 28/3/17 and struck off strength accordingly.	[illegible]

. MAP REF. FRANCE. Sheet 36NW. 1/20000 – 6 – a.

Instructions regarding War Diaries and Intelligence Summaries are contained in F. S. Regs., Part II. and the Staff Manual respectively. Title pages will be prepared in manuscript.

WAR DIARY
~~or~~
~~INTELLIGENCE SUMMARY.~~
(Erase heading not required.)

Army Form C. 2118.

Sheet 6.

Place	Date	Hour	Summary of Events and Information	Remarks and references to Appendices
ARMENTIÈRES (C.28.c.55.45)	26/4/17	a.m. 9.30	Lt. Nelson [?] having reported for duty from Div. Gas School, proceeded to trenches (L'EPINETTE Sector)	[illegible]
"	27/4/17	pm 5.25	171st Bde order No. 10 (Copy No 12) received and extracts made therefrom and sent to each Trench HQ (L'EPINETTE and HOUPLINES) (copies attached)	Appendix Nos [illegible]
"	28/4/17	pm 12.50	Wire received in connection with Brigade Order No 10. (copy attached)	Appendix No. [illegible]
"	29/4/17	–	Sunday – very quiet day.	[illegible]
"	30/4/17	am 8.15	Enemy aeroplane brought down in flames by one of our airmen. Machine fell behind our subsidiary line at C.28.a.70.40: Pilot burnt to death and observer who jumped clear was dead when picked up.	[illegible]
"	"	12 noon	Strength of Battery. 7 Officers and 77 Other ranks.	[illegible]
"	"	–	Authority received on 30/4/17 from Bde H.Q. re Officers on permanent establishment of Light T.M.B. to be struck off strength of their Infantry Battalions (A.G. A/11619/17) of 3/4/17. Following struck off strength of their Infantry Battalions:- Capt H.E. BARROW. Lieut J.W. PYBUS | Lieut H.F. EMRIES [?] 2nd Lt. J.D. JARDINE	

2353 Wt. W2544/1454 700,000 5/15 D. D. & L. A.D.S.S./Forms/C. 2118.

Map Ref. FRANCE Sheet 36 N.W. [illegible] 6 c.

Instructions regarding War Diaries and Intelligence Summaries are contained in F. S. Regs., Part II. and the Staff Manual respectively. Title pages will be prepared in manuscript.

WAR DIARY
or
~~INTELLIGENCE SUMMARY.~~
~~(Erase heading not required.)~~

Army Form C. 2118.

Sheet 5.

Place	Date	Hour	Summary of Events and Information	Remarks and references to Appendices
ERQUINGHEM-LYS. (H.3.d. 55.20)	18/4/17	7.30 pm	Cpl Walker reported for duty from Div. Gas School —	[initials]
"	19/4/17	3.15 pm	L/Cpl McEwan proceeded to Div. Gas School for 4 days Course —	[initials]
"	"	4.30 pm	Brigade Preliminary warning re relief of 10th Australian Light T.M.B. recd. (Copy attached)	Appendix No 3 [initials]
"	20/4/17	5.0 pm	9th Bde Order No 9 (Copy No 11) received, re relief of 10th Australian Brigade in ARMENTIÈRES Sector. (copy attached)	Appendix No. 4 [initials]
"	22/4/17	9.30 am	Capt BARROW and Lieut Eames reported at H.Q. 10th Australian L.T.M.B. and were conducted round the sector.	[initials]
"	"	10.0 am	Sect JARDINE reported to Staff Capt. at Town Major's Office, ARMENTIÈRES, and was shown round the billets.	[initials]
"	24/4/17	2.30 pm	Advance party of the Battery proceeded to HQ. 10th Aust. L.T.M.B. ARMENTIÈRES (C.25.c 55.45)	[initials]
"	"	7.0 pm	In accordance with Brigade Order No 9, the Battery left the billets at ERQUINGHEM and marched to ARMENTIÈRES to relieve the 10th Australian L.T.M.B. in the ARMENTIÈRES Sector. Lieut. EAMES in charge of the right or EPINETTE Sector. Lieut LEONARD in charge of the left or HOUPLINES Sector.	[initials]
ARMENTIÈRES (C.25.c 55.45)	24/4/17	8.0 pm	Completion of relief of 10th Australian L.T.M.B. reported to Brigade H.Q.	[initials]

FRANCE

Map Reference. Sheet 36 NW 1/20000 Edition 6c.

Instructions regarding War Diaries and Intelligence Summaries are contained in F. S. Regs., Part II. and the Staff Manual respectively. Title pages will be prepared in manuscript.

WAR DIARY
or
~~INTELLIGENCE SUMMARY.~~
(Erase heading not required.)

Army Form C. 2118.

Sheet 4.

Place	Date	Hour	Summary of Events and Information	Remarks and references to Appendices
ERQUINGHEM – LYS (H.3.d.85.90)	14/4/17	p.m. 4.0	Cpl Walker proceeded to Div. Gas School for 4 days Course.	[initials]
✓	15/4/17	am 11.30	A working party of 5 NCO's & 8 men proceeded to BOIS GRENIER Sector to work on L.T.M. gun pits and preparation of ammunition.	[initials]
✓	16/4/17	am 10.0	Lieut LEONARD and L/Cpl Vizard reported for duty from Second Army T.M. School.	[initials]
✓	✓	am 11.0	The same working party as yesterday proceeded to BOIS GRENIER Sector to continue work on gun pits and preparation of ammunition	[initials]
✓	17/4/17	am 3.25	Capt. BARRON, Lieut BURFIELD and 13 other ranks, with four guns, assisted 17th Bde Light T.M.B. in support of raid by 71st Infy. Brigade from BOIS GRENIER trenches. Each gun was laid on a different suspected enemy M.G position in INCREASE and INDEX TRENCHES (I. 31. d.). A steady fire was opened from all guns at zero plus 10. Rounds expended 260. Our fire appeared to be effective in keeping down enemy M.G. fire on this flank (RIGHT) of the raid. Enemy retaliated on our positions with some fairly heavy H.E., whiz-bangs, and Rifle Grenades. We suffered no casualties.	MAP. REF 36. NW. 4 1/10,000 BOIS GRENIER Trenches [initials]

2353 Wt. W2544/1454 700,000 5/15 D. D. & L. A.D.S.S./Forms/C. 2118.

Map. Ref. FRANCE. Sheet 36 NW 1/20000 Edition 6c.

Instructions regarding War Diaries and Intelligence Summaries are contained in F. S. Regs., Part II. and the Staff Manual respectively. Title pages will be prepared in manuscript.

WAR DIARY
or
~~INTELLIGENCE SUMMARY~~.
(Erase heading not required.)

Army Form C. 2118.

Sheet 3.

Place	Date	Hour	Summary of Events and Information	Remarks and references to Appendices
RUE MARLE (H.6.d.80.70)	11/4/17	pm. 2.15	Officers & men who took part in last night's operation were relieved.	[illegible]
✓	12/4/17	am. 9.0	Letter No B 3/7 (dated 11/4/17) sent to Divisional Trench Mortar Office re ~~[illegible]~~ suggestions for the forming of a Trench Mortar Corps. (copy attached)	Appendix No 1 [illegible]
✓	✓	am. 11.0	Letter received from the Brigadier General, Commanding 171st Infy. Bde. referring to the raid carried out on night of 10/11th inst. expressing his great pleasure at the manner in which the guns were handled, under circumstances which would have tried older and more seasoned troops, ~~which~~ shows a high standard of discipline and morale. This letter to be read out on "as strong as possible" parade.	[illegible]
✓	✓	pm 9.0	In accordance with 171st Bde Order No 7 of 10/4/17 the section of the Battery holding the Rue du Bois trenches was relieved by the 172nd Bde L.T.M.B.	Appendix 2 [illegible]
✓	13/4/17	pm 2.30	[illegible] Mercer reported for duty from Div. Gas School.	[illegible]
✓	✓	pm 3.0.	The Battery (less ~~the~~ Section in BOIS GRENIER Sector) marched to ERQUINGHEM-LYS (H.3.d.35.20) and took over the billets of the 172nd Bde L.T.M.B.	[illegible]
✓	✓	pm 9.0	In accordance with 171st Bde Order No 7 of 10/4/17 the Section of the Battery holding the BOIS GRENIER trenches was relieved by the 172nd Bde L.T.M.B.	Appendix 2 [illegible]
ERQUINGHEM LYS (H3.d.85.20)	✓	pm 6.0	Orderly Room was opened.	

2359 Wt. W2544/1454 700,000 5/15 D. D. & L. A.D.S.S./Forms/C. 2118.

WAR DIARY
or
~~INTELLIGENCE SUMMARY.~~
(*Erase heading not required.*)

Army Form C. 2118.

Instructions regarding War Diaries and Intelligence Summaries are contained in F. S. Regs., Part II. and the Staff Manual respectively. Title pages will be prepared in manuscript.

Map. Ref. FRANCE – SHEET 36 N.W. 1/20000 Edition 6a.

Sheet 2.

Place	Date	Hour	Summary of Events and Information	Remarks and references to Appendices
RUE MARLE (H.6.d.80.70)	6/4/17	a.m. 7.0.	Four copies of 'BAB' Trench Code No 2, with corrigenda and appendices received from Brigade Headquarters. Two copies of 'BAB' Code No 1 returned (numbers 4749 and 11951 respectively)	
"	7/4/17	a.m. 1.0.	Enemy aeroplane dropped bombs on RUE MARLE and ARMENTIÈRES – no loss of life	
"	8/4/17	a.m. 11.30	Lieut LEONARD and 2 other ranks left for Div. Reinforcement Camp en route for Second Army T.M. School TERDEGHEM for 7 days Course.	
		11.30	Cpl MERCER left for 4 days course at Divisional Gas School	
"		p.m. 3.0.	Lieut PYBUS replaced Lieut. LEONARD in trenches (Rue du Bois Sector)	
"	9/4/17	p.m. 4.30	Cpl Cone returned to HQ. from BOIS GRENIER Sector.	
"	10/4/17	p.m. 2.30	14 other ranks returned to HQ from BOIS GRENIER Sector.	
"	"	p.m. 10.25	Capt. BARROW, Lieut. EAMES and 14 other ranks, with four guns, supported raid by 17 2nd Infy. Bde on enemy's front line at I.31.d (INCREASE TRENCH). Objective for Trench Mortars, enemy's front line at I.31.d.05.30 (INDEX Trench). Fire was kept up for 30 minutes, with intervals, 700 rounds being expended. Our fire was very effective and succeeded in its object of keeping the enemy occupied at that particular point, whilst the raid was in progress. Enemy's retaliation was heavy, but we suffered no casualties.	MAP REF 36.NW.4. 1/10000. BOIS GRENIER Trench map

Volume 3.

WAR DIARY

~~or~~

~~INTELLIGENCE SUMMARY.~~

~~(Erase heading not required.)~~

Army Form C. 2118.

Sheet 1.

Instructions regarding War Diaries and Intelligence Summaries are contained in F. S. Regs., Part II. and the Staff Manual respectively. Title pages will be prepared in manuscript.

MAP REF. FRANCE – Sheet 36 N.W. 1/20000 – Edition 6a.

Place	Date	Hour	Summary of Events and Information	Remarks and references to Appendices
RUE MARLE (H. 6. d. 80.70)	1/4/17	3.0 pm	Cpl Cone T.W. proceeded to DIV. GAS SCHOOL (G. 27. d. 40. 90.) for 4 days Course.	[illegible]
✓	2/4/17		Acting S.M. Hall H. wounded in action by Shrapnel (BOIS GRENIER)	[illegible]
✓	✓	7.0 pm	Lce. Sgt Jones reported for duty from Sec. Army T.M. School, TERDEGEHEM. Report received G.Q.I. (i.e. Good, and Qualified as Instructor.)	[illegible]
✓	3/4/17	? pm	Acting S.M. Hall, died of wounds received in action, at 1st AUSTRALIAN Casualty Clearing Station. ESTAIRES.	[illegible]
✓	✓	6.0 pm	Lce Sgt Jones proceeded to trenches (BOIS GRENIER Sector) to replace Acting S.M. Hall (deceased)	[illegible]
✓	4/4/17	2.0 pm	1 other Rank (241390. Rfn Church) reported for duty, having returned from Base Hospital, and taken on strength of Battery.	[illegible]
✓	5/4/17	7.30 pm	News received that AMERICA declared war on GERMANY.	[illegible]
✓	6/4/17	10.0 am	Cpl Cone T.W. reported for duty from DIV. GAS School.	[illegible]
✓	✓	11.45 am	1 other rank (Rfn Oakes) killed in action by shell which landed on Gun-pit No 4 (BOIS GRENIER Sector). Two other ranks. shell shock (slight)	[illegible]
✓	✓	–	1 other rank (Rfn. Gilligan) evacuated out of Divisional Area to 1st AUSTRALIAN C.C.Stn. and struck off strength accordingly.	[illegible]
✓	✓	3.0 pm	Lieut. Smallpage left to relieve Lieut. Benfield in trenches (BOIS GRENIER Sector). other ranks were relieved also.	[illegible]
✓	✓	6.30 pm	Sec/Lieut. Jardine left to relieve Lieut. PYBUS in Rue du BOIS Sector. 17 other ranks relieved. 21 other ranks also	[illegible]

A5834 Wt. W4973 M687 750,000 8/16 D. D. & L. Ltd. Forms/C.2118/13.

171st Bde. Light T.M.B.

War Diary.

Vol. 3.

April. 1917.

Duplicate.
Copy for Records.

Map. Ref. FRANCE - Sheet 36 NW. 1/20000 6.c.

Instructions regarding War Diaries and Intelligence Summaries are contained in F. S. Regs., Part II. and the Staff Manual respectively. Title pages will be prepared in manuscript.

WAR DIARY

or

~~INTELLIGENCE SUMMARY.~~

~~(Erase heading not required.)~~

Army Form C. 2118.

Sheet 3

Place	Date	Hour	Summary of Events and Information	Remarks and references to Appendices
ERQUINGHEM (H.3.d.85.20)	29/3/17	11.0am	Lieut. Eames, Lieut Burfield and 21 other ranks proceeded to BOIS GRENIER trench sector (H.30 a.) to relieve the 172nd Bde Light TMB.	[initials]
✓	✓	3.0pm.	Capt. Barrow, Lt. Smallpage & Sec. Lieut. Fardine, with remainder of Battery, proceeded to RUE MARLE (H.6.d.80.70) to take over billets of 172nd Bde L.T.M.B.	[initials]
✓	31/3/17	-	Strength of Battery - 7 Officers & 79 other ranks.	[initials]

A5834 Wt. W4973 M687 750,000 8/16 D. D. & L. Ltd. Forms/C.2118/13.

Army Form C. 2118.

WAR DIARY

~~or~~

~~INTELLIGENCE SUMMARY.~~

(*Erase heading not required.*)

Instructions regarding War Diaries and Intelligence Summaries are contained in F. S. Regs., Part II. and the Staff Manual respectively. Title pages will be prepared in manuscript.

Sheet 2.

Place (Map of France Sheet 36 N.W. (Edition 6C) 1/20000)	Date	Hour	Summary of Events and Information	Remarks and references to Appendices
FLEURBAIX	12.3.17	pm 5.0	Capt H.E. Barrow relieved 2/Lt T.D. Jardine in trenches. 20 other ranks were relieved in trenches	[initials]
(H. 21. d.)	"	am 9.0	Lieut Burfield reported at Second Army T.M. School, TERDEGHEM for 7 days Course.	[initials]
"	13.3.17	4.0	Sgt Morris attended Div. Gas School for 3 days Course.	[initials]
"	15.3.17	4.15	1 other rank (Rfn Ugalde) killed in action in trenches (La Boutillerie Sector)	[initials]
"	16.3.17	6.0	Sgt Morris reported for duty from Gas School. Report "Good - passed Gas School.	[initials]
"	17.3.17	am 2.10	1 other rank (Rfn Mason) wounded in trenches.	[initials]
"	18.3.17	11.0 am	Cpl Bond proceeded to Div Reinforcement Camp en route for Second Army T.M. School, TERDEGHEM for 7 days Course.	[initials]
"	"	4.20 pm	1 other rank (Pte Roberts) accidentally wounded whilst walking around trenches of Bde Bombing School (H.21.d.0.1)	[initials]
"	19.3.17	am 10.0	Lieut. Burfield reported for duty from T.M. School, TERDEGHEM.	[initials]
"	"	pm 3.0	Battery relieved in trenches by 170th Bde L.T.M.B. Billets in Fleurbaix also taken over by 170th L.T.M.B.	[initials]
"	"	5.0	Battery left and marched into billets at ERQUINGHEM. LYS (H.4.d.)	[initials]
ERQUINGHEM	"	6.30	Battery billeted in Jute Factory - officers in cottages near by.	[initials]
(H.3.d.85.20.)	24.3.17	am 9.30	Lieut H.F. Eames reported for duty from No 12 Casualty Clearing Stn. HAZEBROUCK.	[initials]
"	"		171st Brigade Relief Orders No 5. (Copy No 9) received.	[initials]
"	25.3.17	am 9.30	Lieut. Pyhus, Lieut Leonard and 23 other ranks proceeded to Rue Marle (H.6.d.9.7) to carry out relief ordered in 171 Bde Order No 5 (para 8) dated 24.3.17.	[initials]

A5834 Wt. W4973 M687 750,000 8/16 D. D. & L. Ltd. Forms/C.2118/13.

VOLUME 2

Army Form C. 2118.

WAR DIARY

or

~~INTELLIGENCE SUMMARY.~~

(Erase heading not required.)

Instructions regarding War Diaries and Intelligence Summaries are contained in F. S. Regs., Part II. and the Staff Manual respectively. Title pages will be prepared in manuscript.

Sheet 1.

Place	Date	Hour	Summary of Events and Information	Remarks and references to Appendices
Map ref FRANCE Sheet 36 Edition 6c) 1/20000				
FLEURBAIX	1/3/17	—	Extract from London Gazette of 27/2/17. "Sec. Lieut to be Temp Lieut — H.F. EAMES. (August 1)	
(H. 21 d.)	"	pm 2.30	Lieut Burfield relieved Lieut Leonard in trenches.	
"	"	5.30	Lieut E. Smallpage and 10 other ranks of 2/5 K.L.R. joined for duty	
"	2/3/17	am 11.0	5 other ranks of 2/6 K.L.R. joined for duty.	
"	3/3/17	—	Strength of unit increased to 7 officers and 84 other ranks, by return of all available men of Reserve Battery. Made up as follows:-	
			Permanent Battery 4 Officers 46 other ranks (establishment)	
			Reserves attached 3 " 38 " (surplus to establishment)	
			Total 7 " 84 "	
"	4/3/17	pm 6.0	2/Lt J.D. Jardine relieved Lieut J.W. Pykes in trenches	
"	5/3/17	4.30	19 other ranks were relieved in trenches. Ref 2nd Army R.O. 614 of 26/2/17 — Instructions were received from 57th Div that "Red Cartridge" must be used by this Unit.	
"	7/3/17	5.0	Lieut Eames relieved Lieut Burfield in trenches	
"	9/3/17	12 noon	Battery attached to 170th Inf. Bde, but remained in present trenches & billets.	
	"	12.15pm	1 other rank wounded at ELBOW FARM (H.35 a 8.3) (Pte Doyle acting as Runner - returning from HQ to trenches)	
	10/3/17	-	Pte Doyle reported "Died of wounds".	
"	11/3/17	5.0pm	Lieut. Smallpage relieved Lieut Eames in trenches. 1 other rank evacuated to Advanced Dressing Stn.	
	"	6.0	Lieut Eames on sick list, evacuated Advanced Dressing Stn.	

171st BDE. LIGHT T. M.B

WAR DIARY

Vol. 2.

MARCH. 1917.

DUPLICATE.

Copy for Records.

Instructions regarding War Diaries and Intelligence Summaries are contained in F. S. Regs., Part II. and the Staff Manual respectively. Title pages will be prepared in manuscript.

WAR DIARY
or
~~INTELLIGENCE SUMMARY.~~
(Erase heading not required.)

Army Form C. 2118.

Sheet 2.

Place	Date	Hour	Summary of Events and Information	Remarks and references to Appendices
STRAZEELE	18.2.17	a.m. 11.30	1 Other rank, suffering from Synovitis Knee, sent to hospital, BAILLEUL.	JJ
✓	19.2.17	9.0	Billeting party of 2 other ranks cycled to SAILLY, sur la Lys, to arrange billets.	JJ
✓	✓	10.0	Lieut. Pybus and 2nd Lt Eames, accompanied by their batmen, and 3420 Sgt Amos and 3705 Gr Wiggins proceeded to FLEURBAIX and reported to 1st New Zealand Brigade for instruction in trench duties. They were sent to 1st N.Z. Bde Light Trench Mortar Battery and 2nd Lt Eames and party went into the trenches (La Boutillerie Sector), Lt. Pybus remaining in L.T.M.B. Billet.	JJ
✓	20.2.17	am 8.45	Battery marched to SAILLY (arriving 1 30 pm.) and billeted in a barn until morning of 22/2/17.	JJ
FLEURBAIX	21.2.17	6.0	Lts Pybus & Eames & party in trenches (La Boutillerie Sector) witnessed raid on German lines by 1st N.Z. Bde.	JJ
SAILLY	✓	–	Resting – during day 2 hours Gas drill carried out.	JJ
✓	✓	9.0	Lieut B.G. Leonard (2/16 K.L.R.), Lieut. S.T. Burfield (2/18 K.L.R.) and 5 other ranks joined for duty.	JJ
✓	22.2.17	8.0	Battery left and marched to FLEURBAIX, taking over billets from 1st N.Z. Bde L.T.M.B.	JJ
FLEURBAIX	✓	11.0	Lieut Leonard and 17 other ranks joined 2/Lt Eames & 3 other ranks in trenches (La Boutillerie Sector) and took over from 1st N.Z. Bde. L.T.M.B.	JJ
✓	26.2.17	pm 4.0	Lieut Pybus and 21 Other ranks relieved 2/Lt Eames & 19 other ranks in trenches.	JJ
✓	25.2.17	am 11.0	10 other ranks of 2/18 K.L.R. joined for duty.	JJ
✓	28.2.17	–	Strength increased during month by return of part of Reserve Battery. Effective strength end of February is 6 Officers and 59 other ranks.	JJ

A5834 Wt. W4973 M687 750,000 8/16 D. D. & L. Ltd. Forms/C.2118/13.

Volume 1

Army Form C. 2118.

WAR DIARY
or
~~INTELLIGENCE SUMMARY.~~

Sheet 1.

Instructions regarding War Diaries and Intelligence Summaries are contained in F. S. Regs., Part II. and the Staff Manual respectively. Title pages will be prepared in manuscript.

171st Inf. Brigade (Erase heading not required.) Light Trench Mortar Battery.

Place	Date	Hour	Summary of Events and Information	Remarks and references to Appendices
PIRBRIGHT CAMP Surrey	12/2/17	am. 10.30	The Battery, consisting of 4 Officers (Capt. H.E. Barrow, 2/6 K.L.R. Lieut J. W. Pybus, 2/7 K.L.R. Sec/Lieut H.F. Eames, 2/5 K.L.R. and Sec/Lieut J.D. Jardine, 2/7 K.L.R.) and 45 other ranks (1 O.R. below establishment) moved off to BROOKWOOD Station (L.&S.W. Rly), taking with them guns and equipment as per A.F. G.1098-243.	[illegible]
BROOKWOOD	"	pm 12.45	Entrained and left for SOUTHAMPTON DOCKS.	[illegible]
SOUTHAMPTON DOCKS	"	3.15	Detrained and embarked on the transport steamer "Manchester Importer".	[illegible]
"	"	6.0	Transport under way.	[illegible]
Le HAVRE	13/2/17	pm. 12.30	Arrived in HAVRE Docks.	[illegible]
"	"	2.0	Disembarked	[illegible]
"	"	7.0	After cleaning out the ship, Battery proceeded to Docks Rest Camp, HAVRE and went under canvas for the night.	[illegible]
"	14/2/17	a.m. 7.0	Left Docks Rest Camp for the Gare des Mérchandises (Point 1) and entrained.	[illegible]
"	"	11.0	Train left the Station and proceeded via ROUEN, ABBEVILLE, ÉTAPLES, BOULOGNE, CALAIS, ST. OMER and HAZEBROUCK to BAILLEUL.	[illegible]
BAILLEUL	15/2/17	pm. 10.0	Detrained and proceeded by road to STRAZEELE (7 miles	[illegible]
STRAZEELE	16/2/17	am 2.0	Arrived and went into billets.	[illegible]
"	17/2/17	—	Resting – Men issued with small box respirators.	[illegible]
	18/2/17	9.0	Officers and N.C.O's received instructions in use of small box respirators from Divisional Gas Officer.	[illegible]

To D.A.G.

3rd Echelon, Base.

Herewith duplicate War Diaries of this Unit for Records from 12th February 1917 to 30th September 1917 – Vols 1 to 8.

171 BRIGADE TRENCH
B12/18
ORDERLY ROOM
14/10/17
MORTAR BATTERIES

Harold E Barrow.
Capt
Cdg 171st L.T.M.B.

171st Bde. LIGHT. T.M.B.

WAR DIARY

Vol. 1.

FEBRUARY. 1917.

DUPLICATE

Copy for Records.

Instructions regarding War Diaries and Intelligence Summaries are contained in F. S. Regs., Part II. and the Staff Manual respectively. Title pages will be prepared in manuscript.

WAR DIARY
or
INTELLIGENCE SUMMARY.
(Erase heading not required.)

Army Form C. 2118.

Sheet 17.

Place	Date	Hour	Summary of Events and Information	Remarks and references to Appendices
ARMENTIÈRES	24/4/17	am. 2.10	Enemy attempted a raid on our EPINETTE Sector at I.5.c 45.31. Party approx 12 strong; They were repulsed, leaving one dead on our wire. Dead man belonged to 21 BAVARIAN Inf Regt. Our L.T.M. gunners "stood to" but were not called upon to open fire.	
✓	✓	2.15	No 306813, Pte DONOVAN wounded accidentally by bomb EPINETTE Sector.	
✓	✓	am 10.0	1 other rank admitted to hosp. with sprained knee	
✓	✓	am 11.45	One gun in action (HOUPLINES Sector) 40 rounds on CENTAUR TRENCH (C 29 c) Direct hit on to parapet and into trench obtained. Half an hour after the shoot, observers saw a stretcher being carried down trench. Retaliation – a few H.E. to right of LONDON ROAD (C.28 d)	
✓	✓	pm 5.30	Lieut LEONARD and 17 OR. left to relieve Sec Lieut JARDINE & party in HOUPLINES trenches.	
✓	✓	✓	15 other ranks left to relieve EPINETTE Sector.	
✓	✓	Am 2-7	Artillery – retaliation was asked for in reply to enemy's fire on area (I.5.c) By 2.35 am, situation normal.	
✓	✓	–	Enemy heavy Minenwerfer threw 9 shells over our front line in vicinity of MUSHROOM (I.10.d) – our retaliation was satisfactory.	
✓	✓	–	Aircraft – owing to fine weather considerable activity prevailed.	

2353 Wt. W2544/1454 700,000 5/15 D. D. & L. A.D.S.S./Forms/C. 2118.

Army Form C. 2118.

Instructions regarding War Diaries and Intelligence Summaries are contained in F. S. Regs., Part II. and the Staff Manual respectively. Title pages will be prepared in manuscript.

WAR DIARY
or
INTELLIGENCE SUMMARY.
(*Erase heading not required.*)

Sheet 16.

Place	Date	Hour	Summary of Events and Information	Remarks and references to Appendices
ARMENTIÈRES	24/5/17	pm 5.30	One Gun in action, HOUPLINES Sector. 30 rounds on to CENSUS TRENCH (C.29.A) damaging wire and parapet. Retaliation – a few pineapples on front line.	
"	"		Aircraft – active all day.	
		pm 7.0	In spite of heavy shelling by his A.A. guns, six of our 'planes flew over enemy lines whereupon his Observation Balloon was hauled down.	
	"	–	Throughout the day, his 'planes made several attempts to cross our lines, but each time were quickly driven back by our A.A. guns	[initials]
"	"	am 3-15	A prisoner was taken on our extreme left. It appears that he was one of a wiring party who misjudged his direction and found himself in some of our disused trenches near the R. LYS. When caught he was making his way back towards his own lines. He belongs to the 11th BAVARIAN INF REGT.	
"	"	–	Attitude of enemy distinctly quiet.	
"	25/5/17	pm 4.0	Lieut. BURFIELD left to relieve Lieut. SMALLPAGE in EPINETTE Sector.	
"	"	6-0	Lieut. PYBUS and batman left for Course with 1st NEW ZEALAND L.T.M.B. at St OMER.	[initials]
"		–	AIRCRAFT – Several of our patrols crossed the enemy lines during the day	
"		–	ARTILLERY – No particular activity to report.	
"		–	VISIBILITY – Good. Very fine weather.	

2353 Wt. W2544/1454 700,000 5/15 D. D. & L. A.D.S.S./Forms/C. 2118.

Army Form C. 2118.

Instructions regarding War Diaries and Intelligence Summaries are contained in F. S. Regs., Part II. and the Staff Manual respectively. Title pages will be prepared in manuscript.

WAR DIARY
or
INTELLIGENCE SUMMARY.
(Erase heading not required.)

Sheet 15.

Place	Date	Hour	Summary of Events and Information	Remarks and references to Appendices
ARMENTIÈRES	23/5/17	am 9.0	Defence Scheme – amended Appendix to IV. rec^d from Bde HQ	
"	"	pm 1.0	Supply Officer, A.S.C. informs us that rations are to be reduced by 5%.	
"	"	pm 1.30	Defence Scheme for medium T.M's rec^d	
"	"	3.30	One gun in action HOUPLINES Sector. 45 rounds at CHICKEN RUN (C.17a) Several direct hits into trench, duckboards and revetments being thrown into the air. Retaliation – About 100 "Pineapples" on front line, 90% landing over 30 yards behind, causing no damage.	
"	"	pm 6.0	Pte Russell reported for duty from Div. Reinforcement Camp.	
"	"	7.0	CAPT. BARROW ~~reported~~ returned to duty from Course at ST. OMER and assumed Command of Battery.	
"	"	–	Artillery – comparatively quiet.	
"	"	–	Aircraft – Observation balloon up behind FRELINGHEIN.	
"	"	–	Visibility – moderate.	

2353 Wt. W2544/1454 700,000 5/15 D. D. & L. A.D.S.S./Forms/C. 2118.

Instructions regarding War Diaries and Intelligence Summaries are contained in F. S. Regs., Part II. and the Staff Manual respectively. Title pages will be prepared in manuscript.

WAR DIARY
or
INTELLIGENCE SUMMARY.
(Erase heading not required.)

Army Form C. 2118.

Sheet 14.

Place	Date	Hour	Summary of Events and Information	Remarks and references to Appendices
ARMENTIÈRES	21/5/17	am 5.30	One gun in action EPINETTE Sector. 12 rounds on to working party at I.5.a. which was dispersed. Retaliation – NIL.	
"	"	pm 3.0	Two guns in action (HOUPLINES Sector) 60 rounds on to enemy front line CENTAUR TRENCH (C.29.c). Results – very good. Two gaps in parapet and several direct hits into trench [illegible] up duckboarding and heavier material. Direct hit on large periscope. Retaliation – not heavy and caused us no casualties.	
"	"	–	Artillery – quiet. CHICKEN RUN was shelled, but nothing else of any importance reported.	
			Enemy – quiet too. Direct hit on junction of FUSILIER and IRISH Avs. (C.1.d)	
"	"	–	Visibility – good.	
"	22/5/17	am 10	Pte Palmer admitted into hospital, suffering from Diarrhoea and debility.	
"	"	–	Artillery – enemy shelled our trench sectors intermittently.	
"	"	–	Aircraft – usual activity	
"	"	–	Visibility – moderate.	
"	23/5/17	am 4.45	One gun in action EPINETTE Sector. 12 rounds were fired on enemy working party near Ruined house (I.5.d.) Party was scattered and a [illegible] damaged. Retaliation – NIL.	

2353 Wt. W2544/1454 700,000 5/15 D. D. & L. A.D.S.S./Forms/C. 2118.

Instructions regarding War Diaries and Intelligence Summaries are contained in F. S. Regs., Part II. and the Staff Manual respectively. Title pages will be prepared in manuscript.

WAR DIARY
or
INTELLIGENCE SUMMARY.
(Erase heading not required.)

Army Form C. 2118.

Sheet B.

Place	Date	Hour	Summary of Events and Information	Remarks and references to Appendices
ARMENTIÈRES	20/5/17	–	Division left II Anzac Corps and Second Army and joined XI Corps, First Army.	
			Corps Commander – Lt. Genl. Sir R.C.B. HAKING KCB.	
			Army Commander – GENERAL Sir H.S. HORNE KCB.	
		pm 1.0.	Copy No 12 of 171st Inf. Bde order No 11 of 20/5/17 received re proposed operation (discharge of gas). See appendix no 4.	Appendix 4.
		pm 2.0	No 20182 Corpl T.W. Cone left for Div. Reinforcement Camp en route to ENGLAND as a candidate for Commission.	[illegible]
		pm 4.0	One gun in action HOUPLINES Sector. 25 rounds on CHICKEN RUN (C.17.a) and 5 on BREWERY (C.17.a). Results – many direct hits into trench and damage to parapet. Enemy 'pineapple' machine, which was retaliating on our rifle grenadiers when we opened fire, was silenced during our second burst of fire – and we continued firing without further interruption.	
		–	Artillery – our 18 pounders were busy during the afternoon, firing on CHICKEN RUN (C.17.a) and FRELINGHEN. Enemy sent a few shells into HOUPLINES – otherwise quiet all day.	
		–	Visibility – indifferent.	
		am 9.30	Aircraft – enemy aeroplane forced back by our guns – dropped smoke [illegible] when crossing his front line.	

Instructions regarding War Diaries and Intelligence Summaries are contained in F. S. Regs., Part II. and the Staff Manual respectively. Title pages will be prepared in manuscript.

WAR DIARY
or
INTELLIGENCE SUMMARY.
(Erase heading not required.)

Army Form C. 2118.

Sheet 12.

Place	Date	Hour	Summary of Events and Information	Remarks and references to Appendices
ARMENTIÈRES	18/5/17.	12 noon 1.0pm	Our Artillery rather more active. CHICKEN RUN locality again shelled during day and retaliation given for enemy "whizz bang" activity between 12 noon and 1.0pm. Enemy artillery activity confined to trench system — no shelling of back areas	
		pm 6.0	Aircraft — 2 enemy planes came over (flying very fast) and made for our observation balloon at NIEPPE. Heavy fire from A.A. guns directed at them. Our left sector report that during the night enemy observation balloon was brought down in flames. Visibility — good.	
	19/5/17	am 9.30 pm 7.30	Lieut EAMES evacuated to Base, BOULOGNE from 2nd AUSTRALIAN C. C. Station. One gun in action EPINETTE Sector. 18 rounds on to suspected Machine Gun Emplacement (I.5.c). Direct hits obtained and breach made in parapet. Retaliation — NIL.	
			Artillery — We shelled enemy lines at I 5 b and I 11 c during the morning. Enemy retaliation to our LTM fire 11.20 am. 8.30pm — shelled SQUARE FARM (I 9 b) — no damage of military importance. Enemy displayed greater activity and directed his fire chiefly on our trench system.	
			Aircraft — 3 observation balloons up over FRELINGHEIN and one over QUESNOY.	

2353 Wt. W2544/1454 700,000 5/15 D. D. & L. A.D.S.S./Forms/C. 2118.

Instructions regarding War Diaries and Intelligence Summaries are contained in F. S. Regs., Part II. and the Staff Manual respectively. Title pages will be prepared in manuscript.

WAR DIARY
or
INTELLIGENCE SUMMARY.
(Erase heading not required.)

Army Form C. 2118.

Sheet 19

Place	Date	Hour	Summary of Events and Information	Remarks and references to Appendices
ARMENTIÈRES	29/5/17	AM. 11.30	Two guns in action HOUPLINES Sector. 26 rounds on to CENSOR'S NOSE, where damage was done to parapet, duckboards and wire. Retaliation – 3 pineapples. Owing to breaking of traversing handle one gun fired only 6 rounds. Artillery co-operated and sent some H.E. and Shrapnel over CENSOR AV. (C 24 c)	(C 23 d)
"	"	PM 4.30	One gun in action EPINETTE Sector. 12 rounds on to new work in enemy front line (I.5.b.). Retaliation – 30 pineapples behind our front line (I.5.a)	
"	"	"	Artillery – enemy normal activity on our trenches.	
"	"	PM 10.15 to 11.15	Aircraft. 5 Planes of ours crossed enemy lines. Loud explosions subsequently heard as if bombs had been dropped.	
"	"	10.35 pm	Gas Projectors were discharged – the enemy put up no lights on the Sector affected (the Brigade front – ARMENTIÈRES Sector) but threw up white Very lights on the flanks. No retaliation.	
"	"	—	Visibility – poor, improving towards evening.	
	30/5/17	AM. 5-0	One gun in action EPINETTE co-operating with one gun HOUPLINES, both firing on CENTAUR TRENCH (C.29.c). Two direct hits on dugouts, corrugated iron and sandbags thrown into the air and several direct hits on trench. Retaliation – 20 H.E. on ORCHARD (C 28 c)	

Instructions regarding War Diaries and Intelligence Summaries are contained in F. S. Regs., Part II. and the Staff Manual respectively. Title pages will be prepared in manuscript.

WAR DIARY
or
INTELLIGENCE SUMMARY.
(Erase heading not required.)

Army Form C. 2118.

Sheet 18.

Place	Date	Hour	Summary of Events and Information	Remarks and references to Appendices
ARMENTIÈRES	27/5/17	–	Pte Donovan evacuated from 3/2nd Westland Field Amb. to 2o 54. C.C. Stn.	
		–	Artillery. quiet day.	
		–	Aircraft Normal activity.	
		–	Visibility – good An abnormally quiet day	
	28/5/17	am 11-10	One gun in action HOUPLINES Sector. 40 rounds on to CHICKEN RUN and CELL TRENCH (C.1)a with very satisfactory results. A large gap made in parapet and judging from his retaliation of 70 pineapples our firing touched a tender spot.	
		pm 5-10	One gun in action EPINETTE Sector 20 rounds on to Support line INCANDESCENT (I 11. a). Retaliation – NIL.	
		pm 11-0	Brigade Secret letter P.205 – "Action to be taken in event of withdrawal of enemy" recd.	
		–	Artillery – FRELINGHEIN again shelled during the day. Otherwise quiet. Enemy shelled HOUPLINES (C 27 a) actively during morning.	
		–	Aircraft – Observation balloons again up at FRELINGHEIN and QUESNOY and PERENCHIES. One aeroplane attempting to cross our lines driven off by our A.A. guns	
			Visibility – again good.	

Instructions regarding War Diaries and Intelligence Summaries are contained in F. S. Regs. Part II. and the Staff Manual respectively. Title pages will be prepared in manuscript.

WAR DIARY
or
INTELLIGENCE SUMMARY.
(Erase heading not required.)

Army Form C. 2118.

Sheet 20

Place	Date	Hour	Summary of Events and Information	Remarks and references to Appendices
ARMENTIÈRES	29/5/17	pm 2.30	4 other ranks left for Div. Reinforcement Camp, en route for course of instruction at FIRST ARMY School of Mortars.	
"	30/5/17	–	Artillery – usual activity on both sides.	
			Aircraft – considerable activity ~~throughout the day~~.	
"	"	am 6.50	Smoke signals dropped by 3 of our aeroplanes	
"	"	–	Visibility – good	
"	"	pm 2.0	Scheme for 'salvage of stores in event of an advance' forwarded to Bde HQ.	
			Rfn Wynne detailed as 'salvage man' in connection with above.	
	31/5/17	am 5.0	Two guns in action HOUPLINES sector. 50 rounds fired on to enemy trench system CENTAUR TRENCH (C.29.a/c). Both guns obtained many direct hits on their targets. Direct hits on dugout – corrugated iron etc thrown in the air. Retaliation – after 15 minutes about 15 pineapples on front line and 20 H.E. on ORCHARD (C.28.b)	
"		pm 6.0	Re shortage in establishment of reserve battery, requirements as follows sent to Bde HQ – 19 others ranks – from 2/5th K.L.R 8; 2/6th 3; 2/7th 3; & 2/8th 5.	
		pm 7.0	Artillery – enemy sent about 6 HE into the town, causing a few casualties to soldiers and Civilians.	

A5834 Wt. W4973 M687 750,000 8/16 D. D. & L. Ltd. Forms/C.2118/13.

Instructions regarding War Diaries and Intelligence Summaries are contained in F. S. Regs., Part II. and the Staff Manual respectively. Title pages will be prepared in manuscript.

WAR DIARY
or
INTELLIGENCE SUMMARY.
(Erase heading not required.)

Army Form C. 2118.

Sheet 21.

Place	Date	Hour	Summary of Events and Information	Remarks and references to Appendices
ARMENTIÈRES	31/5/17	am 10-45 11-30	Artillery – enemy shelled our front line C17c and the ORCHARD (C28c) were shelled with 5.9's & 4.2's. Our artillery replied effectively.	
"	"	–	Aircraft. active all day – about 16 enemy planes attempted to cross our lines at 8-15 pm, but were driven off by planes	
		pm 9.15	Our Observation balloon at NIEPPE brought down in flames by enemy machine, which, in spite of heavy fire from our A.A. guns, returned safely.	
"	"	–	Visibility – good.	
"	31/5/17	–	Effective strength at end of month :– Officers 7 – Other ranks 73. { Includes 1 Officer & 2 O.R. in hospital, 1 " & 5 Other ranks on Courses. Total – 80.	

A5834 Wt. W4973 M687 750,000 8/16 D. D. & L. Ltd. Forms/C.2118/13.

Appendix 1.

Confidential

Appendix No 1.

to

War Diary for May 1917.

of

171st Bde Light T. M. B.

TRANSLATION OF CAPTURED GERMAN OPERATION ORDER FOR THE RAID CARRIED OUT BY THEM ON OUR TRENCHES IN THE EPINETTE SALIENT (36 I 5 central) on night of May 7th/8th 1917.

Bav. Res. Inf. Regt No. 21
I Battalion.

O.U.L. 5-5-1917.
(? Billets at LOMPRET).

Raid "HILDESHEIM".

(A code name for the operation).

1. Object. To ascertain the effect of our artillery fire and to obtain prisoners.

2. Strength of Party.

2 Assault parties	1 W.O.	1 leader.	14 men.
Right flking pty (Covering party		1 L/Cpl	6 "
(Blocking "		1 "	4 "
Left flanking party) Covering party		1 "	3 "
) Blocking "		1 "	4 "
Rearguard		1 leader	7 "
Strength of raiding party	1 W.O.	6 leaders	38 men.

(From notes in a pocket book found on the body of O.C. raiding party, it would appear that the actual composition of the party was as follows:-

Right Covering Party	1 L/Cpl	5 men	(2 revolvers).
" Blocking "	2 "	3 "	(3 ").
" Attack "	1 Cpl.	8 "	(5 ").
Left " "	1 L/Cpl	7 "	(5 ").
" Blocking "	1 Cpl.	4 "	(3 ").
" Covering "	2 L/Cpls	3 "	(2 ").
Rear-guard	-	3 "	

This would make the total strength of the raiding party 42. The revolvers were probably automatic pistols.)

3. Assembly. The raiding party will form up in readiness in front of the foremost trench of the EPINETTE salient. It will begin to work up to this position. 30 minutes before the bombardment begins and is to be so arranged that the assault party is in the centre and the two blocking and covering parties on the flanks. The rearguard will at once take up the position assigned to them (see sketch).

When going forward into the assembly position a white tape will be laid to mark the way back.

4. Action of Artillery, Trench Mortars and Machine Guns.

Destructive artillery fire on the enemy's trench sectors 405 - 410 - 415 - 445 - 450 from Zero minus 25 minutes to Zero minus 20 minutes.

~~N.B. by Int:~~ The above figures refer to points marked on the accompanying sketches reproduced from the originals found on the body of the O.C. raid).

From Zero - 20 to zero - 10 there will be an interval.

From Zero - 10 to zero - 5 hurricane bombardment of the above-mentioned trenches.

From Zero - 5 to zero development of the box barrage as per sketch.

As the apex of the EPINETTE salient at point 430 is absolutely necessary as a place of assembly for the raiding party, bombardment of this point itself should be avoided.

From Zero - 10 to zero - 5 all available trench mortars will direct their fire into the trench sector 420-440.

From Zero - 5 to zero the trench mortars will assist in forming the box-barrage at points 410 and 450.

Machine guns will be on the alert.

(Paragraph 4 was subsequently altered as follows:-)

Para. 4.......

Para. 4 of the raid "HILDESHEIM" is to be altered as follows:-

Zero Hour - 25 Destructive bombardment begins) 5 minutes destructive
- 20 " " ends) bombardment.
- 10 Intense bombardment begins) 10 minutes hurricane bombardment
-+ 0 " " ends) with co-operation of L.T.Ms. on points 420-440.
+ 25 Destructive bombardment begins)
+ 45 " " ends) 20 minutes destructive fire.

Artillery barrage is as per attached sketch.

At Zero hour the L.T.Ms. will lift on to points a - 415 - b (as shown in sketch) to form the box-barrage. At Zero + 15 the L.T.Ms. will cease fire.

The machine guns in this sector will be on the alert.

5. Entry of Party into Enemy's Trenches.

On the artillery barrage lifting at Zero - 5, the raiding party will advance from the jumping off position, the assault party and the two flanking parties will as far as possible simultaneously enter the enemy's trenches between points 420 and 440.

The right flanking party will block the road immediately south west of point 420.

The left flanking party will be at point 440.

The assault party will as rapidly as possible seize any English still in the trenches and any war material that may be found. As soon as this has been done, the O.C. Raiding Party will give the password "URLAUB" ("leave") which will be the order to withdraw.

The flanking parties will be responsible for covering the retirement.

Should the enemy in the meantime have placed a barrage on his own trenches, the raiding party will remain in the apex of the EPINETTE salient until the fire abates. A decision will rest with the O.C. raiding party as the situation dictates.

6. Clothing and Equipment.

For the Assault Party: lace boots, puttees, bayonet, automatic pistol, cap, hand-grenades in sandbags, and wire-cutters.

For the flanking parties ~~hand-grenades,~~ rifles; otherwise as for the Assault Party.

The blocking parties will take with them wire hedge-hogs (gooseberries) for blocking trenches.

Letters and documents will be taken away from the members of the raiding party.

(Note by Int: O.C. Raiding Party who was killed in our raid had in possession 3 copies of the Raiding Instructions and a set of maps. Papers found on another man killed identified the 9th Bav. Pioneer Coy.

7. Mixcallaneous. Sectors 'a' and 'b' will be ready for immediate action during the operation.

The Company Commander in sector 'b' will, after the party has gone forward, detail men to guide any wounded to the aid post and escort prisoners to the rear.

Telephonic communication between the Command Post "NEUE WELT" - Sector 'a' - centre group - will be maintained throughout the entire operation.

Telephone messages respecting the raid are forbidden.

Watches will be synchronised at 9 p.m.

(Sgd) V. SAVOYE.

(Note by Int: The exact location of the Command Post 'NEUE WELT' is not known but it is believed to be the battalion H.Qrs.)

German Names. House at 36 I 5 c 8.8 TORBOGEN-HAUS ("Arched gateway house").
" " 36 I 5 a 25.65 LONDON-HAUS.
" " 36 I 5 a 4.7 DOVER-HAUS.

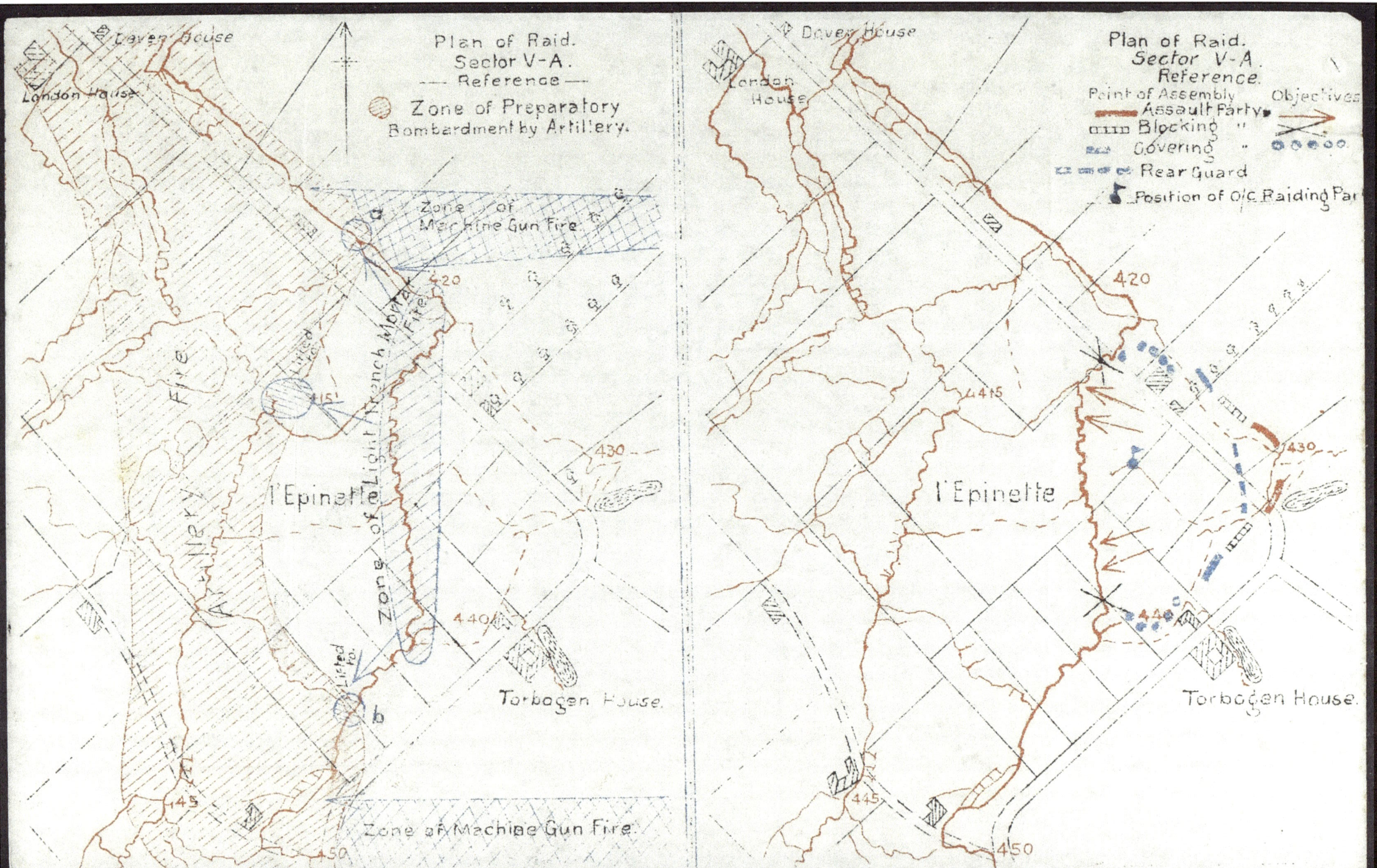

Plan of Raid.
Sector V-A.
— Reference —
Zone of Preparatory
Bombardment by Artillery.
Dover House
London House
Artillery
Fire
Zone of Machine Gun Fire
Zone of Light Trench Mortar Fire
Lifted to.
Lifted to.
15'
a
b
420
430
440
445
450
l'Epinette
Torbogen House.
Zone of Machine Gun Fire.
Plan of Raid.
Sector V-A.
Reference.
Point of Assembly
Objectives
Assault Party
Blocking "
Covering "
Rear Guard
Position of O/C Raiding Par
Dover House
London House
420
4415
430
440
445
450
l'Epinette
Torbogen House.

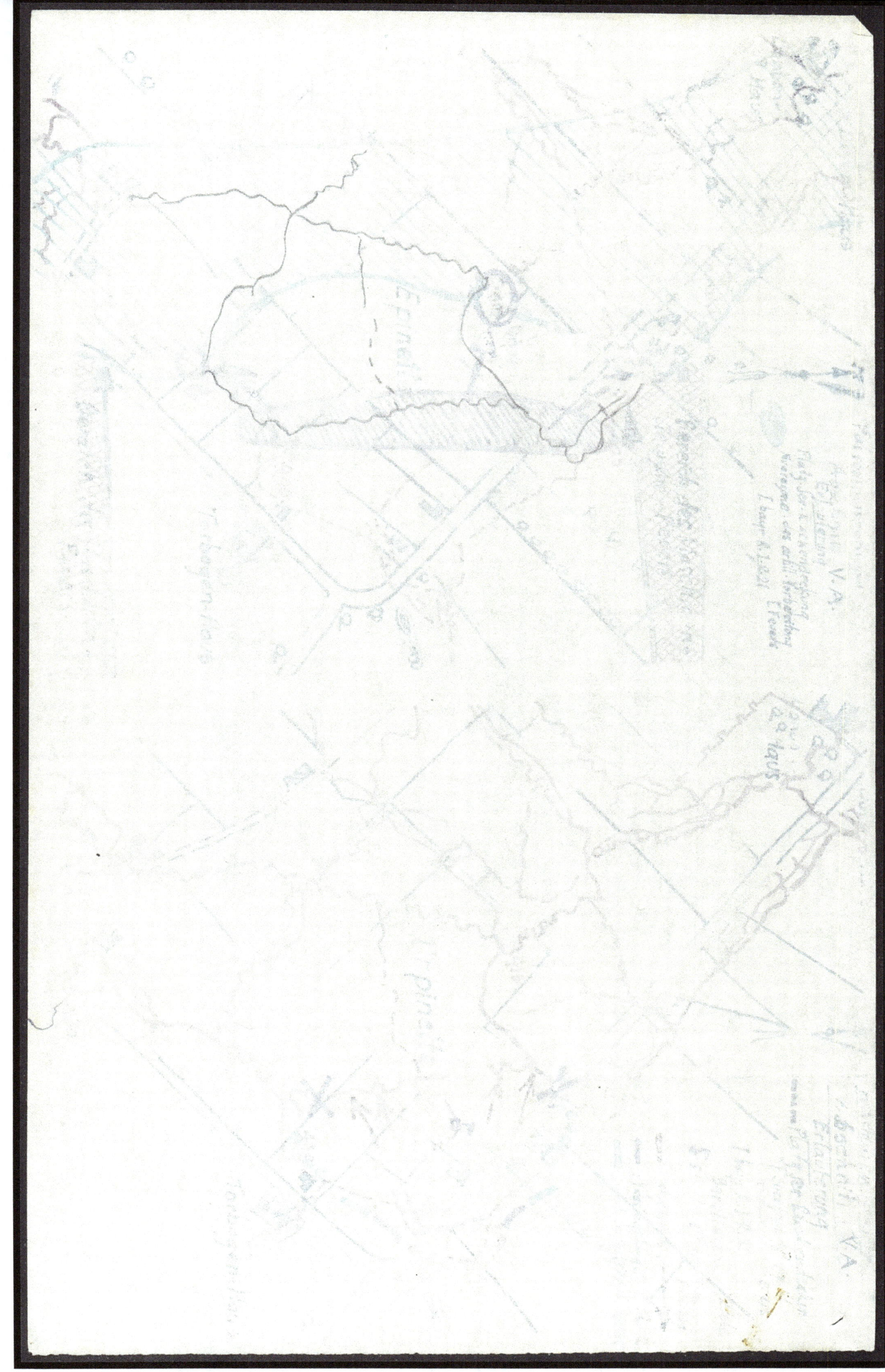

Abschnitt V.A
420
430
440
445
450
L'Epinotte
Ferhogen Haus

INTELLIGENCE CIRCULAR A.Z.12.

57th Div.Headquarters,
9th May 1917.

The following further notes are issued regarding the enemy raid on the Left Sector on the evening 7th/8th May.-

1. The enemy preliminary bombardment was intense from the outset and appears generally to have conformed to the orders issued, a copy of which is reproduced below, and it is noticeable that this new Division in the line appears to make far greater use of trench mortar and machine gun fire.

2. Our troops in the HOUPLINES Sector state that the dust was very thick and it was extremely hard to see any distance. The heavy Minnie barrage that was put down both at 8.p.m. and at 1.30.a.m. when the enemy made his attempts to enter the line, was very heavy, and machine guns swept the parapet throughout the operation.

3. During the second bombardment the enemy put up five green VERY lights on the junction of EPINETTE and RUE du BOIS. These signals are thought to have been an indication of the extreme flank ofthe bombardment.

A most efficient type of night signalling lamp was captured from the enemy, and it was used, it is thought, by him in place of a telephone to maintain communication between the raiders and the enemy lines.

4. Although there is no very definite evidence as to the strength of the party raiding HOUPLINES , it is believed that about 20 of the enemy succeeded in entering our lines at that point, and only a few of the EPINETTE raiding party succeeded in gaining entrance.

With regard to this latter party, it is thought that, in addition to the assault party and the two flank parties, there were besides, two other parties remaining out in N.M.L. to protect the flanks from a counter attack.

Ralph [signature] Captain,

for Lieut. Colonel,
General Staff, 57th Division.

... ...

5th May 1917.

21st RESERVE BAVARIAN INFANTRY REGIMENT.

1st BATTALION.

C O N F I D E N T I A L.

PATROL OPERATION - HILDESHEIN.

1. Object.- To take prisoners and to work out our artillery plans.

2. Composition:- Two Assault Parties, consisting of 1 Leader (?N.C.O.) 14 men.
The covering party, covering the patrol to the right to prevent approach of enemy - 1 L/Cpl. 4 men.

Left .....

P.T.O.

Left covering party, consisting of 1 N.C.O. and 3 men; and 1 Cpl. and 4 men.
Reserve: 1 Leader (? Officer) and 7 men.

Strength of the Patrol - 6 leaders and 38 men.

3. ASSEMBLY: The patrol will take up a position in front of the front line trenches in the EPINETTE SALIENT. They will begin working to this position 30 minutes before the commencement of the Artillery fire, and it will be carried out in such a manner that the Assault Party is in the middle of the two covering parties on the flanks.

Reserve Party will at once take up position as laid down in sketch.

Whilst proceeding to the point where they are to lie in wait, the patrol will leave behind a white tape to show them the way back.

4. ORDERS FOR ARTILLERY. The Artillery will fire on Points 405, 410, 415, 445 and 450 in the enemy trenches from 25 minutes before ZERO to 20 minutes before ZERO.
From 20 minutes before ZERO to 10 minutes before ZERO there will be an interval. From 10 minutes before ZERO to five minutes before ZERO, there will be a barrage fire on the trench system shown in sketch.
From 5 minutes before ZERO to ZERO Artillery fire, as shown in sketch, to prevent reinforcements of the enemy.
As it is absolutely necessary to obtain possession of the point of the EPINETTE SALIENT, Point 430, for the assembly of the parties comprising the patrol, an attempt will be made by bombardment to drive people out of the point of the Salient.
From 10 minutes before ZERO to 5 minutes before ZERO, every available Minenwerfer will bring fire to bear on trenches 420 and 440.
From 5 minutes before ZERO to ZERO, the Minenwerfers will be responsible for preventing an approach of reinforcements by fire on points 410 and 450.

Machine guns will hold themselves in readiness to fire.

5. ENTRANCE OF THE PATROL IN THE ENEMY LINE.: On the Artillery barrage lifting at 5 minutes before ZERO, the patrol will advance from the point of assembly. The assault parties and the two covering parties will, if possible, break into the enemy trenches at the same time, between points 420 and 440.
Right Covering Party will be responsible for preventing the enemy approaching Point 420.
Left Covering Party will perform the same duty at point 440.

The Assault Party will deal with any Englishmen in the trenches as quickly as possible. As soon as this has been accomplished, the patrol leader will give the password "URLOUB" which will be the order to retire.

The Covering Parties will be responsible for the covering of the withdrawal.

If the enemy ....

If the enemy has in the meanwhile barraged our own trenches, the patrol will remain in the apex of the EPINETTE SALIENT until the fire has ceased. This is left to the discretion of the patrol leader.

6. CLOTHING & EQUIPMENT. Assault party - Shoes, bayonet, revolver, cap, bombs (in sandbags) and wirecutters.

Covering parties - Rifle, and everything else carried by the Assault Party.

All letters and documents will be taken away from the patrol before the operation.

7. MISCELLANEOUS. All ranks in Sectors A & B will stand to during the operation.

Company Commander in Section "B" will be responsible for the evacuation of the wounded to the aid post, and will attend to the disposal of the prisoners.

Telephonic communication will be maintained between NEUE WELT and Sector "A" during the operation, and also the middle group.

All telephone conversation with regard to the patrol is forbidden. ZERO hour will be made known at 9.p.m..

(signed) von Savoye.

... ...

6th MAY 1917.

21st RES.BAVARIAN INFANTRY REGIMENT - 1st BATTALION.

Sheet No 4
Operation HILDESHEIN is altered as follows:

Time.

Minus 25 - Destructive Bombardment begins, lasting 5 minutes.

Minus 20 - End of Destructive Fire.

- 10 minutes interval.

Minus 10 - Barrage begins)A 10 minutes bombardment (barrage)
)with light minenwerfers at points
ZERO. - End of barrage.)420 and 440.

Plus 25 - Destructive fire begins)
) 20 minutes destructive fire
Plus 45 - End of Destructive fire.)

- Artillery action as per attacked sketch.
- At ZERO light minenwerfers will fire on points 415
x and 16 as per sketch as barrage.
- Up to plus 15 light minenwerfer fire will continue.
- M.Gs. in this sector will hold themselves ready to fire.

****

V.A.

Erläuterung

V.A.

Erläuterung

Epinal

T-bogen-Haus

Epinal

Erläuterung
420
415
L'Epinette
430
410
Forhogen Haus
445
450

IS. 73.
8/5/17.

ENEMY OPERATION night of 7th/8th May 1917.

p.m.
7.30. Hostile artillery opened N. of R. LYS.
7.35. Heavy barrage put down on C.16.1 to C.17.2 front & support line IRISH AVE. and C.Ts.
8.0. Gas Alarm - Strombos horns sounded Left Co. of Left Battn. (HOUPLINES C.17.c/30.40 to C.17.a/0.2) raided by party of 35 of whom 20 gained entrance. Communication with this part of line was cut by bombardment.
8.20. Hostile barrage "side-stepped" along EPINETTE front, until when
8.45. Enemy fire concentrated on our front, support & C.Ts. from I.5.1. to I.5.5.
8.50. Second gas alarm sounded.
9.0. S.O.S. called for from C.23.4 & 5. All the line was heavily engaged from C.23.5 to I.5.1.
9.10. Enemy raiding party entered between I.5.3 and I.5.1.
9.13. Our guns put down a heavy barrage.
9.35. Hostile fire slackened.
9.40. Hostile fire on whole left sector ceased.
10.15. Whole line where enemy had raided reported normal.
a.m.
1.25. Heavy rifle & M.G. fire on I.10.1 to I.16.3 fron & support.
1.35. Heavy T.M. barrage also put down.
1.45. Barrage lifted and concentrated on centre section.
1.52. All reported quiet.

p.m.
7.40. Gas alarm passed from left.

8.30 to 9.30. Gas cloud passed over subsidiary line of RUE DU BOIS sub-sector causing no casualties.

a.m.
12.45 Enemy box barrage in front, support & subsidiary lines, combined M.G., T.M., & artillery on I.15.1 & I.15.2.

1.20. Smoke seen coming from enemy lines in RUE DU BOIS sub-sector. S.O.S. sent up to check suspected raid. No enemy approached our lines, being repelled if raid attempted under cover of smoke screen by our combined fire. Our casualties: 1 killed, 1 wounded.

3.0. Situation normal.

p.m.
8.45. Enemy S.O.S. CORDONNERIE appears to be one green flare. Enemy response to his S.O.S. was feeble opposite this sector throughout the night.
9.40. Part of our artillery co-operated with right flank division minor operation on enemy FAUQUISSART section.

10.0. Our artillery fired in response to red enemy S.O.S. about N.9.4. Soon stopped after expenditure of 92 rounds.

NOTE. It would appear that the enemy's artillery opposite the right sector was fully employed in co-operating in the raids on our centre and left, and in assisting to repel the raid carried out by our right flank Division at 9.40. p.m..

APPENDIX 4.2.

AWARDS OF THE MILITARY MEDAL TO N.C.O'S AND MEN OF THE 57th DIVISION. (Contd.)

No.306051 - Pte.Frederick EASTHAM, "H" Battalion.

At .... on the night of 7th May 1917, this man was in charge of No.9 Lewis Gun Team. Four of his team including Nos.1 & 2 were killed by a shell, the remaining man being wounded. He assisted the wounded man, and carrying his gun directed him along the duck-boards. He then returned to the fire bay and despite the fact that he was blown twice off the fire step, he worked the gun single-handed until the enemy were almost on top of him. He then retreated out of the fire bay and opened fire from the rear bay, thus preventing the enemy from entering the fire bay and considerably delaying the enemy's entrance by their having to get in another part of the line.

No.241337 - Cpl.George BOND, 171st Light Trench Mortar Battery. ("F" Bn.)

At............... on the night of the 7th May 1917, this N.C.O. displayed great gallantry and initiative during the raid by the enemy. When word was received at the right Sec.H.Q. that the line had been entered by the enemy, he at once went straight up through the enemy's barrage, brought his gun into action and kept it in action under heavy fire from "Minnenwerfer" until the enemy were driven out. He set a fine example and showed great skill in the handling of his gun team. On a previous occasion he shewed a fine example when his gun pit had been blown in on top of him, by keeping his gun in action.

No.266875) Cpl.William James KELLY, 171 st Light T.M.Battery. ("G" Bn.)

At............... on the night of 7th May 1917, this N.C.O. displayed great gallantry and initiative during a raid by the enemy. He was at his left section H.Q. when the enemy opened a heavy barrage and brought his gun into action on the gap in the line the gun was laid on. Notwithstanding the gun pit being partially blown in he kept his gun team in action throughout the operation and set a fine example to his section besides rendering valuable aid. He has previously distinguished himself by his gallant conduct.

No.357758 - Pte.Andrew Semple GETTY, "L" Battalion.

After a raid of the......Brigade from the -------- Sector on the night of the 10Th/11Th April 1917, when wounded were out in "No Man's Land", Pte.GETTY continually went out and assisted to bring in the wounded under shell, machine gun and rifle fire ; he set a magnificient example throughout.

No.241031 Rfn.Joseph MADDEN, "N" Battalion.

For conspicuous bravery at......................... on the morning of April 26th 1917, A dug- out in the front line was blown in by heavy shell fire burying one man. Rfn.MADDEN worked for one and a half hour's under continuous shell fire to rescue the buried man. He was exposed to direct observation from the enemy's lines from his waist upwards.

The undermentioned N.C.O's were awarded the Military Medal when serving in other Divisions :-

No.49198 - Sgt.F.H.RUSSELL, 285th Bde.,R.F.A.
No.96437 - Sgt.F.COGGAN, do
No.21541 - C.S.M.GODWIN W. 170th Machine Gun Company.

Volume 5.

War Diary

of

171st Bde Light Trench Mortar Battery.

for

June, 1917.

MAP REF. FRANCE 36 NW. 1/20000 Edition 6 F. | 36 NW 2 & NE 1 (parts of) Edition 7 a. 1/10000.

Instructions regarding War Diaries and Intelligence Summaries are contained in F. S. Regs., Part II. and the Staff Manual respectively. Title pages will be prepared in manuscript.

WAR DIARY
or
INTELLIGENCE SUMMARY.
(Erase heading not required.)

VOLUME 5.

Army Form C. 2118.

Sheet 1.

Place	Date	Hour	Summary of Events and Information	Remarks and references to Appendices
ARMENTIÈRES	1/6/17	am 9.0	Lieut PYBUS returned to duty from course with 1st NEW ZEALAND L.T.M.B.	
(C25 c 55.45)	"	—	During the morning, enemy shelled our back areas (chiefly ERQUINGHEM-LYS)	
"	"	pm 5.0	One gun in action (L'EPINETTE Subsector) firing 18 rounds on to head of enemy trench (TWINE ALLEY - I 5.d.) sandbagging and debris being thrown up. Retaliation – a few "min-jars" (medium T.M's) to left of our communication trench (PLANK AV.) – no damage.	
"	"		Aircraft – active throughout the day.	
"	"	pm 8.15	Squadron of 6 to 10 aeroplanes patrolling. Four enemy machines manoeuvred to attack 6 of ours. They were driven off by our anti aircraft fire.	
"	2/6/17	pm 12.30	3 other ranks from 7/8 KLR reported for duty and taken on strength of reserve battery	
"	"	5.0	3 other ranks from 7/7 KLR reported for duty, and taken on strength of reserve battery	
"	"	pm 4.30.	Lieut SMALLPAGE relieved Lieut. BURFIELD in L'EPINETTE Subsector.	
"	"	7.2	3 guns in action HOUPLINES Subsector, firing 100 rounds on to large concrete work at C.29 a and c. Several rows of sandbags displaced and gaps made in parapet. Retaliation confined to 6 pineapples.	
"		—	Aircraft – enemy patrolled his own lines but did not venture to cross ours. Our aircraft active all day.	

A5834 Wt. W4973 M687 750,000 8/16 D. D. & L. Ltd. Forms/C.2118/13.

Same map ref.

Instructions regarding War Diaries and Intelligence Summaries are contained in F. S. Regs., Part II. and the Staff Manual respectively. Title pages will be prepared in manuscript.

WAR DIARY
or
INTELLIGENCE SUMMARY.

(*Erase heading not required.*)

Army Form C. 2118.

Sheet 2.

Place	Date	Hour	Summary of Events and Information	Remarks and references to Appendices
ARMENTIÈRES	3/6/17	pm 6-0	In conjunction with Medium T.M's, one gun in action (L'EPINETTE Subsector) firing 12 rounds on INANE ALLEY (I.5.d.) enemy communication trench. Retaliation – 4 [illegible]	
"	"	pm 5.30	Lieut. PYBUS, S.M. Amos and 15 other ranks left to relieve Lieut. LEONARD and party	
"	"	5.30	L/Sgt McGain and 11 other ranks left to relieve L'EPINETTE trench party.	
"	"	5.30	A large fire was observed in rear of FRELINGHEIN (C.11.c)	
"	"	6.30	Aircraft. one of our planes, patrolling the enemy lines was attacked by 4 Boche planes. One wing was severed and the machine fell [illegible] one occupant being thrown out before it had descended far. It fell about C.12 – central.	
"	"	9.20	Enemy machine attempted to bring down an observation balloon, N.W. of the town. The observers escaped in parachutes and balloon and enemy machine escaped intact.	
"	"	10.20	Four of our machines crossed enemy lines and explosions as of dropped bombs were subsequently heard.	
	4/6/17	–	No guns in action today.	
"	"	am	Artillery – enemy showed much activity shelling suspected battery positions in the town and also NOUVEL HOUPLINES (C.27a)	
"	"	–	Aircraft – active throughout the day, enemy machines several times crossing our lines but being driven off by our Anti-aircraft guns.	
"	–	–	Visibility – fair. Snipers inactive on both of our subsectors.	

A5834 Wt. W4973 M687 750,000 8/16 D. D. & L. Ltd. Forms/C.2118/13.

Army Form C. 2118.

Instructions regarding War Diaries and Intelligence Summaries are contained in F. S. Regs., Part II. and the Staff Manual respectively. Title pages will be prepared in manuscript.

WAR DIARY
or
INTELLIGENCE SUMMARY.
(Erase heading not required.)

Sheet 3.

Place	Date	Hour	Summary of Events and Information	Remarks and references to Appendices
ARMENTIÈRES.	5/6/17	am 10.30	2 other ranks reported for duty from 7/6 (Rifle) Bn K.L.R and were taken on strength of reserve battery.	
"	"	am 9.0 to 2.30 pm	Two guns in action L'EPINETTE Subsector retaliating to 'pineapples' and 'Bangers' which were silenced by about 2-30 pm.	
"	"	pm 6.0	Two guns in action HOUPLINES Subsector, firing 60 rounds from rear of HOBBS FARM (C 23.a) on to enemy front line (C.17.c). Parapet blown in and considerable damage done. Retaliation – 6 pineapples.	
"	"	7.0	Enemy sent about a dozen High Explosive shells in vicinity of our billets (C.25.c 55/45). No casualties were sustained by the battery but 1 officer and 5 other ranks of the infantry battalion in reserve (7/8th King's Liverpool) were wounded.	
"	"	pm 11.0	Enemy recommenced the shelling of the town and continued till about 3.0 am 6/6/17 – some 600 shells were fired. No damage to our personnel or billets.	
"	"	–	Aircraft. Slight activity – a patrol of 7 enemy machines flew along our lines going South. One of our SOPWITH planes flew very low over enemy line and was not fired upon.	

A5834 Wt. W4973 M687 750,000 8/16 D. D. & L. Ltd. Forms/C.2118/13.

Instructions regarding War Diaries and Intelligence Summaries are contained in F. S. Regs., Part II. and the Staff Manual respectively. Title pages will be prepared in manuscript.

WAR DIARY
or
INTELLIGENCE SUMMARY.
(Erase heading not required.)

Army Form C. 2118.

Sheet 4.

Place	Date	Hour	Summary of Events and Information	Remarks and references to Appendices
ARMENTIÈRES	6/6/17	am 8.30	Scheme submitted to Brigade HQ re action of L.T.M.'s in event of withdrawal by enemy on our front.	
"	"	10.0	7 other ranks reported for duty from 2/5th King's L'pool Regt. and taken on strength of reserve battery.	
"	"	pm 6.0	171st Bde Order No 13 ~~[illegible]~~ received under P.235. Operation order re discharge of GAS from our front.	
"	"	—	L'EPINETTE – one gun in action, retaliating to enemy 'pineapple' machine. 'Pineapple' ceased fire.	
"	"	—	Aircraft – very quiet all day.	
"	7/6/17	am 3.10	~~Second~~ Army (on our left) attacked the MESSINES–WYTCHAETE ridge, capturing the villages of MESSINES, WYTCHAETE and OOST-TAVERNE, about 25 guns, many machine guns and trench mortars and over 3500 prisoners.	
"	"	—	Artillery – enemy very active against our back areas especially against the town, the N.E end of which received the most attention.	
"	"	am 5.30	Enemy observation balloon seen to break loose from direction of QUESNOY.	
"	"	—	Our Artillery heavily shelled FRELINGHIEN (C11 c&d) and HOUPLINES trench system throughout the day.	

Instructions regarding War Diaries and Intelligence Summaries are contained in F. S. Regs., Part II. and the Staff Manual respectively. Title pages will be prepared in manuscript.

WAR DIARY
or
INTELLIGENCE SUMMARY.

(Erase heading not required.)

Army Form C. 2118.

Sheet 5.

Place	Date	Hour	Summary of Events and Information	Remarks and references to Appendices
ARMENTIÈRES	7/6/17	am	One gun in action L'EPINETTE Subsector retaliating to enemy pineapples & [illegible]	
"	"	pm 3.30	One other rank (HOUPLINES) wounded by shrapnel in left hand.	
"	"	3.0pm to 6.0pm	Enemy artillery very active, throwing some 300 shells into HOUPLINES. The Bridge at C.27.d.40.50 (by HOUPLINES CHURCH) was probably the objective.	
"	"	pm 11.0	Aircraft – enemy plane flying low dropped two small bombs near Battalion HQ (C.22.c). Enemy aeroplane activity otherwise confined to his own lines. Our own very active, 36 planes up at the same time between 5/7.30 am. Visibility good.	
"	8/6/17	am 10.30	One other rank (HOUPLINES Sub-sector) wounded, (head, neck & arm). HE. (a 4.2") burst near our No 4 gun pit (CAMBRIDGE Av. (C.17.c))	
"	"	am 11.30	One gun in action in L'EPINETTE Subsector, retaliating to pineapples from INCANDESCENT (I.5.c)	
"	"	—	In the afternoon, one gun in action (HOUPLINES Sub sector). In retaliation to 2 pineapples, five rounds were fired. 60 pineapples in reply, four shots in answer which provoked another 40 pineapples. Enemy apparently then ran out of pineapples as he resorted to HE. Shrapnel & one minnie.	

Instructions regarding War Diaries and Intelligence Summaries are contained in F. S. Regs., Part II. and the Staff Manual respectively. Title pages will be prepared in manuscript.

WAR DIARY
or
INTELLIGENCE SUMMARY.
(Erase heading not required.)

Army Form C. 2118.

Sheet 6.

Place	Date	Hour	Summary of Events and Information	Remarks and references to Appendices
ARMENTIÈRES	8/6/17	–	Artillery, enemy still active, HOUPLINES being heavily shelled by 5.9s.	
"	"	–	Aircraft – active, altho' visibility poor, owing to ground mist, which rendered observation difficult.	
"	"	7.25 am	Six of our planes engaged four of the enemy and brought down one. One of our planes was brought down in the evening near LE BIZET (C.13.d)	
			Five Albatross planes brought down	
"	"	8.10 pm	2 enemy planes down and one of ours at DIG Cabal.	
"	"	–	Enemy's attitude during the past few days on this sector has been quiet, except for the shelling of back areas.	
"	9/6/17	6 A am	One of our machines brought down by AA guns in rear of enemy lines.	
"	"	4.55 pm	Enemy machine flew low over HOUPLINES, being fired on by rifles.	
"	"	–	A quiet day, visibility poor.	
"	"	–	Throughout the day & night, the town and environs were intermittently shelled.	
"	9/6/17	6.0	Appendix II to Bde Order No 14 received. Bde Order No 14 re "action in event of enemy withdrawal" now complete.	

A5834 Wt. W4973 M687 750,000 8/16 D. D. & L. Ltd. Forms/C.2118/13.

Instructions regarding War Diaries and Intelligence Summaries are contained in F. S. Regs., Part II. and the Staff Manual respectively. Title pages will be prepared in manuscript.

WAR DIARY or INTELLIGENCE SUMMARY.

(Erase heading not required.)

Army Form C. 2118.

Sheet 1.

Place	Date	Hour	Summary of Events and Information	Remarks and references to Appendices
ARMENTIÈRES	10/6/17	–	Throughout the day, 50 rounds fired in retaliation from L'EPINETTE Sub-sector.	
"	"	pm 3.30	24 rounds in conjunction with medium T.M's at I.11.A. causing damage to enemy trenches	
			20 rounds on I.5.C. in retaliation to pineapples.	
			6 " " I.5.d. where movement was observed.	
"	"	pm 5.30	Lieut BURFIELD relieved Lieut SMALLPAGE in L'EPINETTE Subsector.	
			ARTILLERY – enemy active on HOUPLINES Trench system with 5.9's during the morning.	
			During the night enemy again shelled the town in vicinity of C.25.a.7.7. where a large fire was started by hostile shelling & burned for some 5 or 6 hours throughout the night (from 10 pm to 4 am)	
			Visibility again poor. Aircraft – inactive	
"	11/6/17	am 1.5	Prisoner captured in HOUPLINES Subsector, near the River LYS – one of a patrol of four, fired on by a sentry. Remaining three disappeared & prisoner gave himself up. Identification – normal – 14th BAVARIAN Inf Regt.	
"	"	pm 5.15	L'EPINETTE Sector relieved by 2/Lt. Towns & 14 other ranks.	
"	"	5.20	HOUPLINES " " " 2/Lt JARDINE & 17 "	
"	"	9.25	After unusual activity on the left Company front of our HOUPLINES Subsector (i.e. just South of the RIVER LYS – the enemy opened up with a hurricane bombardment	

... Casting

A5834 Wt. W4973 M687 750,000 8/16 D. D. & L. Ltd. Forms/C.2118/13.

Army Form C. 2118.

Instructions regarding War Diaries and Intelligence Summaries are contained in F. S. Regs., Part II. and the Staff Manual respectively. Title pages will be prepared in manuscript.

WAR DIARY
or
INTELLIGENCE SUMMARY.
(Erase heading not required.)

Sheet 8.

Place	Date	Hour	Summary of Events and Information	Remarks and references to Appendices
ARMENTIÈRES	11/6/17	pm 9-25	(contd). --- lasting 20 minutes, after which a party of the enemy, estimated at about 20/30 strong entered our line just south of the river. They were immediately ejected by our posts, who pursued them into No man's Land. Four of the enemy were left dead in our line and one officer was brought in from out wire, i.e. 5 dead in all. Our casualties were 1 R.E. (Special Coy) Officer killed & 2 R.E. other ranks ~~killed~~ wounded. 5 other ranks of 7/7th K.L.R. (battalion in line) wounded. The L.T.M.B. did not open fire as the enemy barrage was to the left of our S.O.S. lines.	
		9.55	Situation again NORMAL. Identification of ~~enemy~~ enemy dead - 14 Bavarian I.R. (normal)	
		—	Aircraft - usual patrols were up and fired upon by enemy AA.	
		am 9.0	Guns. Enemy machine flew low over our line and fired upon by Lewis guns.	
		—	Artillery - our howitzers active against enemy trench system just south of the river (HOUPLINES Subsector)	
		pm 9.25	In answer to S.O.S. from left Company (HOUPLINES) a barrage was put on enemy front line CELIA TRENCH within one minute of commencement of enemy barrage. (C17a)	
		—	Visibility - fair	

A5834 Wt. W4973 M687 750,000 8/16 D. D. & L. Ltd. Forms/C.2118/13.

Instructions regarding War Diaries and Intelligence Summaries are contained in F. S. Regs., Part II. and the Staff Manual respectively. Title pages will be prepared in manuscript.

WAR DIARY
or
INTELLIGENCE SUMMARY.
(Erase heading not required.)

Army Form C. 2118.

Sheet 9.

Place	Date	Hour	Summary of Events and Information	Remarks and references to Appendices
ARMENTIÈRES	12/6/17	pm. 12.30	Artillery - enemy shelled vicinity of billet with Shrapnel, causing no damage.	
〃	〃	1-0	1 other rank (Pte Croot) wounded by Shrapnel in streets of town.	
〃	〃	2.30	HOUPLINES - retaliation gun fired 6 rounds in response to call against 'pineapples'.	
〃	〃	—	EPINETTE - 〃 〃 10 〃 〃 〃 〃 〃 〃 do	
〃	〃	3-45	do - one gun in action from I.11.c. - target, enemy line at I.7.a (INCENSE) 30 rounds fired with good results. Enemy retaliation consisted of 2 rifle grenades during our firing. At 4.0 pm, 10 'minnies' on right of sector & 30 pineapples in vicinity of the gun. Further, some 10 whizzbangs and 3 'minnies' on Le PORT EGAL FME (I.10.b.). Our artillery replied and silenced him for the time being. Later (at 4.35 pm) he again fired with 'whizz-bangs' on CENTRAL AV. area.	
〃	〃	—	Artillery - enemy active all day on EPINETTE trench system.	
〃	〃	—	Aircraft - 6 enemy planes which crossed our lines during the morning were heavily fired upon ~~by~~ our AA guns and withdrew. Visibility - Good.	
〃	13/6/17	pm 2-0	4 other ranks proceeded to First Army School of Mortars for course of L.T.M's.	
〃	〃	3-0	3 〃 〃 returned from — do — and reported that Pte (Act/LCpl) Howard had been accidently wounded in the head (8/6/17) whilst attending the course.	
〃	〃	3-45	1 Other rank reported for duty from 2/6 (Rifle) Bn. K.L.R. and taken on strength of Battery	

Instructions regarding War Diaries and Intelligence Summaries are contained in F. S. Regs., Part II. and the Staff Manual respectively. Title pages will be prepared in manuscript.

WAR DIARY
or
INTELLIGENCE SUMMARY.
(Erase heading not required.)

Army Form C. 2118.

Sheet 10

Place	Date	Hour	Summary of Events and Information	Remarks and references to Appendices
Armentières	13/6/17	pm 6-0	1 other rank reported for duty from 2/5 Bn. K.L.R. and taken on strength of Battery.	
			HOUPLINES.	
"	"	1-20	One gun in action from Loc. 16. 10 rounds fired. Retaliation 5 pineapples.	
"	"	4-30	— do — 15 " " " 3 "	
"	"	5-45	Retaliation gun fired 30 rounds on to enemy front line (CENTRAL TR.) causing damage to trench and parapet & wire. Enemy retaliation – NIL.	
"	"	6.15	One gun in action from Loc. 11. on to enemy front line (CENSUS TR.) causing damage to trench and parapet and direct hit on dug-out. Suspected pineapple machine also shelled. } Retaliation. NIL.	
			EPINETTE.	
"	"	pm	Retaliation gun at (I5C30.20) front line, fired 10 rounds during day on INANE Supports.	
"	"	7.30	One gun in action from GAP F on to suspected machine gun emplacement at I.5.d.0.4. 15 rounds fired. Retaliation – NIL.	
"	"	11.0	Gas was successfully discharged from the Brigade front. Enemy's attitude quite normal. He increased the number of Very Lights & opened short bursts of rifle & M.G. fire.	
	14th	am 12-30	Gas again discharged. Normal.	
	15th	am 11.30	Aircraft – 5 of our planes were engaged by 21 enemy planes. Both sides returned homewards after a short fight.	
"	"	—	Artillery – enemy showed less activity, but he still continues to search for Battery positions in ARMENTIERES.	

A5834 Wt. W4973 M687 750,000 8/16 D. D. & L. Ltd. Forms/C.2118/13.

Instructions regarding War Diaries and Intelligence Summaries are contained in F. S. Regs., Part II. and the Staff Manual respectively. Title pages will be prepared in manuscript.

WAR DIARY
or
INTELLIGENCE SUMMARY.
(Erase heading not required.)

Army Form C. 2118.

Sheet 11.

Place	Date	Hour	Summary of Events and Information	Remarks and references to Appendices
ARMENTIÈRES	14/6/17	am 3-0	HOUPLINES Sector. One gun in action from Loc. 16 (left of IRISH Av) 12 rounds fired Retaliation – 4 pineapples	
✓	✓	7.30	— do — 12 ✓ ✓ ✓ 23 ✓	
✓	✓	11-30	EPINETTE Sector. One gun in action from I10b [illegible] Target – trench behind enemy salient at I11a. Rounds fired, 40. Results satisfactory, trench material thrown up. Retaliation 8 'whizzbangs' behind our support line and about 15 'minenwerfers' behind front line. This shoot carried out in conjunction with medium T.M.s.	
✓	✓	pm 6-0	HOUPLINES One gun in action from Loc 11. 30 rounds expended against enemy 'pineapple' machine about C 23 c 95-15 (CENSUS TR.) Results good, retaliation, NIL.	
✓	✓	11-40	One gun in action from Loc 16. 20 rounds Retaliation 20 pineapples	
✓	✓	pm 2-30	— do — 12 ✓ do 3 HE and 1 shrapnel	
✓	✓	4-15	— do — 15 ✓ do 25 pineapples.	
✓	✓	4-15	— do — Loc 14 (behind HOBBS FARM. C 23 A) 36 rounds on to wire of CELT TR. Retaliation – 40 pineapples, 6 whizz-bangs. Results good, coils of wire seen in air	
✓	✓	—	During the day, our retaliation gun responded to calls from front line, fired about 30 rounds. (C.28 d – TRAMWAY) firing on enemy front line (CENTRAL TRENCH)	
✓	✓	pm 4.30	After our 4.15 pm shoot from Loc 16 the last pineapple of enemy retaliation landed by the gun wounding the team (3 other ranks, Ptes Lynch, Hickman & Cottrell – all slightly)	
✓	✓	—	Artillery – Ours fairly active during day, both counter battery and trench targets being engaged.	
✓		—	enemy fairly active. 5" battery registering on our right centre Company (HOUPLINES).	
✓		—	Heavy artillery less active against the town.	

A5834 Wt. W4973 M687 750,000 8/16 D. D. & L. Ltd. Forms/C.2118/13.

Army Form C. 2118.

WAR DIARY
or
INTELLIGENCE SUMMARY.
(Erase heading not required.)

Instructions regarding War Diaries and Intelligence Summaries are contained in F. S. Regs., Part II. and the Staff Manual respectively. Title pages will be prepared in manuscript.

Sheet 12.

Place	Date	Hour	Summary of Events and Information	Remarks and references to Appendices
ARMENTIÈRES	15/6/17	—	Following report from R.A. GHQ. re 3" Stokes T.M.s "Collars are inclined to slip. During a barrage on enemy front line trench, a collar slipped, causing a gun to fire some 40 yards short. This would have had serious effect on our own infantry. As already advocated, I am still of opinion that one or two studs should be screwed into the barrel of the gun to receive them. This would save any chance of the collar slipping. Please say if defect is frequently noticed in your Army." — Our B.5/46 of 14/6/17 to Headquarters, 171st Inf. Bde reads as follows: "The slipping of the collar in the Stokes 3" T. Mortar has been a frequent occurrence with us. Possibly one or two studs screwed into the barrel of the gun would be sufficient to prevent this defect."	
		pm 6.45	One gun in action from loc 16 (HOUPLINES Sector) fired 6 rounds. Retaliation about 30 pineapples. The object of this shoot was to test the presence of the enemy in the sector opposite us, as owing to our operations north of the River LYS (i.e. the MESSINES AREA) it was thought probable that the enemy would attempt a withdrawal. The object was soon attained. Enemy replied almost immediately, though except for this, he had been very quiet throughout the day.	
		—	EPINETTE — two ~~T.M.s~~ guns in front line all day for retaliation against enemy trench machines (e.g. T.M.s, "pineapples" etc.). Fired 25 rounds. One gun obtained direct hits on screen in INANE TRENCH.	

A5834 Wt. W4973 M687 750,000 8/16 D. D. & L. Ltd. Forms/C.2118/13.

Army Form C. 2118.

WAR DIARY
or
INTELLIGENCE SUMMARY.
(Erase heading not required.)

Instructions regarding War Diaries and Intelligence Summaries are contained in F. S. Regs., Part II. and the Staff Manual respectively. Title pages will be prepared in manuscript.

Sheet 13.

Place	Date	Hour	Summary of Events and Information	Remarks and references to Appendices
ARMENTIÈRES	15/6/17 (Contd)	–	Information received vide D.A.G. List No 789/790 of 9/10th June 1917 that Sec/Lieut. H.F. EAMES was transferred to ENGLAND (sick) per H.S. "St Patrick" 4/6/17 and struck off strength from that date.	
"	"		ARTILLERY – our own fairly active; enemy's, quieter.	
"	"	pm 1.0	Enemy registered on our front and support line (CELT SYSTEM) HOUPLINES Sector.	
"	"	–	Aircraft. Normal. Visibility, fair.	
	16/6/17	am 4.30 to 9.30	HOUPLINES – Loc 16. one gun in action, 12 rounds fired. Retaliation 5 pineapples.	
"	"	pm 3.0	do do 5 do do 5 do	
"	"		do do do 4 do do 2 do and 1 minenwerfer.	
"	"	12 noon	do (C.28.d) Retaliation gun fired 3 rounds in response to call.	
"	"	2.15pm	do do do 6 do (Enemy replied with 20 [illegible]).	
"	"	3.0pm	do Loc 8. One gun in action, registering on C29a 90/25 (junction of two enemy communication trenches. 12 rounds fired. Retaliation, NIL.	
		–	do Enemy artillery very active on IRISH Av. and front line. The communication trench was blown in on two separate occasions.	
			EPINETTE – two retaliation guns in front line fired 30 rounds during day	
"	"	pm 6.0	Enemy observation balloon near QUESNOY brought down in flames by two of our planes.	
"	"	–	Visibility – Good	
		3.30	1 other rank [illegible] (Armourer) accidentally wounded (EPINETTE) whilst removing cartridge from container of shell. The cartridge exploded, blowing off tops of fingers & thumb of left hand.	

A5834 Wt. W4973 M687 750,000 8/16 D. D. & L. Ltd. Forms/C.2118/13.

Instructions regarding War Diaries and Intelligence Summaries are contained in F. S. Regs., Part II. and the Staff Manual respectively. Title pages will be prepared in manuscript.

WAR DIARY
or
INTELLIGENCE SUMMARY.
(Erase heading not required.)

Sheet 14.

Army Form C. 2118.

Place	Date	Hour	Summary of Events and Information	Remarks and references to Appendices
ARMENTIÈRES	16/6/17 (contd)	pm 8-45	HOUPLINES One gun in action (Loc 16) 9 rounds fired, Retaliation - NIL.	
	17/6/17	am 4-30	HOUPLINES One gun in action (Loc 16) 30 rounds fired, Retaliation - NIL.	
		am 2-18	One gun (retaliation gun, C28d) fired 9 rounds in response to call. Retal. NIL.	
		6-0	do do fired 20 rounds on to working party at C29c 50/75 (CENTAUR TR), scattering the party. Enemy retaliated with H.E. on our Communication trench (LONDON ROAD) and in vicinity of gun, wounding 1 other rank (Cpl Bentley) slightly in left thigh.	
		am 9-45	One gun in action (Loc 16) 6 rounds fired - Retaliation - About 10 "Whizz bangs" behind our front line doing no damage.	
		pm 2-30	One gun in action (Loc 16) 18 rounds fired, retaliation - NIL.	
		1-30 pm	Note. Whilst carrying up ammunition for this shoot, 1 other rank (Pte Turner) was slightly wounded in neck & left shoulder by H.E. shell which fell in front line close by him, causing him slight shell shock also.	
			EPINETTE Retaliation policy continued, three guns firing in front line during the day and firing about 50 rounds, chiefly on enemy support line (INCANDESCENT and INCARNATE)	
			Visibility - good - More movement observed in enemy back areas.	

A5834 Wt. W4973 M687 750,000 8/16 D. D. & L. Ltd. Forms/C.2118/13.

Army Form C. 2118.

WAR DIARY
or
INTELLIGENCE SUMMARY.
(Erase heading not required.)

Instructions regarding War Diaries and Intelligence Summaries are contained in F. S. Regs., Part II. and the Staff Manual respectively. Title pages will be prepared in manuscript.

Sheet 15.

Place	Date	Hour	Summary of Events and Information	Remarks and references to Appendices
ARMENTIÈRES	17/6/17 (contd)	pm 8.30	HOUPLINES One gun (Loc 16) fired 12 rounds – retaliation – NIL	
		8.30	" (Loc. 11) fired 35 rounds on enemy front line (Junction of CENSUS/CENTAUR trenches (C 29a 73.50) Results good, trench badly damaged. Retaliation – after half an hour, a burst of whizzbangs on ORCHARD.	
		–	Artillery – Enemy shelled the town throughout the day, (probably searching for battery positions). Otherwise fairly quiet on [illegible]	
	18th	am 4.30	HOUPLINES One gun in action (locality 16) fired 12 rounds, retaliation NIL	
		noon 12	– do – – do – 15 – do – NIL	
		pm 9.0	– do – – do – 14 rounds on CELL RESERVE. Retaliation – after ½ an hour 12 medium minenwerfers behind front line in vicinity of communication trench (IRISH AV.)	
		am 11.30	Retaliation gun (C 28 d) fired 6 rounds in response to call. Enemy did not reply.	
		pm 1.45	– do – 6 – do – Retaliation – about 18 HE in vicinity of gun; only damage being telephone wire cut.	
		pm 7.20	One gun in action from Gap L. firing 30 rounds on to new work in CENSUS TRENCH (C 23 c 91/35 to 80/70) Results good and retaliation, NIL.	
		–	EPINETTE Three guns in front line during day fired about 50 rounds in retaliation to enemy trench machines.	
		pm 5.30	Lieut SMALLPAGE relieved Sergeant BUFFIELD in EPINETTE Sector. 1 Other rank reported for duty from hospital and retaken on strength of battery.	
		–	Artillery – normal. Aircraft – considerably more active over the town. Visibility – good.	

A5834 Wt. W4973 M687 750,000 8/16 D. D. & L. Ltd. Forms/C.2118/13.

Army Form C. 2118.

WAR DIARY
or
INTELLIGENCE SUMMARY.
(Erase heading not required.)

Sheet 16.

Instructions regarding War Diaries and Intelligence Summaries are contained in F. S. Regs., Part II. and the Staff Manual respectively. Title pages will be prepared in manuscript.

Place	Date 1917	Hour	Summary of Events and Information	Remarks and references to Appendices
	June	am	HOUPLINES	
ARMENTIÈRES	19th	10.30	One gun in action from locality 16 fired 15 rounds, retaliation, NIL	
	"	am 3.30	— do — 16 " 18 " " NIL	
	"	pm 12.30	— do — locality 11 " 15 " " NIL Target enemy front line (CENSUS TR. C29a7/6).	
	"	pm 2.0	— do — " 11 " 20 " Target enemy machine gun emplacement in CENSUS TRENCH (about C23c95/05). Direct hits obtained. Retaliation – after 15 minutes about 30 HE (4.2") on front and support line behind Loc. 11. Our artillery (18 pounders) replied with about 100 rounds, silencing the enemy.	
	"	–	EPINETTE – during day 30 rounds were fired at a snipers post (I5c8.2) 3 loopholed plates. Two were blown up and a hole made in the third. Retaliation – NIL	
	"	pm 5.30	do – trench party relieved by Sgt McBain & 14 other ranks.	
	"	5.30	HOUPLINES – Lieut. LEONARD and party relieved Sec Lieut. JARDINE and party.	
	"	–	Artillery – quiet. Aircraft – more active than usual. Visibility – good	
		am	HOUPLINES	
	20th	4.45	One gun in action from locality 16. 20 rounds fired into CELL SUPPORT TR. Retaliation – NIL.	
	"	11.50	— do — 16 15 — do — do – NIL	
	"	7.40	— do — 16 10 — do — do – NIL.	
	"	–	EPINETTE. One gun in retaliation fired 20 rounds on cook-house at I11a.6/10. Several direct hits obtained, corrugated iron, wood and sandbags seen in the air. Artillery – more active than usual, the whole brigade front receiving attention. Aircraft – also more active. The enemy continues to search for Battery positions in the town. Enemy T.M's quiet.	

A5834 Wt. W4973 M687 750,000 8/16 D. D. & L. Ltd. Forms/C.2118/13.

Instructions regarding War Diaries and Intelligence Summaries are contained in F. S. Regs., Part II. and the Staff Manual respectively. Title pages will be prepared in manuscript.

WAR DIARY
or
INTELLIGENCE SUMMARY.
(Erase heading not required.)

Army Form C. 2118.

Sheet 17

Place	Date	Hour	Summary of Events and Information	Remarks and references to Appendices
ARMENTIÈRES	21/6/17	–	As a result of our increased activity with L.T.M's, the enemy has practically ceased to use his 'pineapple' machines on our sector, and the practice of using light T.M's for retaliation has been most successful.	
"	"	8.30 am	One gun in action (Loc.16). 15 rounds fired, retaliation – NIL.	
"	"	1.30 pm	– do – (Loc.6). 10 – do – do – NIL.	
"	"	7.10	– do – (Loc.6). 10 – do – do – NIL.	
"	"	–	Epinette – fired 20 rounds on suspected light M.G. emplacement. Several hits scored on the structure.	
"	"	–	Artillery – active during day. 200 rounds on CENTRAL TRENCH between 7 & 8 pm. Wire cutting for special operation.	
"	"		Aircraft – Both sides fairly active on patrol work.	
"	"	8.0 am	– do – – enemy observation balloon brought down by one of our aeroplanes.	
			Visibility – good	
"	22/6/17	1-0 am	HOUPLINES. In support of a raid on CENTAUR TR. (C.29.a) by 3 Officers & 100 other ranks of 2/6th [illegible] the K.L.R. we had three guns in action, firing 100 rounds each as follows:–	See Appendix No. 1.
			No 1 gun – front line (INDIA) C.29.c 25/30. Target CENTAUR TRENCH (enemy front line) C 29 c 55.70	
			No 2 " – do (GAP K) C 29 a 05/45. " CENSUS TRENCH (– do –) C 29 a 80.65	
			No 3 " – do (Loc.12) C 23 c 20/05. " CENSUS TRENCH (e.f.l. & M.G. emplacement) C 23 c 95.05	
"	"	"	EPINETTE – 3 guns fired 165 rounds, creating a diversion by bombarding INANE TRENCH.	

Instructions regarding War Diaries and Intelligence Summaries are contained in F. S. Regs., Part II. and the Staff Manual respectively. Title pages will be prepared in manuscript.

WAR DIARY
or
INTELLIGENCE SUMMARY.
(Erase heading not required.)

Army Form C. 2118.

Sheet 18.

Place	Date	Hour	Summary of Events and Information	Remarks and references to Appendices
ARMENTIÈRES	21/6/17	am 4.45	One gun in action from Loc 16. Fired 10 rounds. Retaliation 10 H.E on RIVER AVENUE.	
"	"	pm 5.0	do Loc 16. " 14 " " do 45 small H.E. on support line. Enemy firing from D.7.a.	
"	"	–	During day, retaliation gun (C.28.d) fired 30 rounds in response to calls.	
"	"	–	do do (EPINETTE) " 24 " " reply to 2 pineapples from Bde.	
"	"	–	Aircraft – very quiet, though visibility good.	
"	"	–	Artillery – Enemy again very active. NOUVEL HOUPLINES (C.27.a.7.2) shelled by day and night.	
"	"	–	Our co-operation in the minor enterprise of yesterday proved very successful and his trenches were very badly damaged at the points bombarded by our guns.	
	22/6/17	am 7.30	Retaliation gun (C.28.d) fired 16 rounds in response to call.	
		12.15pm	One gun in action from Loc 10. 15 rounds fired. Retaliation NIL	
		5.55pm	do Loc 16. 10 " " do 3 H.E. on front line	
"		–	EPINETTE – during the day, about 90 rounds were fired, chiefly in retaliation. 50 rounds expended in conjunction with medium TMs. One gun firing on I.5.c.7.0 one gun firing on INANE TR. from I.5.d.0.4 to d.2.5	
"		9.0am to 2.0pm	Enemy artillery active in vicinity of Section HQrs FUSILIER LANE (HOUPLINES Sector)	
"		7.15pm	Completed scheme for collection of Salvage in event of an advance, rec'd from Bde HQ.	

A5834 Wt. W4973 M687 750,000 8/16 D. D. & L. Ltd. Forms/C.2118/13.

WAR DIARY
or
INTELLIGENCE SUMMARY.
(Erase heading not required.)

Army Form C. 2118.

Instructions regarding War Diaries and Intelligence Summaries are contained in F. S. Regs., Part II. and the Staff Manual respectively. Title pages will be prepared in manuscript.

Sheet 19.

Place	Date	Hour	Summary of Events and Information	Remarks and references to Appendices
ARMENTIÈRES	24/6/17	am 20	Gas was successfully discharged from our HOUPLINES sector – enemy attitude normal.	
"	"	2-10	Enemy opened heavy barrage of artillery and minenwerfer on our front line (EPINETTE Sector) and LOTHIAN, CENTRAL and PLANK Avs. and on support line between LOTHIAN and PORTEGAL (I.5.c III a & c). Our S.O.S. sent up 2-15 am and artillery opened 2-18 am. Our S.O.S. guns (L.T.M.) opened fire immediately S.O.S. was sent up and fired 145 rounds on their S.O.S. lines. An enemy raiding party attempted to raid our line South of the MUSHROOM, but were repulsed by our Lewis gun fire. Battalion in line (7/5 K.L.R.) suffered casualties as follows:- Killed – 1 Officer & 2 Other ranks; Wounded – 7 Other ranks	
"		am 4-0	Artillery – enemy high velocity large calibre gun fired about 12 shells into the town. About 2 or 3 secs. elapsed between report and explosion. This gun is supposed to be a 5.9" naval gun.	
"		am 6-20	HOUPLINES – one gun in action from loc. 10 fired 20 rounds on to CENTAUR Row and Trench with good results. (Gaps in parapet, & sandbagging & trench material thrown in air) Retaliation – 36 pineapples and a few H.E. in vicinity of LONDON ROAD (C.29.c) after 5 minutes.	
"		pm 2-0	One gun in action Loc 8, firing 20 rounds on to CENTAUR TR. C.29.c. Retaliation – after 15 minutes, about 10 whizzbangs doing no damage.	
"		4.35	Two guns in action from Loc 13 – 40 rounds fired at CENT TR. – with good results. Retaliation after 30 minutes – 9 pineapples & 10 whizzbangs from direction of C.23.b.	

A5834 Wt. W4973 M687 750,000 8/16 D. D. & L. Ltd. Forms/C.2118/13.

Instructions regarding War Diaries and Intelligence Summaries are contained in F. S. Regs., Part II. and the Staff Manual respectively. Title pages will be prepared in manuscript.

WAR DIARY
or
INTELLIGENCE SUMMARY.
(Erase heading not required.)

Army Form C. 2118.

Sheet 20.

Place	Date	Hour	Summary of Events and Information	Remarks and references to Appendices
ARMENTIÈRES	24/6/17	–	HOUPLINES – during the day retaliation gun (C28d) fired 15 rounds in response to calls.	
"	"	pm 9-0	One other gun reported for duty from hospital and taken on strength) Battery (reserve)	
"	"	–	Artillery – active by day and night. The town and back areas shelled by 5-9's.	
"	"	noon 12	Aircraft – Enemy plane brought down one of our observation balloons.	
"	25/6/17	am 7-15	HOUPLINES: One gun in action from loc 16. 16 rounds fired. Retaliation – 8 pineapples and a few HE from direction of C.17c.	
"	"	pm 2-0	— do — 14 — do. Retaliation – NIL.	
"	"	pm 4.30	Two — do — loc 8. 30 — do. One pineapple machine put out C29c 80-90. Another at C29a 60.20 unsuccessfully tackled. Retaliation – 16 'whizzbangs' from direction of D.25 or 26 – 20 pineapples.	
"	"	am 1.52.	Artillery – enemy shelled vicinity of billets, evidently searching for gun positions in RUE BAYARD (C 25 c 55-45). Enemy active on our HOUPLINES trench system. Aircraft – normally active – weather conditions good.	
"	26/6/17	am 11-0	HOUPLINES: One gun in action from loc 16. 15 rounds fired – Retaliation, 12 'pineapples'.	
"	"	pm 2-0 to 6-0	Retaliation gun (C28d) fired 65 rounds on to CENTAUR TR and SUPPORT. Enemy replied with 27 whizzbangs – (no pineapples)	

A5834 Wt. W4973 M687 750,000 8/16 D. D. & L. Ltd. Forms/C.2118/13.

Army Form C. 2118.

WAR DIARY
or
INTELLIGENCE SUMMARY.
(Erase heading not required.)

Sheet 21.

Instructions regarding War Diaries and Intelligence Summaries are contained in F. S. Regs., Part II. and the Staff Manual respectively. Title pages will be prepared in manuscript.

Place	Date	Hour	Summary of Events and Information	Remarks and references to Appendices
	1917 June			
ARMENTIÈRES	26th	–	EPINETTE. About 90 rounds fired by three guns on INANE DRIVE (I.5.C.7.1) with good results. Retaliation – NIL	
"	"	–	Artillery enemy showed increased activity with heavy artillery. Both on our trench systems and back areas.	
"	"	pm 10.25	Aircraft Very active, several planes flying high crossed our lines. Two machines crossed our lines (EPINETTE) returning about 11.0 pm	
"	"	pm 5-30	Sec Lieut. BURFIELD relieved Lieut. SMALLPAGE in L'EPINETTE Sector.	
"	27th	am 5.0 to 6.0	Enemy aeroplanes dropped bombs on the town. Much civil damage, but none of military importance	
"	"	am 10.0	One gun in action from loc 6. 10 rounds fired, which provoked heavy retaliation to the extent of 10 light minenwerfers, 50, 4.2's and 4.5" "whizzbangs".	
"	"	–	Retaliation gun (C.28.d) fired 20 rounds during the day in response to calls.	
"	"	pm 3-10	EPINETTE – two guns in action in conjunction with medium T.M's. One at I.10.d.05/10 fired 30 rounds on iron plate in INCH about I.17.a.05.40. Another gun at I.10.b.70.30 fired 30 rounds on INCARNATE with good results. Enemy retaliated heavily for the latter guns shoot with 77 m.m. & 10.5 cm on & behind our supports by CENTRAL Av.	
"	"	am 11.0	One gun fired 22 rounds on INCANDESCENT. Large holes made in parapet. Enemy retaliated with rifle grenades & whizzbangs.	
"	"		Enemy Artillery considerably active on both sectors. The town shelled more heavily than usual.	

A5834 Wt. W4973 M687 750,000 8/16 D. D. & L. Ltd. Forms/C.2118/13.

Instructions regarding War Diaries and Intelligence Summaries are contained in F. S. Regs., Part II. and the Staff Manual respectively. Title pages will be prepared in manuscript.

WAR DIARY
or
INTELLIGENCE SUMMARY.
(Erase heading not required.)

Army Form C. 2118.

Sheet 22.

Place	Date	Hour	Summary of Events and Information	Remarks and references to Appendices
	1917 June			
ARMENTIÈRES	27th	pm 5.30	Lieut J.W. PYBUS and 17 other ranks relieved Lieut. LEONARD & party in HOUPLINES Sector	
"	"	"	L/Sgt Jones and 15 – do – L/Sgt McGain & party in EPINETTE "	
"	28th	am 11.15	EPINETTE. One gun in action fired 10 rounds on iron plate in INCANDESCENT (about I.5.c.55.05) and obtained direct hits. In action later on, fired another 10 rounds smashing parapet in INCANDESCENT.	
"		4	One gun in action fired 30 rounds on INCH TRENCH. Enemy retaliated with minenwerfers and pineapples to right of gun.	
		pm 5.15	One gun in action fired 30 rounds on INCARNATE TR. (about I.11.c.60.95) parapet knocked in and hits on suspected M.G. emplacement. Retaliation – 1 pineapple & 2 'minnies'.	
		pm 3.0	HOUPLINES. 25 rounds expended in registering on CENTAUR TR. at C.29.a.40.00 and 40.20 from new retaliation pit (C.28.d.80.65). Retaliation – 20 pineapples from CENTAUR SUPPORT at C.29.c.85.85 also 10, 4.2"s and 12 "Whizzbangs".	
		5.30	One other rank wounded by pieces of H.E. shell which burst by gun pit (C.28.d.80.65) (Pte Cookson)	
		–	Four other ranks returned to duty from Course at First Army School of Mortars	
		–	G.R.O. 2304 of 25/6/17 re L.T.M. Batteries received. A.F.B. 213 rendered for new permanent Battery from this date.	
		–	Artillery – back areas again heavily shelled (both the town and HOUPLINES)	
			Aircraft – quiet. Weather, dull & wet. Visibility poor	

A5834 Wt. W4973/M687 750,000 8/16 D. D. & L. Ltd. Forms/C.2118/13.

Instructions regarding War Diaries and Intelligence Summaries are contained in F. S. Regs., Part II. and the Staff Manual respectively. Title pages will be prepared in manuscript.

WAR DIARY
or
INTELLIGENCE SUMMARY.
(Erase heading not required.)

Army Form C. 2118.

Sheet 23.

Place	Date 1917	Hour	Summary of Events and Information	Remarks and references to Appendices
ARMENTIÈRES	June 29th.	–	EPINETTE – No 1 gun in support line (I 10 d 05.10) fired 20 rounds on INCH. Retaliation NIL.	
			2 " " front line (I.11 c 1.9.) " 20 " " INCARNATE TR + SUPPORT. Retaliation – NIL.	
			3 " " " (I.5.c.25.20) " 20 " " INCANDESCENT. Retaliation – 8 HE.	
			4 " " " (I.5.c.85.31) " 20 rounds on INANE. Retaliation: – NIL	
"	"	pm 3-30	HOUPLINES – In conjunction with medium T.M's, one gun in action from GAP H. Target – suspected 'pineapple' machine. 30 rounds fired with good results, several direct hits into trench. Retaliation – 18, 4.2's.	
"	"	pm 7-0	– Two guns in action – One from Loc 16. objective suspected pineapple machine at C17c 80.95. Ammn expended 25. Retaliated almost immediately – 15 pineapples, 9 rifle grenades, 3 minniewerfer (light). One gun from GAP J. objective, C29a 65.15. 25 rounds fired. Retaliation – after 10 minutes in vicinity of LONDON ROAD, 20, 5.9's	
"	"	pm 2-0	Four other ranks proceed to First Army School of Mortars, CLARQUES (nr ST. OMER) for course of L.T.M's.	
"	"	–	Aircraft – normal activity. Artillery, still increased activity, both on trench systems and back areas, the town being again shelled.	

Army Form C. 2118.

Instructions regarding War Diaries and Intelligence Summaries are contained in F. S. Regs., Part II. and the Staff Manual respectively. Title pages will be prepared in manuscript.

WAR DIARY
or
INTELLIGENCE SUMMARY.
(Erase heading not required.)

Sheet 24.

Place	Date	Hour	Summary of Events and Information	Remarks and references to Appendices
	1917 June		EPINETTE.	
ARMENTIÈRES	30th.		No 1 gun fired 22 rounds from GAP A on suspected snipers post in INCH TRENCH. Direct hits obtained, post smashed up. Retaliation – 3 minenwerfers and 21 small H.E.	
			2 Gun fired 20 rounds from Support Line (I 10 b 65.20) on INCARNATE, smashing in the parapet. Retaliation – about 15 77mm shells.	
			3 gun fired 25 rounds from I 5 c 35/50, {15 on INCANDESCENT SUPPORT and 10 on – do – TRENCH. Retaliation – 8 HE. (77mm)	
			4 gun fired 25 rounds from I 5 C 55/40 {15 on INANE ALLEY and 10 " INCANDESCENT TRENCH} Retaliation NIL.	
			HOUPLINES.	
			One gun in action from Loc 16 during the day fired 20 rounds, and enemy replied with 18 whizzbangs and 15 pineapples.	
"	"	pm 3-0	One gun in action from GAP J. on C. 29 a 80 30 (junction of CENTAUR ROW & CENSUS SUPPORT. 25 rounds fired with good results. Retaliation on LONDON ROAD and in direction of gun 30 whizzbangs.	
"	"	pm 6-30	One gun in action from GAP H. objective C 29 c 80.70, junction of CENTAUR SUPPORT and CENTRAL AV. 25 rounds fired. Retaliation almost immediately 15, 4.2" in vicinity of LONDON ROAD, also 3 medium minenwerfers. NOTE – This is the first appearance of a medium minenwerfer in this particular sector for the last two months.	

A5834 Wt. W4973 M687 750,000 8/16 D. D. & L. Ltd. Forms/C.2118/13.

Instructions regarding War Diaries and Intelligence Summaries are contained in F. S. Regs., Part II. and the Staff Manual respectively. Title pages will be prepared in manuscript.

WAR DIARY
or
INTELLIGENCE SUMMARY.
(Erase heading not required.)

Army Form C. 2118.

Sheet 25.

Place	Date	Hour	Summary of Events and Information	Remarks and references to Appendices
	1917 June			
ARMENTIERES	30th	–	Artillery – still very active on back areas, the town, HOUPLINES and CHAPPELLE D'ARMENTIERES being heavily shelled. HOUPLINES in particular has been badly damaged lately.	
			Strength of Battery at end of month.	
			Officers 6. Other ranks 81.	
			Taken on strength – do – 19	
			Struck off " Officers 1 do 11.	
		–	Copy No 13 of Brigade Order 14 – re withdrawal of Enemy complete with appendices received from Bde HQ.	

[signature] Major R.F.
for Bde LTM B.
30/6/17.

Appendix

To

Volume 5

War Diary

of

171 Bde Light Trench Mortar Battery.

June, 1917.

WAR DIARY – June, 1917

Appendix No. 1

Copy No 1.

Operation Orders No 1.

171st Bde Light T. M. B.

Ref. maps.
Sheet 36 NW. 2 & NE. 1. (parts of)

17/6/17.

1. Information – From information obtained by patrols the CENTAUR TRENCH (C. 29. a & c) is held by the enemy.

2. Intention – It is intended to make a raid on zero day at zero hour on CENTAUR TR. between points C. 29. a. 43. 05 and 29. a. 64. 42.

Objects (a) to continue a harassing policy & prevent the enemy from withdrawing troops.
(b) To kill & capture as many as poss: of the enemy.
(c) To capture and destroy war material.
(d) To obtain identifications & gain information regarding enemy's system of defence.

3. Support – The raid will have artillery, trench mortars and Vickers guns to support them.

4. L.T.M's – The battery will support the raid as follows:–

A. HOUPLINES Subsector.

No. 1 Gun.	Position.	C. 29. c. 25. 30.	Target.	CENTAUR TR. C. 29. c. 55. 70.
2	"	C. 29. a. 05/45.	"	CENSUS TR. C. 29. a. 80. 65.
3	"	C. 23. c. 20. 05.	"	" (M.G. emplacement) C. 23 c. 95. 65.

Time Table as follows:–

Zero.	No 3 gun. rapid barrage.
" +5.	Nos 1 & 2. Slow "
" +21	Nos 1, 2, & 3. rapid barrage till end of operation which will be judged by slackening of our artillery fire.

B. L'EPINETTE To create a diversion, three guns of this sub-sector will bombard INANE TRENCH from zero till end of operation, as follows:–
No 1 gun. I. 5. d. 30. 70. Nos. 2 & 3 – I. 5. d. 00. 50.

Harold E. Barrow.
Capt.
Cdg. 171st Bde L.T.M.B.

For further information, see attached Special Operation Order of 2/6 K.L.R.

CODE.

RATIONS LATE.	Postpone Operations --minutes.
THIRSTY.	Cancel Operations.
TOAST.	Increase barrage.
REST.	We are returning.
BILLET.	All in.
BLANKETS.	Killed.
STEAMER.	Wounded.
ADRIFT.	Missing.
Squealers.	Prisoners.
STUT.	Parker's Party.
BOMBER	Clarkes Party.
RUBBER	Moseley's Party.
HENLEY.	O.C. Raid.
SNAPS.	Entered enemy's line.
GINGER.	Heavy opposition.
TREACLE.	Light do
RETURN SENT.	All going well.
HUNGRY.	No Boshe found.
STARVING.	Lengthen Barrage 70 yards.

....

SECRET

2/6TH (RIFLE) BATTALION "THE KING'S"(LIVERPOOL REGIMENT.)

SPECIAL OPERATION ORDERS.

Copy No 9

16th June 1917.

Ref: Maps
Sheets 36 N.W. 2 and N.E. 1 (Parts of)
Sketch Map.
Aeroplane Photographs.

1. INFORMATION. From information obtained by Patrols the CENTAUR TRENCH is held by the Enemy.

2. INTENTION. It is intended to make a Raid on Zero Day at Zero hour on CENTAUR TRENCH, between Points C.29.a.43.05. and C.29.a.64.43. and Penetrate to his Support Lines - CENTAUR SUPPORT at C.29.a.79.30. to C.29.a.68.12. and searching CENTAUR ROW C.T. also to search CENTAUR LANE and establish a block at C.29.a.59.22.

   Objects of the Raid are :-
   (a) To continue a harassing policy, and prevent the Enemy from withdrawing Troops.
   (b) Killing and capturing as many of the Enemy as Possible.
   (c) Capturing and destroying War Material.
   (d) Obtaining identifications, and gaining information regarding the Enemy's system of defence.

3. ARTILLERY, VICKERS GUNS and TRENCH MORTAR SUPPORT.
   The Raid will have Artillery, M.T.M.B., L.T.M.B. and Vickers Gun Support - vide Appendix "A".
   The Battalion in the Line will act as Supports.

4. COMPOSITION OF RAIDING PARTY. The Raid will consist of 3 Officers and 100 Other Ranks, divided into three Attacking Parties, under the Command of 2nd Lt: C.T.Steward, and will be organised as follows :-

   THE ATTACKING PARTY ON THE RIGHT. - "PARKERS PARTY" - Lieut: Parker and 20 Other Ranks willenter CENTAUR TRENCH at C.29.a.42.17.
   1 N.C.O. and 6 men will work along the Trench to the Left for about 30 yards and establish a block, leaving 2 men on the Parapet to warn the Centre Attacking Party.
   1 N.C.O. and 2 men will work to the Left of the Strong Point suspected at about C.29.a.42.10.
   Lieut: Parker and the remainder of the Party (2 NCOs and 8 men) will work along to the right, sending 1 N.C.O. and 2 men to the right of the suspected Strong Post whilst Lieut: Parker, 1 N.CO and 6 men work further along the Trench and establish a block at C.29.a.43.05.

   THE CENTRE ATTACKING PARTY - "CLARKES PARTY". 2nd Lt: C.W.Clarke and 16 Other Ranks.
   2nd Lt: Clarke will remain outside the Enemy Trench to maintain communication with O.C.Raid.
   This Party will enter CENTAUR TRENCH at C.29.a.50.30. and will leave 2 men on the Parapet to warn the Left Attacking Party.
   The remainder of the Party (3 N.C.Os and 11 men) will work to the Right, sending 1 N.C.O. and 4 men down CENTAUR LANE to form a block at C.29.a.59.22., the rest (2 N.C.Os and 7 men) continuing along CENTAUR TRENCH until they reach

the two Parapet men left by the Right Attacking Party. If Enemy are not found or all are disposed of they will form a Parapet Party.

LEFT ATTACKING PARTY - "MOSELEY'S PARTY."
2nd Lt: O.V.Moseley and 31 Other Ranks.
"Moseley's Party" will enter CENTAUR TRENCH at C.29.a.32.41.
1 N.C.O. and 8 men will work to the left to clear suspected Strong Point and establish a block at about 50 yards.
1 N.C.O. and 6 men will work to the Right to clear Trench as far as "A" Co's Parapet men.
1 N.C.O. and 4 men will clear Travel Trench to the Left.
1 N.C.O. and 4 men will work down CENTAUR ROW clearing Dug-out on Right, then down C.T., clearing out suspected Dug-out at C.29.a.73.36.
If all is reported clear they will proceed to junction of Trench at C.29.a.79.30. and establish a block.
2nd Lt: Moseley, 1 N.C.O. and 6 men will follow this Party to search CENTAUR SUPPORT to C.29.a.68.12.

Each Party will be accompanied by 2 Scouts, 2 Bridgemen 3 Matmen and 2 Stretcher Bearers and in addition the Centre Party will have two Signallers and 2 Runners. These will form a covering Party for attacking Troops and will be the last to withdraw, bringing Bridges and Mats with them.

"B" Co: 2/6th K.L.R. will find a Lewis Gun Team as Covering Party at C.29.a.45.65.

5. TIME TABLE. 10.0 p.m. - Scouts will examine and report on Enemy's wire.
Zero - 20 mins - Parties will assemble. {C.28.b.96.34 to C.29.a.25.80. Positions marked by sign boards.
Zero - 10 mins - Parties will form up in N.M.L. in front of our Trenches.
Zero - 5 mins - Bridges will be laid across Stream.
Zero - 3 mins - Parties will be formed up across Stream, awaiting Barrage from C.29.a.46.65 - C.29.a.10.26.
Scouts will return to Stream, having laid tapes to Gaps.
Zero.......... Artillery Barrage.
Zero Plus 2 mins - Barrage lifts at rate of 100 yds a minute - vide Appendix "B"
Zero Plus 3 mins - Raiders enter Trench at C.29.a.42.17., C.29.a.50.30., and C.29.a.62.41.
Zero Plus 16 mins - "Moseley's Party" leaves CENTAUR SUPPORT.
Zero Plus 19 mins - "Clarke's Blocking Party" leaves CENTAUR LANE.
Zero plus 20 mins - "Moseley's Party" and "Clarke's Blocking Party" withdraw from Enemy Trenches.
Zero Plus 23 mins - All Parties withdraw from Enemy Trenches.

6. SIGNALS. "Moseley's Party" and "Blocking Party" at C.29.a.59.22 will rely on watches for time of return.
Signal for withdrawal - Green Very Light followed by Red, fired by O.C. Raid from Front Line.
To postpone Barrage 60 minutes a Rocket shewing White - Green - White will be sent up by O.C.Raid and from Bn: H.Q.

7. COMMUNICATIONS. Telephone to be laid from O.C.Raid, - C.29.a.15.57. to O.C. Covering Party and from O.C.Raid to Battalion Headquarters.

LIAISON OFFICER. A/286 Bty: will be with O.C.Raid and establish communication with O.C.Bty: and through him to the Howitzers.

O.C.Raid will send all reports to Battalion Headquarters.

8. RENDEZVOUS. Parties will return by same routes across N.M.L. In event of Hostile Barrage they will,

(a) take cover in N.M.L.
(b) do do under our own Parapet.

Enemy Barrage may be expected on LONDON ROAD - TRAMWAY and SPAIN AVENUE.

Parties will return by TIMARU - PANAMA and WESSEX AVE:

9. IDENTITY. All faces will be blacked.

All Papers or other marks of Identification will be removed.

All Ranks will wear a label tied to the second top button of the Jacket, bearing Regtl: No: Rank, Name and Religion only.

Check Station will be established in Front Line - C.29.a.20.10 - C.29.a.33.70 - C.28.b.90.42.
Labels will be collected at Junctions of Avenues and SUBSIDIARY LINE.
Labels of Stretcher Cases will be collected at A.D.S.

11. EQUIPMENT. Vide Appendix "C".

12. SYNCHRONISATION OF WATCHES. All Watches will be synchronised with the Brigade Headquarters at 9.0 a.m. and 7.0 p.m. and at Battalion Headquarters at Zero - 3 hours

In the event of any mistake IN TIME Artillery time will be taken.

13. CASUALTIES. ADVANCED DRESSING STATION - near junction of VANCOUVER and GLOUCESTER AVENUE.
Stretcher Cases will go via SOUTH AFRICA and PRETORIA - on cessation of Hostile Barrage via LONDON ROAD and TRAMWAY.
R.A.P. - TISSAGE DUMP.
Walking Cases via TIMARU - PANAMA and WESSEX AVE:. to Battalion Headquarters in the Line.

(sgd) C.E.Wurtzburg.
Captain and Adjutant, 2/6th (Rifle) Bn: Liverpool Regiment.

Copies to :-

No: 1 Retained.
2)
3) War Diary.
4. O.C.Raid.
5.)
6.) H.Q., 171st Inf: Bde:
7)
8. O.C.Left Group R.A.
9. O.C., 171st Bde: L.T.M.B.
10. O.C. 171st Bde: M.G.C.
11 & 12

7. COMMUNICATIONS. Telephone to be laid from O.C.Raid, - C.29.a.15.57. to O.C. Covering Party and from O.C.Raid to Battalion Headquarters.

LIAISON OFFICER. A/286 Bty: will be with O.C.Raid and establish communication with O.C.Bty: and through him to the Howitzers.

O.C.Raid will send all reports to Battalion Headquarters.

. RENDEZVOUS. In the event of heavy Enemy Barrage being put on N.M.L. during withdrawal, Raiders will take cover in N.M.L. untilmover.

If Barrage is put on C.T. cover must be taken in Front Line.

Immediately Raiders return to our Lines they will make their way via GLOUCESTER AVENUE to the Subsidiary Line, where they will be accommodated for the night.

9. IDENTITY. All faces will be blacked.

All Papers or other marks of Identification will be removed.

All Ranks will wear a label tied to the second top button of the Jacket, bearing Regtl: No: Rank, Name and Religion only.

2nd Lt: F.E.Evans will collect these Labels at C.28.b.35.80.

Labels of Stretcher Cases will be collected by Lieut: F.C.Bowring at junction of Tramway and Subsidiary Line.

. COUNTERSIGN. - will be arranged.

11. EQUIPMENT. Vide Appendix "C".

12. SYNCHRONISATION OF WATCHES. All Watches will be synchronised with the Brigade Headquarters at 9.0 a.m. and 7.0 p.m. and at Battalion Headquarters at Zero - 3 hours

In the event of any mistake IN TIME Artillery time will be taken.

. CASUALTIES. ADVANCED AID POST on LONDON ROAD - TRAMWAY C.28 d.80.60.

R.A.P. - TISSAGE DUMP - Walking cases via GLOUCESTER AVENUE.

Stretcher cases by Tramway.

. PRISONERS. Prisoners and all identifications to be sent to Battalion Headquarters in the Line.

(sgd) C.E.Wurtzburg.

Captain and Adjutant, 2/6th (Rifle) Bn: Liverpool Regiment.

Copies to :-

No: 1 Retained.
2)
3) War Diary.
4. O.C.Raid.
5.)
6.) H.Q., 171st Inf: Bde:
7)
8. O.C.Left Group R.A.
9. O.C., 171st Bde: L.T.M.B.
10. O.C. 171st Bde: M.G.C.
11. [illegible]

APPENDIX "A"
ARTILLERY.

CANCEL PARAGRAPHS 1, 2 and 3. and SUBSTITUTE :-

1. ARTILLERY. 18 PDRS: 6 Guns A/286 Bde: R.F.A.
4 Guns 376th Bty: A.F.A.
2 Guns 376th Bty: A.F.A.
2 Guns B/286th Bde: R.F.A.
Commanded by MAJOR W.H.BROOKES M.C.,

From Zero to Zero, plus 2 mins. a preliminary bombardment on Enemy Front Line Trench from C.29.c.43.00. to 70.50., then 1 creeping lift at 100 yards per minute to a cross-country barrage :-

A/286 Bde: R.F.A.	Enemy Front Line Trench C.29.c.55.70 to Trench Junction C.29.c.77.97.
376th Bty: A.F.A.	Trench Junction C.29.a.89.47 to Front Line Trench C.29.a.75.60.
½ Section 376 Bty: A.F.A.	) Trench Junction C.29.a.
1 Section B/286 Bde: R.F.A.	) 95.25 to Trench Junction C.29.a.89.47.

where this barrage is to remain until the end of the operation.

1 Section C/286 Bde: R.F.A. will barrage CENTAUR SWITCH from C.29.c.77.97. to C.29.a.98.25 from Zero to end of Operation.

4.5." HOWS: 2 Hows D/286 Bde: R.F.A. will barrage from Zero to end of Operation, Trench Junction C.29.b.10.80., C.29.d.05.55.
A third Howitzer of D/286 Bde: R.F.A. will neutralise Trench Mortar Emplacement at C.29.c.65.88 from Zero to Zero plus 2 minutes.
At Zero plus 2 minutes this Howitzer will lift to Trench Junction C.29.c.85.70. and remain there until the end of Operations.

2. RATES OF FIRE.

	18 PDRS:
Zero to plus 2 mins.	6 rounds per gun per minute, Shrapnel only.
Plus 2 mins to plus 5 mins.	3 rounds per Gun per min., Shrapnel and H.E.
Plus 5 mins to end of Operation.	2 rounds per Gun per min. Shrapnel and H.E.
	4.5" HOWS:
Zero to plus 2 mins.	2 rounds per How. per minute
Plus 2 minutes to end of Operation.	1 round per How per minute

3. TRENCH MORTARS. "Z" Medium Trench Mortar Bty: will cooperate in the operation by :-
(1) 1 Mortar neutralise Machine Gun at C.23.c.80.65.
(2) 1 Mortar barrage Trench Junction C.29.a.99.75.
Rate of fire - 1 round per Mortar per 2 minutes, from Zero to end of Operation.
"Z" Trench Mortar Bty: will know the end of the Operations by cessation of Artillery barrage.

APPENDIX "A" (cont.)

4. L.T.M.B. CANCEL PARAGRAPH UNDER HEADING "TARGETS" and SUBSTITUTE.

TARGETS.

No: 1 Gun. C.29.a.50.75.
No: 2 Gun. C.29.a.80.70.
No: 3 Gun. C.23.c.90.02.

VIDE MAP ATTACHED.

CANCEL PARAGRAPH UNDER HEADING " TIME TABLE" and substitute :-

TIME TABLE.

Zero. No: 3 rapid barrage.
Zero plus 5. Nos: 1 + 2 slow barrage.
Zero plus 31. Nos: 1,2 and 3 - rapid barrage until end of Operation.

DIVERSION. 3 Guns will bombard INANE TRENCH from Zero until end of Operations.
No: 1 Gun. I.5.d.30.70.
Nos: 2 & 3 Guns. I.5.d.00.50.

5. VICKERS GUNS.

Position.	Target.
(a) 2 Guns. C.23.c.20.00.	From C.23.c.80.70. To C.29.a.75.75.

5. VICKERS GUNS. - Paragraph (a) for :-

1 Gun. C.29.c.12.75.	From C.29.c.99.20. To C.29.c.40.90.
read :-	
1 Gun C.29.c.12.75.	From C.29.c.99.20. To C.29.c.43.80.

Paragraph (b) cancel :-

1 Gun I.9.b.10.10.	CENTRAL SUPPORT - C.29.c.90.2. To C.29.d.40.10.
	C.29.d.27.82.
1 Gun C.28.c.65.85.	4 HALLOTS FARM - C.23.d.22.70.
1 Gun. C.23.c.75.20.	Junction of trenches at C.29.b.8032.
1 Gun. C.22.a.70.25.	Junction of Trenches at C.29.b.39.30.

TIME TABLE. All Guns open at ZERO plus 4 minutes. Should hostile M.G. Fire commence before that time Guns detailed in (a) above will commence firing at once.

All Guns will cease fire with Artillery.

APPENDIX "A" (cont.)

T.M.B. - TARGETS.

No: 1 Gun.	C.29.a.72.50. juntion CENTAUR and CENSUS TRENCHES.
No: 2 Gun.	C.29.c.50.75. CENTAUR TRENCH.
No: 3 Gun.	C.29.a.95.25 juntion CENTAUR ROW and CENTAUR SWITCH.

VIDE MAP ATTACHED.

TIME TABLE.

Zero plus 5.	Nos: 1 and 2 Guns slow Barrage.
Zero plus 16.	No: 3 Gun slow Barrage.
Zero Plus 21.	Nos: 1.2 and 3 rapid Barrage until the end of Operation.

DIVERSION. 3 Guns will bombard INANE TRENCH from Zero until end of Operations.

No: 1 Gun. I.5.d.30.70.
Nos: 2 & 3 Guns. I.5.d.00.50.

5. VICKERS GUNS.

Position.		Target.
(a) 2 Guns.	C.23.c.20.00.	From C.23.c.80.70. To C.29.a.75.75.
1 Gun.	C.29.c.13.75.	From C.29.c.99.20. To C.29.c.40.90.
(b) 1 Gun.	I.9.b.10.10.	Central Support - C.29.c.90.75. To. C.29.d.40.10.
1 Gun,	I.9.b.3.7.	Track C.29.c.90.75. - C.29.b.40.30.
1 Gun.	I.3.d.36.52.	Search Track C.29.b.20.10 - C.29.b.40.30.
1 Gun	I.4.a.53.80.	Barrage CENTRAL AVENUE at C.29.d.27.82.
1 Gun	C.28.c.65.85.	4 HALLOTS FARM - C.23.d.22.70.
1 Gun.	C.22.c.75.20.	Junction of trenches at C.29.b.8032.
1 Gun.	C.22.a.70.25.	Junction of Trenches at C.29.b.39.30.

TIME TABLE. All Guns open at ZERO plus 4 minutes. Should hostile M.G.Fire commence before that time Guns detailed in (a) above will commence firing at once.

All Guns will cease fire with Artillery.

APPENDIX "B"

PARKER'S PARTY.

2 Scouts.
2 Bridgemen.
3 Matmen.

"A" Party.	
1 Officer and 10 O.R..	1 Officer.
	3 Bayonet men.
	2 Bombers.
	1 Rifle Grenadier.
Right Strong Point clearing Party.	(2 Bayonet men and 1 Bomber.
	(1 Bomber.
"B" Party.	
2 N.C.Os and 8 men.	2 Bayonet men.
	1 Bomber.
	1 Rifle Grenadier.
	1 Carrier.
	2 Parapet men.
Left Strong Point clearing Party.	(2 Bayonet men.
	(1 Bomber.

2 Stretcher Bearers.

....

CLARKE'S PARTY.

2 Scouts.
2 Bridgemen.
3 Matmen.

"A" - Main Assault Party.	
1 N.C.O. and 8 men.	2 Bayonet men.
	1 Bomber.
	1 Carrier.
	1 N.C.O.
	1 Bomber.
	1 Carrier.
	1 Spare Man.
	1 Rifle Grenadier.
"B" .C.T.Block.	
1 N.C.O. and 6 men.	2 Bayonet men.
	1 Bomber.
	1 Carrier.
	1 N.C.O.
	2 Parapet men.

1 Officer.
2 Signallers.
2 Runners.
2 Stretcher Bearers.

....

MOSELEY'S PARTY.

2 Scouts.
2 Bridgemen.
3 Matmen.

"A" Party.	
1 N.C.O. and 6 men.	3 Bombers.
	1 Rifle Grenadier.
	2 Bayonet men.
	1 N.C.O.

P.T.O.

<u>"B" Party.</u>
<u>1 N.C.O. and 6 men.</u>

2 Bombers.
1 Rifle Grenadier.
3 Bayonet men.
1 N.C.O.

<u>"C" Party.</u>
<u>1 N.C.O. and 4 men.</u>

1 Bomber.
1 Rifle Grenadier.
2 Bayonet men.
1 N.C.O.

<u>"D" Party.</u>
<u>1 N.C.O. and 4 men.</u>

1 Bomber.
1 Rifle Grenadier.
2 Bayonet men.
1 N.C.O.

<u>"E" Party.</u>
<u>1 Officer and 6 O.R.</u>

1 Officer.
2 Bombers.
1 Rifle Grenadier.
3 Bayonet men.
1 N.C.O.

2 Stretcher Bearers.

....

APPENDIX "G"

EQUIPMENT.

All Ranks will wear plain suits and trousers, puttees, steel waistcoats, shrapnel collar, steel helmet, box respirator and canvas tally label. In addition they will carry respectively :-

	Revolvers	.45 Amm.	Watch	Torch	Knob Kerries	Rifle & Bayonet	S.A.A.	Bombs	Bomb Carrier	Rifle Grenades	Cup Discharger	Blank Ammun.	Wire Cutters	Gloves	Wire Breakers	Telephone	Cable
Officers.	1.	24	1.	1.	1.			2									
N.C.Os.			1.	1.		1.	50	4							1.		
Scouts.	1.	24.	1.					2					1	1.			
Bridgemen.	1	24						4					1.				
Matmen.	1.	24.						4.					1				
Signallers.	1.	24		1.				4.								1.	350x
Runners.						1.	50	4							1.		
Bombers.					1.			10									
Carriers.						1.	50	12	1.						1.		
Rifle Grenadiers.						1.	50			10	1	20			1.		
Bayonet men.				1.		1.	50								1.		
Stretcher Bearers.	1	24						4									
Parapet men.						1.	50	6							1		

****

SECRET. COPY NO. 11

SPECIAL INSTRUCTIONS for S.O.S.,

- Night of 21st/22nd June, 1917 -

....

1. From 12.00 midnight on the 21st/22nd June 1917, until completion of Raid, i.e., when Artillery have been notified "FINISHED", the S.O.S. will only be acknowledged by request on telephone, or by written message.

2. O.C., 2/6th Liverpool Regiment will be responsible for notifying Units in the Line that Operations are completed.

ACKNOWLEDGE.

J.O. Huntley

2nd Lieut. Acting
Brigade Major.
171st Infantry Brigade.

ISSUED AT 9 p.m., 20.6.1917, to :-

Copy No. 1. B.G.C.,
2. Brigade Major.
3. 57th Division.
4. Left Group Artillery Commander.
5. 2/6th K.L.R.,
6. 57th Divisional Artillery.
7. 2/5th K.L.R.,
8. 2/7th ,,
9. 2/8th ,,
10. O.C. Raid.
11. 171st L.T.M.B.
12. 171st M.G.Coy.
13. 173rd ,,
14. War Diary.
15. ,,
16. File.

<u>SUBJECT:</u> <u>War Diaries</u>.

57th (W. Lancs.) Division
SECRET
No. 6 66
Date 15 8 17

D.A.G.,

3rd Echelon.

War Diary for 171st Infantry Brigade L.T.M.Battery for month of July is forwarded.

D.H.Q.
15/8/1917.

Major-General.
Commanding 57th Division.

57

HQ 171 Infy Bde
App to Vol 6
July 17

WAR DIARY

Vol. 6.

July 1917.

171st BRIGADE, LIGHT TRENCH MORTAR BATTERY.

MAP REFERENCES
① FRANCE. Sheet 36 N W 1/20,000 Edition 6c.
② TRENCH MAP. HOUPLINES. 36 NW 2 and NE 1, parts of. 1/10,000 Edition 7a.
③ BOIS GRENIER - 36 NW 4. 1/10,000. Edition 6d.

Instructions regarding War Diaries and Intelligence Summaries are contained in F. S. Regs., Part II. and the Staff Manual respectively. Title pages will be prepared in manuscript.

WAR DIARY
or
INTELLIGENCE SUMMARY.
(Erase heading not required.)

VOLUME 6.

Army Form C. 2118.

Sheet 1.

Place	Date 1917	Hour	Summary of Events and Information	Remarks and references to Appendices
ARMENTIÈRES (C 25 c 55-45)	July 1st.	am. 1-30 2-30	Enemy artillery shelled the town with high velocity gun (prob 5.9" calibre), several shells falling in vicinity of Billet (the usual damage to houses - no military damage)	
		2-10	Under cover of an artillery barrage, an enemy raiding party of about 40 (in three separate parties) succeeded in obtaining a momentary footing in our lines (L'EPINETTE Sub-sector). Encounter took place between these men & our posts, who without further assistance drove them out, leaving 1 badly wounded prisoner in our hands.	
		2-20	In response to S.O.S. our Nos 3 & 4 guns (EPINETTE) and No 5 gun (HOUPLINES) fired over 200 rounds in front of raided sector. No 4 gun-team sustained two Casualties:- Pte TAYLOR R.W. and 306363 Pte TOBIN J. both wounded. Pte TAYLOR, who was in charge (latter badly wounded in throat & neck) refused attention and ordered his team to continue firing. Pte TOBIN, who was wounded in 6 places, carried on firing, until no longer able to. He then went to HQ. with report, leaving the No 3 (Pte GORMAN) in charge. The next day (2nd) Pte TAYLOR died of wounds. re Pte TOBIN, who was awarded the Military Medal, the following is republished from Divisional orders "No 306363, Pte JACK TOBIN, (2/8 KLR) & 171st Bde L.T.M.B. - At ___ on the night of 30th June/1st July 1917 this man displayed great gallantry and initiative during the raid by the enemy. After his No 1 had been wounded and he himself had been wounded in 3 places in the arm and 3 places in the leg he continued firing his gun onto the front of the raided sector. When the ammunition had been expended he went to report and to get Stretcher bearers, leaving the unwounded man of the team to attend to his No 1. During the raid 105	

A5834 Wt. W4973 M687 750,000 8/16 D. D. & L. Ltd. Forms/C.2118/13.

Army Form C. 2118.

WAR DIARY
or
INTELLIGENCE SUMMARY.
(Erase heading not required.)

Sheet 2.

Instructions regarding War Diaries and Intelligence Summaries are contained in F. S. Regs., Part II. and the Staff Manual respectively. Title pages will be prepared in manuscript.

Place	Date	Hour	Summary of Events and Information	Remarks and references to Appendices
ARMENTIERES	1/7/17		---- rounds were fired from the gun into the front of the raided sector". The G.O.C. 57th Division congratulates the above named on the receipt of the award for his gallantry. (Div. Routine Order 1036 of 1/7/17)	
"	"	–	EPINETTE – during the day 60 rounds were fired on enemy front and support lines, drawing some 30 HE (77mm) in retaliation.	
"	"	am 6.0	HOUPLINES – 20 rounds fired on CENTAUR TR. at C29a 40.20 drew 18, 4.2's and 14 5.9's in retaliation. 20 rounds from another gun drew only 6 pineapples.	
"	"	–	Enemy planes active – flying low over EPINETTE sector inspecting damage caused by enemy barrage during raid. Visibility – indifferent.	
	2/7/17	–	During day 100 rounds on various targets in EPINETTE sector, retaliation normal. 50 rounds during day from HOUPLINES Sector – retaliation – pineapples only.	
	"	–	Artillery – our guns heavily shelled PERENCHIES and also did useful counter-battery work. – Quiet on enemy trench system.	
	"	–	Artillery – enemy. not so active on trenches, but back areas heavily shelled (ARMENTIERES, + HOUPLINES)	
			Aircraft – two of our planes engaged an enemy plane over FRELINGHEIN and brought it down in enemy lines (C.18). Enemy aircraft very active flying high over the town and low over our trenches in both sectors.	
"	"	pm 10.30	3 bombs dropped on the town – no material damage.	

Instructions regarding War Diaries and Intelligence Summaries are contained in F. S. Regs., Part II. and the Staff Manual respectively. Title pages will be prepared in manuscript.

WAR DIARY
or
INTELLIGENCE SUMMARY.
(Erase heading not required.)

Army Form C. 2118.

Sheet 3.

Place	Date	Hour	Summary of Events and Information	Remarks and references to Appendices
ARMENTIÈRES	3/7/17	–	Two Copies (NOS. 540, 541) of BAB Trench Code No 3 received from HQrs 171st Brigade	
		–	During the day, 80 rounds expended from EPINETTE Sector – retaliation normal, (some 70 rounds of 77mm (HE)	
			50 rounds from HOUPLINES Sector – much damage to enemy trench at C29c 8050	
		am 3.30	One other rank wounded, in retaliation to our shoot.	
		pm 2.0	do — sent to First Army Rest Camp.	
			Artillery – no unusual activity on our part. Enemy continued his activity on our trench system in HOUPLINES Sector, also on back areas, doing an appreciable amount of damage in the town.	
		–	Aircraft. our planes more active. ~~[illegible]~~ flying over enemy trenches. At	
		11.50 am	forced an enemy plane to retire in direction of QUESNOY. Continued enemy activity – planes flying low over our trenches and also over the town.	
	4/7/17	–	During the day, 70 rounds fired from EPINETTE Sector – retaliation heavier. Enemy 77mm (HE) 6 minenwerfers and 6 [illegible]	
			[illegible] C29a 45.25 (CENTAUR TRENCH)	
		–	96 rounds from HOUPLINES Sector (30 on to enemy [illegible] front line) retaliation slight, only 50 HE over gun pits and front line.	
		pm 6.30	One extra copy (NO. 542) of BAB Trench Code No 3. recd	
		–	Artillery – our normal activity against enemy trench system in both sectors. Enemy more active than usual on EPINETTE trenches – front line and supports being heavily shelled by HE (4.2") at I5a. Back areas again heavily shelled (ARMENTIÈRES and HOUPLINES in particular.)	
			Aircraft – quiet owing to very low visibility.	

A5834 Wt. W4973 M687 750,000 8/16 D. D. & L. Ltd. Forms/C.2118/13.

Instructions regarding War Diaries and Intelligence Summaries are contained in F. S. Regs., Part II. and the Staff Manual respectively. Title pages will be prepared in manuscript.

WAR DIARY
or
INTELLIGENCE SUMMARY.
(Erase heading not required.)

Army Form C. 2118.

Sheet 4.

Place	Date	Hour	Summary of Events and Information	Remarks and references to Appendices
ARMENTIÈRES	5/7/17	-	Information rec'd from base ~~that~~ 265912 Cpl BENTLEY was transferred to ENGLAND, Wounded on 23-VI-17 and is struck off strength accordingly.	
		-	241112 LeCpl (unpd) TERRY A.N. promoted paid Corporal as from 23-VI-17 to fill a vacancy.	
		-	During day 80 rounds fired from EPINETTE Sector. Retaliation, about 20 "minnies" silenced by our 18 pounders.	
			HOUPLINES Sector 25 rounds on to CENTAUR TR. at C.29.a 40.20 drew 4 HE and 12 "whizz-bangs". 30 rounds from retaliation gun drew no reply from the enemy.	
		-	Artillery - Usual trench activity on our part. Enemy considerably more active on our trench systems and also on back areas.	
		-	Aircraft - More activity on our part and less activity on enemy's. Enemy observation balloons up during day.	
	5/7/17	5.0 pm	Both trench parties relieved. 2/Lt JARDINE relieved Lt PYBUS in HOUPLINES	
	6/7/17	-	During day 90 rounds were fired from EPINETTE in conjunction with Heavy and Medium trench mortars. Considerable damage done to enemy parapets & trench Revetting thrown in the air.	
		-	90 rounds on various targets from HOUPLINES Sector - Retaliation very slight. Artillery - Co-operated with our Heavy, Medium & Light T.M. Btys. Enemy quiet until roused by our T.M. fire, when he retaliated with about 250, 4.2" and 5.9"s on our EPINETTE trenches.	

A5834 Wt. W4973 M687 750,000 8/16 D. D. & L. Ltd. Forms/C.2118/13.

Army Form C. 2118.

Instructions regarding War Diaries and Intelligence Summaries are contained in F. S. Regs., Part II. and the Staff Manual respectively. Title pages will be prepared in manuscript.

WAR DIARY
or
INTELLIGENCE SUMMARY.
(Erase heading not required.)

Sheet 5

Place	Date	Hour	Summary of Events and Information	Remarks and references to Appendices
ARMENTIÈRES	6/7/17	(Cont'd)	Enemy minenwerfers active on both sectors, firing about 100 rounds (heavy). Granatenwerfer fired 100 rounds from LE 4 HALLOTS FARM (C 23 d) on K front line trench about C 23 a 45.70. Many fell short of our line. Aircraft – renewed activity on both sides. About 10.30 am an enemy machine appeared to be forced down at (D 1 d) Back areas again heavily shelled and especially the South & South West parts of the town where shells of all calibres up to 11 inches fell, doing considerable damage to the Civilian population.	
	7-7-17	–	During day, about 50 rounds on various targets (EPINETTE) do – 108 – (HOUPLINES sector) – including 20 rounds at 6.0 am on enemy support line (CELIA. C 1 a 80.30) Result – much damage to track also one Bosche seen in the air. (blown up) Artillery – in retaliation to enemy, our guns fired 150 rounds (18 prs & 4.5 Hows) on to CELIA SUPPORT in C 1 a. Enemy very active especially with his whizzbang batteries. Continued shelling of our back areas (HOUPLINES) during early evening and the town during the night (very heavy about 2-30 am (8/7/17) Aircraft – normal activity – Visibility low during the morning, clearing up late afternoon.	
	8/7/17	–	HOUPLINES – no guns in action, day spent in preparing emp^ts. EPINETTE – 100 rounds fired during the day, 50 in cooperation with the [illegible]. The enemy artillery replying vigorously to this sheet with 30 b40 – 5.9" and about 12 minenwerfers behind the MUSHROOM	

A5834 Wt. W4973 M687 750,000 8/16 D. D. & L. Ltd. Forms/C.2118/13.

Instructions regarding War Diaries and Intelligence Summaries are contained in F. S. Regs., Part II. and the Staff Manual respectively. Title pages will be prepared in manuscript.

WAR DIARY
or
INTELLIGENCE SUMMARY.
(*Erase heading not required.*)

Army Form C. 2118.

Sheet 6

Place	Date	Hour	Summary of Events and Information	Remarks and references to Appendices
ARMENTIÈRES	8.7.17	(Contd)	Enemy artillery activity chiefly directed against our trenches. The support line in C.8.d. was shelled by 12.5.9s and 25 4.2s and numerous whizzbangs. Aircraft – very little activity – visibility – very poor. Apart from artillery activity – a quiet day. The quietest day for over a month in ARMENTIÈRES.	
	9.7.17		EPINETTE – guns fired about 90 rounds with good results & received some 6 whizzbangs & 16 HE in retaliation HOUPLINES – do 208 ✓. Retaliation to all shoots amounted to over 630 whizzbangs, some heavy minenwerfers and some light minenwerfers. Artillery Our guns more active. About 4.30 pm. some 200 rounds on CENTAUR (C29a) by our 18 pounders. CELIA and CELL also shelled. Between 5 & 6.30 pm – over 200 on INANE support (I5d) and CENTRAL (C29c) Enemy – generally quiet on EPINETTE trenches, but very active in retaliation to our HOUPLINES shoots Aircraft – inactive. Visibility bad. Observation consequently difficult.	
	10.7.17	am. 1-30	Gas was released from Cylinders and projectors were fired from various points of our front. The enemy sounded horns and gongs, bombed his own wire, opened rapid rifle and M.G. fire, but did not send up any unusual number of Very lights.	
		am. 9.0	11 copies of BAB Code No 2 (Nos 11668/69/70/71) returned to Brigade Hqrs.	
		noon	HOUPLINES – 40 rounds on to CENTAUR TR. and SUPPORT in C29c with good results. Retaliation 15 H.E. and 1 minenwerfer on ORCHARD (C28d). Our artillery cooperated by firing 15 rounds (4.5" Howitzer) and 30 – 18 pounders.	

A5834 Wt. W4973 M687 750,000 8/16 D. D. & L. Ltd. Forms/C.2118/13.

Instructions regarding War Diaries and Intelligence Summaries are contained in F. S. Regs., Part II. and the Staff Manual respectively. Title pages will be prepared in manuscript.

WAR DIARY
or
INTELLIGENCE SUMMARY.
(Erase heading not required.)

Army Form C. 2118.

Sheet 7.

Place	Date	Hour	Summary of Events and Information	Remarks and references to Appendices
ARMENTIÈRES	10/7/17	–	Epinette – during the day, 30 rounds were fired on INCLEMSE TRENCH (in I 17 a)	
"	"	–	Artillery – our "4.5" Howitzers fired on C 18 a 48.98 & neutralized a "minenwerfer" reported to be firing from that spot.	
			Enemy artillery less active on back areas, but more aggressive on trench system. The shelling of the town and of HOUPLINES was less, being confined to areas around battery positions.	
"	11/7/17	am 3-45	The four guns of EPINETTE Sector fired 120 rounds on various targets in enemy front line and communication, with good results. Retaliation – NIL.	
		pm 8.0	Epinette – another 24 rounds fired – Target, screens at I. 5. b. 3.8.	
		–	HOUPLINES – active – about 120 rounds fired on various targets with very satisfactory results. Retaliation in all, nearly 200 H.E.s (chiefly 4.2" and 77 mm)	
		–	Artillery – enemy very active against our trench system of the left subsector (HOUPLINES) especially C 17 a & c. C 16 d C 23 b and C 22 a. Fire of a destructive nature and distributed fairly evenly over this sector. Normal aerial activity. Visibility high.	
	12/7/17	–	Epinette – usual activity – 90 rounds on various targets (INANE – I 5 c. 75 20) where hurdles have been put up – front line at I. 11. a. 3.1 – also fired upon)	
			HOUPLINES – no guns in action. Enemy continues to be active with his heavy minenwerfer against the left company sector and an offensive [illegible] in loc. 16 (C 17 c 35.90) Enemy ground has been over the front line [illegible] 50 to 100 yards.	

Army Form C. 2118.

WAR DIARY
or
INTELLIGENCE SUMMARY.
(Erase heading not required.)

Instructions regarding War Diaries and Intelligence Summaries are contained in F. S. Regs., Part II. and the Staff Manual respectively. Title pages will be prepared in manuscript.

Sheet 8

Place	Date	Hour	Summary of Events and Information	Remarks and references to Appendices
ARMENTIÈRES	12/7/17	–	Aircraft – an enemy plane was brought down intact by one of our machines (in B.24.d central). Pilot was wounded and the Observer (unhurt) surrendered to 2 men of the 7/5th K.L.R. who had previously been signalled to by our aeroplanes.	
	13/7/17	am 3.30	EPINETTE – All guns in action, firing 100 rounds on INTENSE AV. (I.1.a) INANE ALLEY (I.1.a) and suspected movement in INCARNATE and INANE Trenches (I.1.c). No retaliation to this shoot at the time, but usual artillery activity throughout the day, several shells falling near our gun positions.	
		pm 3.0	HOUPLINES – One gun in action to attempt to draw fire from 'minnie' suspected at DEBRIS FM (C.17.d). Artillery (4.5" Hows) stood by to fire on 'minnie' if required, but enemy did not open fire. One gun in action against CENTRAL TR. (C.29.c) drew fire from minnie located as at C.29.b.10.00. Aircraft – enemy dropped bombs on the town, doing no damage except the wounding of one civilian horse.	
	13/7/17	pm 5.30	Both our trench parties relieved – HOUPLINES by Lt Leonard and Lt O'Rourke, EPINETTE by Lt Jones and 13 – do	
	14/7/17	–	Epinette – 65 rounds fired (30 in conjunction with Medium T.Ms. – on target, INCARNATE I.1.a)	
		–	HOUPLINES – CENTRAL TR (C.29.a.9.3) and suspected T.M. Emplacement at C.29.b.30.65 fired upon. Several direct hits on trench, but owing to difficult observation, it is not certain whether the target was hit.	

A5834 Wt. W4973 M687 750,000 8/16 D. D. & L. Ltd. Forms/C.2118/13.

Instructions regarding War Diaries and Intelligence Summaries are contained in F. S. Regs., Part II. and the Staff Manual respectively. Title pages will be prepared in manuscript.

WAR DIARY
or
INTELLIGENCE SUMMARY.
(Erase heading not required.)

Army Form C. 2118.

Sheet 9.

Place	Date	Hour	Summary of Events and Information	Remarks and references to Appendices
ARMENTIERES	14th July 17	7.06 10.30	Artillery – hostile batteries (5.9s" and 4.2s") firing with aeroplane observation, shelled the town, shells falling at 3 second intervals. HOUPLINES was shelled at the same time. In the line his activity on our extreme left (HOBBS FARM (C 23 a) to the River LYS (C 16 b) was very marked – method adopted being intense intermittent fire, four barrages being placed on our front and support line (C 17 a. and c). Considerable damage was done to our trenches. These barrages may be due to enemy nervousness and apprehension of offensive action on this front, for he made no attempt to follow these barrages with an infantry assault	
"	15/7/17	– noon	Capt H.E. BARROW proceeded on leave. Operation Order No 18 (71st Inf Bde) – re para 6. Scheme for support by 71st Light T.M.B. forwarded to Headquarters, 71st Brigade. (see Appendix 1 attached)	Appendix 1
"	"	"	Epinette. – during the day several targets were engaged – breach made in parapet of INCH (I 11 ?) – recent repairs to INANE and INCANDESCENT fired on & smashed down again. 80 rounds fired.	Maps as referred to in order
			Houplines. – 60 rounds fired on to enemy front line at C 29 c. 60 70 and a Trench Mortar Emplacement at C 23 d. 10 30.	
			Artillery – hostile batteries again active on our HOUPLINES trenches, doing considerable damage to communication trenches, (CAMBRIDGE and IRISH Avenues)	

A5834 Wt. W4973 M687 750,000 8/16 D. D. & L. Ltd. Forms/C.2118/13.

Army Form C. 2118.

WAR DIARY
or
INTELLIGENCE SUMMARY.
(Erase heading not required.)

Instructions regarding War Diaries and Intelligence Summaries are contained in F. S. Regs., Part II. and the Staff Manual respectively. Title pages will be prepared in manuscript.

Sheet 10.

Place	Date	Hour	Summary of Events and Information	Remarks and references to Appendices
ARMENTIÈRES	16/7/17	am 2-10	HOUPLINES. The enemy, under cover of a very heavy barrage, attempted a raid on our trenches (C.17.a & c). This was vigorously repulsed and the enemy retired leaving 3 prisoners. The prisoners are unintelligent of low morale and surrendered willingly. Raiding party composed of Regimental STORMTRUPP of the 11th Res. Bavarian Inf. Regt. One of our S.O.S. guns was blown up by direct hits and the team (3 other ranks killed) the other gun was damaged - barrel pierced by shell pieces. Number of rounds fired by S.O.S. gun unknown. The pit and ammunition dump both blown up.	
		am 6-0	40 rounds fired on to enemy communication trench (CENTRAL AV. C.29.d.40.85) Several direct hits into trench throwing up earth and duckboards. NO retaliation.	
			EPINETTE - 65 rounds on enemy front line (INCH (I.16.b) and INCANDESCENT (I.5.c))	
		-	Artillery - moderately active and always confined to our left sector trenches (C.17 a and c and C.16.d) The town and HOUPLINES were again shelled	
	17/7/17	pm 5.0	Lieut BURFIELD relieved Lieut SMALLPAGE in EPINETTE Sector	
		-	EPINETTE - INCH TRENCH (I.16.d) and INCARNATE (I.16.c) were again fired on, 50 rounds being expended. Enemy did not retaliate.	
			HOUPLINES - 50 rounds fired on to CENTRAL TRENCH (C.29.d.10.99) and CONCRETE HOUSE (C.22.c.99.80) Enemy retaliated with a few (about 15) H.E.s doing no damage.	
		-	Artillery - hostile battery engaged one of our Field Batteries in the town (C.25.b). Considerable material damage was done. Later he searched for our heavy guns with a high velocity gun (5.9 inch) but without success.	

A5834 Wt. W4973 M687 750,000 8/16 D. D. & L. Ltd. Forms/C.2118/13.

Army Form C. 2118.

WAR DIARY
or
INTELLIGENCE SUMMARY.
(Erase heading not required.)

Instructions regarding War Diaries and Intelligence Summaries are contained in F. S. Regs., Part II. and the Staff Manual respectively. Title pages will be prepared in manuscript.

Sheet 11

Place	Date	Hour	Summary of Events and Information	Remarks and references to Appendices
ARMENTIÈRES	18/7/17	–	EPINETTE. 60 rounds fired during the day on various targets, to which the enemy replied with a few "whizzbangs" (77 mm).	
			HOUPLINES. 45 rounds fired on enemy support line (C 29 d 20.40) doing some damage, (several direct hits). Enemy replied with 9 small HE. (77 mm)	
			Our trench headquarters of the left sector (FUSILIER Av. C 16 d 10.10) has been heavily shelled lately. During enemy raid on night of 17/18th, the ammunition dump and cork house were both blown up. Repair work is being carried out and a temporary dump made further along the trench. Enemy continues to shell intermittently and occasionally register a direct hit.	
	19/7/17	–	EPINETTE. 60 rounds expended, chiefly on INCH TRENCH and support line (about I 6 b 7.4) and INCANDESCENT TRENCH and support line (about I 11 a 60.65). No retaliation received.	
			HOUPLINES. 40 rounds fired on to CENTRAL SUPPORT line (C 29 c 2.3). Several hits along trench. Enemy replied with 35 HE (4.2" field gun). One shot landing just in front of gun, no damage done.	
	20/7/17		EPINETTE. 80 rounds expended on INCH TR. at I 17 a 1.5. Enemy replied with "minnewerfers" in CHARDS FARM sector.	
			One gun in this sector was damaged by a premature burst, the shell exploding at the muzzle of the gun killing the No 1 of the team and wounding the No 2. All precautions re preparation	

Army Form C. 2118.

Instructions regarding War Diaries and Intelligence Summaries are contained in F. S. Regs., Part II. and the Staff Manual respectively. Title pages will be prepared in manuscript.

WAR DIARY
or
INTELLIGENCE SUMMARY.

(Erase heading not required.)

Sheet 12

Place	Date	Hour	Summary of Events and Information	Remarks and references to Appendices
ARMENTIERES	20/7/17	–	– – – of ammunition and care of gun had been taken and the explanation of the accident is difficult. Possibly the abnormal pressure caused by using Green cartridge and 3 ballastite rings may have burst the "base plate" of the shell, giving the propellant flash access to the explosive in the shell. The Gun team concerned were trained and very capable gunners and no blame can attach to them.	
		–	HOUPLINES. 45 rounds on enemy's front line (C 29 c 60.60 and C 23 c 90.50) doing some considerable damage to the trench. Enemy replied with 70 77mm H.E. shells and 3 minenwerfers. The majority of enemy shells were well over our line and did no damage whatever.	
	21/7/17	–	EPINETTE – 30 rounds fired on INCH SUPPORT at about I 6 b 4.9.5 with good result. Retaliation nil	
	–	–	HOUPLINES – 60 rounds on enemy front line at C 29 a 20.25 and C 29 a 90.95. Enemy replied with 40 small H.E. shells on our front line and communication trenches (LONDON ROAD and TRAMWAY – C 28 d) Enemy artillery again active in vicinity of our left trench 4.9.5 (C 16 d)	
	22/7/17	5.30 Am	Both trench parties relieved. 3 other ranks sent to XI Corps School of Mortars for Course.	

A5834 Wt. W4973 M687 750,000 8/16 D. D. & L. Ltd. Forms/C.2118/13.

Instructions regarding War Diaries and Intelligence Summaries are contained in F. S. Regs., Part II. and the Staff Manual respectively. Title pages will be prepared in manuscript.

WAR DIARY
or
INTELLIGENCE SUMMARY.
(Erase heading not required.)

Army Form C. 2118.

Sheet 13

Place	Date	Hour	Summary of Events and Information	Remarks and references to Appendices
ARMENTIERES	22/7/17	–	EPINETTE – 50 rounds fired on INCH and INCARNATE (I 7 a 1.5 and I 11 a 40.70). Good results. Enemy replied with "pineapples" and many 77 mms (HE)	
			HOUPLINES. Enemy aircraft very active all day over the trenches of this Sector	
✓	✓		Artillery – The town again heavily shelled, and the last two days guns of heavy calibre (11 inch rover) have been employed. Targets in the town are chiefly the billeting areas. Much damage caused to civilians and property.	
✓	23/7/17	–	1 other rank wounded (slightly gassed) in EPINETTE Sector.	
			EPINETTE. 30 rounds on INCH (traversed from I 7 a 10.55 to I 7 a 00.30)	
			30 " " INCARNATE and head of communication trench.	
			The medium T.M.s were firing at the same time and enemy replied with some HE "77 mms", 10 pineapples & about 6 – 4.2s."	
			HOUPLINES. 40 rounds from 2 guns on the enemy front line (C 29 c 80.50 – C 29 a 30.80) considerable damage to parapet and trench. Enemy retaliated with 12, HE and 10 "pineapples" in vicinity of gun positions.	
			40 rounds from 2 guns on the front line at C 29 c 50.75 and C.T. at C 29 a 65.45 (CENTAUR Row). Several direct hits obtained. Enemy retaliated with 11 minenwerfers and 10 small HE on the BAB M. and SPAIN AV. (communication trench)	
		–	Artillery. Although visibility was poor, enemy continued to concentrate his fire on battery positions in the town (two guns being damaged)	

A5834 Wt. W4973 M687 750,000 8/16 D. D. & L. Ltd. Forms/C.2118/13.

WAR DIARY
or
INTELLIGENCE SUMMARY.
(*Erase heading not required.*)

Army Form C. 2118.

Instructions regarding War Diaries and Intelligence Summaries are contained in F. S. Regs., Part II. and the Staff Manual respectively. Title pages will be prepared in manuscript.

Sheet 14.

Place	Date	Hour	Summary of Events and Information	Remarks and references to Appendices
ARMENTIERES	24/7/17.	5 pm	2/Lt Jardine relieved Lt Leonard in HOUPLINES Sector	
"	"	6.30 am	1 other rank slightly wounded in the town.	
"	"	—	EPINETTE 45 rounds fired on INCH and INCHMATE (I 1) a. 15 60 and I 11 a. 40 10) with good result. Retaliation — 1 HE only.	
			HOUPLINES 40 rounds from one gun on to junction of CENTAUR Road and [illegible] at C 29 a. 80 35. Retaliation, Nil.	
"	"		Artillery. Enemy shelling of the town was slightly less intense.	
"	25/7/17		No guns in action. Preparations completed for participation in raid by the 2/8th (Irish) Bn K.L.R.	
			Artillery. hostile activity with 5.9s and guns of small calibre in the centre of the town and near the ASYLUM (I 2 a) where a fire broke out.	
"	26/7/17	2.0 am	1550 rounds fired in support of raid by 2/8th K.L.R. as per attached Appendix No II. Our casualties numbered 2 killed and 3 wounded. One gun and team destroyed by direct hits on pit.	
"	"		Artillery. enemy minenwerfers played a large part in answering his S.O.S. for our raid this morning. Their fire was very erratic and came down to a considerable extent on his own front line. It seems possible that these T.Ms had only recently come into this sector and had not had time to register.	
			The object of creating a diversion near the [illegible] (C 17 a) was very successful.	

Instructions regarding War Diaries and Intelligence Summaries are contained in F. S. Regs., Part II. and the Staff Manual respectively. Title pages will be prepared in manuscript.

WAR DIARY
or
INTELLIGENCE SUMMARY.
(Erase heading not required.)

Army Form C. 2118.

Sheet 15

Place	Date	Hour	Summary of Events and Information	Remarks and references to Appendices
ARMENTIÈRES	27/7/17	–	None of our guns in action. Casualties, nil	
"	"	–	Artillery. Hostile batteries of light calibre again active round the town, and some increase in "Minenwerfer" activity on our left sector.	
"	28/7/17	–	Work continued during day on new ammunition dump at our left sector H.Q. (C.16.d)	
"	"	–	Artillery – Enemy continues to be very active in shelling the town and HOUPLINES. Heavy T.M's (minnies) more active on our left sector trenches (especially C.17 a & c and C.23 a): HOUPLINES Sector.	
	29/7/17	from 12 midnight to 3.30 am	Enemy artillery most active on the town and HOUPLINES, both places suffering a severe bombardment but especially the town with Gas shells and H.E. Great numbers of the civilian population and many military were sent to the Hospitals (gassed). See Divisional Intelligence attached	Appendix 2
"	"		Our casualties numbered 3 other ranks (gassed)	
"	30/7/17	–	Further casualties as a result of gas bombardment – 1 Officer (Lt BURFIELD) and 12 other ranks. All the orderly staff and the Q.M. Staff suffered (all evacuated to hospital). The mens billet and the Officers billet were badly smashed by H.E. and gas shells and many orderly room papers lost in the debris. A gun team on their way up to the HOUPLINES trenches became affected & were evacuated from the Regimental Aid Post.	
	31/7/17	–	2 other ranks evacuated to hospital (gassed)	

A5834 Wt. W4973 M687 750,000 8/16 D. D. & L. Ltd. Forms/C.2118/13.

Instructions regarding War Diaries and Intelligence Summaries are contained in F. S. Regs., Part II. and the Staff Manual respectively. Title pages will be prepared in manuscript.

WAR DIARY
or
INTELLIGENCE SUMMARY.

(Erase heading not required.)

Sheet 16

Army Form C. 2118.

Place	Date	Hour	Summary of Events and Information	Remarks and references to Appendices
ARMENTIÈRES	31/7/17	–	TOTAL EFFECTIVE STRENGTH at end of month.	
			5 Officers 40 Other ranks.	
			Capt Barrow returned from leave on 29th and Lieut PYBUS proceeded on leave.	
			2/Lt BURFIELD struck off strength as wounded (gas) and	
			28 other ranks — do — do.	
			3 do absent on duty (Course at XI Corps School of Mortars)	
				[illegible] Lt R.F.A.

D. D. & L., London, E.C.
(A7883) Wt. W809/M1672 350,000 4/17 Sch. 52a Forms/C/2118/14

APPENDICES

to

WAR DIARY

for

JULY, 1917.

VOLUME 6

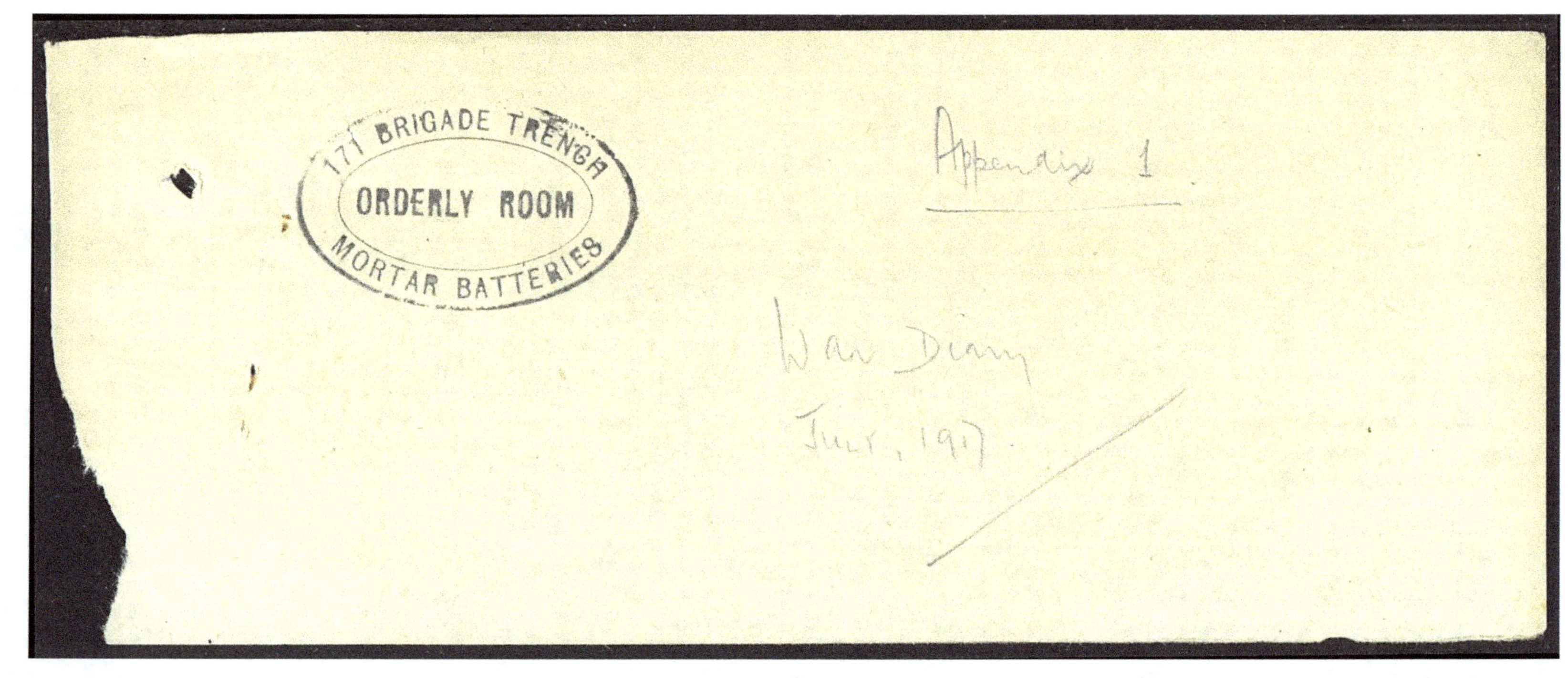

171 BRIGADE TRENCH
ORDERLY ROOM
MORTAR BATTERIES

Appendix 1

War Diary
July, 1917

SECRET. COPY NO. 5

Ref. Map.
36 NW.2 & NE (part of)
,, 4. 1:10.000.

171st BRIGADE ORDER NO. 18.

.... 3rd July, 1917.

SUBJECT. 1. A Raid upon the enemy's Trench System in L'EPINETTE SUBSECTOR will be carried out by the 2/8th Battn. K.L.R.

INTENTION. 2. At Zero on "Z" day, The Raid will be carried out in order to :-
(a) Effect a demonstration to assist Operations elsewhere.
(b) Inflict Casualties.
(c) Destroy war material, and damage enemy trenches.
(d) Obtain Identification.

GENERAL IDEA. 3. Under cover of an Artillery Barrage, the Raiding Party will enter the enemy's lines between :-
I.5.c.93.34 - I.5.d.25.60
and penetrate as far as the Support Line, inflicting as much damage as possible in a limited time.

DETAIL. 4. The Raid will be carried out by approximately 3 Officers and 100 Other Ranks.

ARTILLERY. 5. O.C., Left Group Artillery will draw up a programme for Wire-Cutting and the support of this Enterprise, on the lines indicated in this Office No. P.370 of 29.6.1917.

L.T.M.Bs. 6. O.C., 171st L.T.M.B., will prepare Orders in co-operation with Artillery scheme.

M.G.COMPANY. 7. O.C., 171st M.G.Company will draw up M.G. programme to suit scheme. O.C., 173rd M.G.Company will place guns at his disposal.

R.E., 8. O.C., 421st Field Company, R.E., will assist in preparing the necessary 'jumping-off' place. 'Jump-Off' either from our line or from a tape line. Arrangements for parties of Sappers with Mobile Charges to blow in dugouts, demolish M.G.Emplacements, etc., are to be made.

COMMUNICATION. 9. 171st Brigade Signal Officer will arrange special communication between 'Jumping-Off' place, Battalion HdQrs and Brigade HdQrs.

CODE NAME. 10. This Operation will be referred to in future as TOGO.

ACKNOWLEDGE.

E. Alexander
Captain, Brigade Major.
171st Infantry Brigade.

ISSUED AT 6 p.m., to :-

Copy No. 1. B.G.C.,
2. Brigade Major.
3. Staff Captain.
4. 2/8th K.L.R.,
5. 171st L.T.M.B.,
6. 171st M.G.Company.
7. 173rd ,,
8. Left Group, R.A.,

Copy No. 9. M.T.M.Commander (through Left Group Commander)
10. 421st Field Co, R.E.,
11. War Diary.
12. ,,
13. Brigade Signalling Officer.
14. 57th Division.) For
15. C.R.A., 57th Divn.) information.

MAP REF
3/SNW 4
1/10,000

171 Bde Light Trench Mortar Battery

Operation Orders No 5 — 13th July 1917

<u>Scheme</u>

On Z day at zero hour the battery will support raid by the Infantry on INANE trench system.

The guns of the L T M B will fire on the following targets

GUN	OBJECT	TARGET	RATE OF FIRE
No 1	Suspected M G	I 5 c 15 50	
No 2	To thicken barrage on front line	I 5 b 45 00	Zero to +2 – 20 per minute
No 3	Blocking CT	I 5 d 45 80	+2 to +30 – 10
No 4	Strong point	I 5 d 60 85	+30 to +35 – 20
No 5	do do	I 5 d 45 76	
No 7	Blocking CT	I 11 a 80 85	
No 6	M G	I 5 c 75 20	Zero to +½ – 20 rounds
–	Front line block	I 5 c 65 15	Zero +2 to zero +35 – 10 rds per minute
No 8	To thicken barrage	I 11 a 60 62	Zero to +35 – 10 per minute

TOTAL – 3220.

Copy No 2.

Harold E Barrow (?)

Captain
Commanding,
171st Bde Light T.M.B

Copy 1.

SPECIAL OPERATION ORDER
171st Bde L. T. M. B. (HOUPLINES Sub-sector)

Map ref. TRENCH MAP – HOUPLINES 36 NW2 & NE1 (part of) 1/10000 Edition 7c.

On Z day at zero hour, two guns will be in action from Loc 16 (C 17 c)

① Object – (a) to assist operation by 2/8 KLR in EPINETTE Sub sector by creating a diversion.
(b) to annoy the enemy and damage his trench system.

② Intention – the guns will fire as per attached Appendix A.

③ Synchronization – a watch will be synchronised at left Coy. HQrs at 11-0 pm on 25th inst. Watches of NCO's i/c guns will be synchronised by this watch.

Copy 1 – To HQrs 171 LTMB.
2 – OC. Bn. in line.
3 – " left Coy.
4 – retained.

25-7-17

J. Jardine 2/Lt.
OC Left Sect.
171 LTMB.

APPENDIX A to Special Operation order of 25th July 1917

No 1 gun – from C 17 c 35-90.

(a) zero – 5. ~~to~~ zero – 4 — 20 rounds rapid (green – 300x) on junction of CELL TR. & CELL ROW. (C 17 c 85-60)

(b) Zero to zero + 30 — slow bursts of five on front line traversing between C 17 c 85.60 – 300x and C 17 c 80.80 – 250x (green) until ammⁿ is finished (i.e. 80 rounds)

No 2 gun – from C 17 c 30-95.

(a) Zero – 5 ~~to~~ to zero – 4 — 20 rounds rapid (green – 250x) on junc. of CELL TR. and CELL AV. (C 17 c 80-93)

(b) Zero to zero + 15 — 30 rounds in bursts of five – vertical searching of CELL AV. up to 300x green.

(c) Zero + 15 to zero + 30 — 50 rounds slow fire (yellow 220x) on front line at junction of CELL [illegible]

[signature] 7/17

171 BRIG. TRENCH ORDERLY ROOM MORTAR BATT. R.G.A.

Appendix 2.

War Diary

July 1917.

Appendix 2.

CONFIDENTIAL.

57th DIVISIONAL DAILY BULLETIN, No. 18.
Period of 24 hours ending 6 a.m., 29/7/1917.

(Not to be taken forward of Company Headquarters.)

****

1. ARMENTIERES suffered a severe bombardment during the night. During the day the enemy engaged some of our battery positions in the centre section and shelled our C.T's and F. & S.L. of the Left Section. Otherwise hostile fire was normal. We carried out a successful raid on the CORDONNERIE front capturing prisoners. Visibility was poor throughout the day.

2. The German artillery was on the whole less active during the day. On the Right he confined his attention chiefly to back areas and was not so active as during the preceding period. During the day the Centre Section was fairly quiet except for some Minnie activity between 6.30 and 8 p.mp in reply to our T.M. shoot. On the Left the enemy put some 4,2's on to IRISH AVENUE and the trenches in the vicinity, and there was a general increase of activity in the EPINETTE sub-section. It was however at night that the German artillery was most active, and more damage was done both to buildings and communications, and more casualties inflicted, than at any previous time since the Division has been in that Section of the front. As early as 4,20 p.m. there was a ten minutes intense bombardment on RUE de LILLE and RUE MARLE; at 5.20 p.m. this fire was switched on to TISSAGE DUMP and continued for an hour. At 12 midnight the enemy opened a most intense fire of gas and H.E., exceeding in volume all recent bombardments, which was of a most deliberate character. At 12.15 a.m. there was a lull, and then the fire was continued with quarter-hour intervals between shoots, the fire being directed not against Battery positions, but on all the quarters of the town suitable for billetting. Fire slackened off in intensity after 2.30 a.m., but was continued at intervals all through the remainder of the night. The gas cloud caused by the shells was exceedingly dense and a large number of men were affected in billets before they could get their respirators on. The Headquarters of the Right Brigade were forced to take full precautions as a gas cloud drifted intact over that area from ARMENTIERES between 1.30 and 3.30 a.m.; this affords ample evidence of the volume of gas shells employed in last night's bombardment. The German Command evidently concentrated the fire of all their available guns, and by searching out the billetting areas of the town on an organised system of fire the enemy's belief that the town is being used to concentrate large numbers of troops seems to be confirmed. ARMENTIERES and its environs continue to be shelled this morning, guns of heavy calibre being once again in action.

3. On the FLEURBAIX Section a company raiding party consisting of 4 Officers and 135 O.R. left our lines at 10.30 p.m. with the object of obtaining identifications within the enemy's lines near ROUGES BANCS. The advanced parties of our raid encountered a part of an enemy raiding party in N.M.L. who were about to attack our lines. According to prisoners' statements the strength of the whole enemy party was 2 Officers and 89 O.R. As soon as our advanced section of about 30 men saw these Germans, they at once charged having a hand to hand fight in N.M.L. in which they were speedily joined by the remainder of our raiding party. The enemy ran away and passed within his old F.L. systems. In the meanwhile the programme of the raid was adhered to as far as possible, the scattered parties of Boches being dealt with as and when they appeared, and in the majority of cases the enemy put up a good

/ fight considering...

fight considering how completely he must have been taken by surprise. Our men in every case held the ground they had occupied and met the Germans with the bayonet inflicting severe casualties on him. Our raiding parties returned to our lines shortly after 1 a.m. having driven the Germans back across N.M.L. and caused them to seek cover in their intermediate line which it is now confirmed by prisoners is to all intents and purposes the E.F.L. We took three prisoners - two being wounded (one having since died) and from their statements it appears probable that the 38th Landwehr Division still remains in the line, their regiment the 101st R.E.R. of the 219th Division being on their left.
A full account of the examination of these two men will be issued in due course.

D.H.Q. RALPH GLYN, Captain,

28th July,1917. for Lieut-Colonel,
General Staff, 57th Division.

....

WEATHER FORECAST - Noon 28/7/1917 to Noon 29/7/1917.

Wind variable. Mainly light but gusty at times. Further Thunderstorms likely. Fair - bright intervals. Changeable Temperature. Visibility becoming good. Morning mist.
Temperature 60 to 80 degrees.

....

CONFIDENTIAL.

57th DIVISIONAL DAILY BULLETIN, No. 20.
Period of 24 hours ending 6 a.m., 30/7/17.

(Not to be taken forward of Company Headquarters)

****

1. Right Section quiet. Centre Section hostile artillery active in retaliation to T.M. shoots. ARMENTIERES and back areas of Centre Section again continuously shelled by day and night. Fewer gas shells. A Company raiding party from the Right Battalion again penetrated as far as RUE DES TURCS and returned without incident. Visibility bad.

2. The Germans continued their policy of bombarding ARMENTIERES and causing as much destruction to billetting areas as possible. There was a slightly smaller proportion of gas shells than on the night of the 28th - 29th. The vicinity of NOTRE DAME came in for especially heavy shelling. The civil population sustained a good many casualties from gas poisoning, and since the French Civil Authorities left the town some weeks ago all these civilians have to be dealt with through our medical organisation. There have been one or two cases where French individuals have behaved with courage and coolness, thereby greatly assisting the British Authorities in what has been a most difficult task. As has been the case recently the troops in the line of the Left Section have had a very quiet time, the enemy's attention being mainly concentrated on Armentieres and back areas. A few rounds were put into BAC St. MAUR and on certain cross roads of the Right and Centre sections.

3. The artillery of the Right and Centre groups was active in continuation of the programme shoots of tactical points. On account of the low visibility that lasted all day little movement was noticed, but where seen was promptly fired on. Our patrols report that fewer working parties were heard especially on the Left Section front. Covered by a patrol of 20 men, a working party, engaged in the repair of a gap cut by our artillery opposite the BOUTILLERIE salient, was located by one of our patrols of the Right Section who after lying within 15 yards of the covering party managed to get back to our lines in spite of the attempts of the German covering party to surround them, and turned L.G. fire on the spot where the work was being done. During the day some men were observed near BAS MAISNIL carrying cylinders measuring about 3' x 2'. There is some work going on near WATER FORT and it is desirable that this portion of the line be kept under close observation, as from aeroplane photographs it is clear that from LES CLOCHERS to BAS MAISNIL through CHATEAU RICHE the enemy intends to construct some very strong work.

4. A raiding party of a company of the Right sub-section again searched the enemy's lines for a period of four hours and to a depth of over four hundred yards near FARM DE MOUQUET and RUE DES TURCS. The enemy, probably aware that a similar enterprise had been carried out by a company two nights previously, though not re-occupying his forward trenches kept FARM DE MOUQUET and the ground in rear well lit up by flares. This fact together with the "bad going" of the shell pitted ground full of water as a result of yesterday's thunderstorms made progress very slow. Some delay was also caused through a break in the telephone wire preventing the supporting party receiving the "all clear" signal and so not going on as early as they might have. No enemy were encountered.

/ :3/ NED SWITCH.....

NED SWITCH and NEEDLE support were both thoroughly reconnoitred and found to be unfit for use. As our party was leaving the old enemy F.L. the Germans put eight light Minnies about the point of exit. He was also reported to have fired whizz-bangs into his old Front Line a few minutes later. This reconnaissance is useful in showing that the enemy has apparently given up any idea of re-occupying his old Front Line, and that he is aware of our practice of patrolling well within his lines, which he will attempt to meet by lying up in his old trenches, keeping the ground well illuminated by lights, etc., and having some of his guns on night lines to barrage that part of N.M.L. which was once his old Front Line System.

The enemy is still very alert on the whole of the Centre Front as well as opposite HOUPLINES.

D.H.Q.

RALPH GLYN, Captain,

30th July,1917.

for Lieut.-Colonel,
General Staff, 57th Division.

....

WEATHER FOFECAST - Noon 30/7/17 to Noon 31/7/17.

Wind W. or N.W. 10 to 15 m.p.h. changing later to N. and afterwards probably to N.E. Overcast with some showers, perhaps thunderstorms. Probably a bright interval towards night, then temporarily overcast again. Afterwards gradually fair. Cool. Visibility indifferent becoming good.
Temperature 60 rising to 70.

....

CONFIDENTIAL.

57th DIVISIONAL DAILY BULLETIN, No. 21.
Period of 24 hours ending 6 a.m., 31/7/1917.

(Not to be taken forward of Company Headquarters.)

****

1. German Artillery bombarded ARMENTIERES HEAVILY during the day, and were active on parts of the RUE DU BOIS Sub-section. The Right Section was quiet. The enemy attempted a Raid in the early hours of the 30th on HOUPLINES Sub-section, but were seen and driven off. Visibility was very low.

2. Yesterday ARMENTIERES was again heavily bombarded, battery positions as well as billeting areas being shelled chiefly by 5.9's and 8". In addition to further serious damage caused to the town, the enemy put down a short barrage on the banks of the River LYS at intervals during the day. The LE BIZET bridge was broken down, and the banks were a good deal cut up. The trench system was quiet except for a barrage bombardment in which MINNIES and 77 mms. predominated, on the F.L. at the at the junction of the two Sub-sections, and a box barrage put down on JAPAN AVENUE - WILLOW WALK & PLANK AVENUE ROAD at about 2-30 a.m. At 2-45 a.m. the enemy came over in two parties and attempted to enter our lines in C.23.a & c. The enemy whose total strength is reported as about twenty were spotted and driven back by Machine and Lewis Gun fire. Everything was reported quiet by 3-10 a.m. It now appears that at 9-15 a.m. yesterday morning, the 30th, a party of 7 of the enemy entered our lines on the EPINETTE SALIENT, their presence there being discovered by the outbreak of rifle fire. On our trench patrols hurrying to the spot the enemy was found to have retired. In no case was any identification obtained either by ourselves or the enemy.

3. The enemy on the Centre Section continued to devote most of his attention to shelling RUE MARLE, the outskirts of ARMENTIERES, and certain roads of back areas. The trench beside LILLE ROAD was broken down at different points. Otherwise the enemy fired mainly in retaliation to our T.Ms. and had some success by the use of gas shells and by obtaining direct hits he silenced for a time two batteries which had done very good work. On the whole there was a noticeable absence of Minnie fire. The enemy on this Section maintains a very watchful attitude, and where our fire had cut gaps in his wire, it was noticed that he put down occasional bursts of fire, fired a great many Very lights, and bombed his own wire at INCREASE and showed other signs of nervousness. Our patrols report that the wire cutting on the Centre* had been attempting to repair the damage done, one wiring party being located at INCISION. This systematic wire shooting on the BOIS GRENIER Section always produces better results than when carried out on any other part of the Divisional Front for the reason that it is in this section (almost throughout its entire length) a matter of importance to the Germans to maintain the wire in good order, as there is not the depth of ground available in rear, and they have had therefore to establish themselves well forward. The German artillery is also so disposed as to enable it to promptly and heavily retaliate to our T.M. shoots. The Ridge Line being the main defensive position of the enemy, and of particular importance where it most closely approaches the LILLE FORTRESS LINE, which is opposite the Centre Brigade Front, the forward defences become of greater proportionate importance.

*has been satisfactory and the enemy

/ 4. Two raiding ...

4. Two raiding parties were organised by the Right Brigade having as their objective the thorough reconnaissance of the enemy's forward defences opposite the right half of the BOUTILLERIE Sub-section. Contact was not obtained with the enemy, and our patrols returned without loss, having proved that the enemy does not hold his Front or Support Line at NED, and that his line was held near NEAT, and that its garrison was very much on the alert. This may be due to the fact that wire-cutting having to be carried out in a short period gave the enemy a clue to our intention; or more likely, that the Germans will hold this Section of their F.L. system until such time as the new works near BAS MAISNIL and OLGA SWITCH allow for a readjustment of the line.

D.H.Q., RALPH GLYN, Captain,

31/7/17. for Lieut-Colonel,
General Staff, 57th Division.

....

WEATHER FORECAST - Noon 31/7/17 to Noon 1/8/17.

Wind N. or N.E. 10 to 15 miles per hour. Mainly overcast. Some rain or drizzle likely. Gradually improving later. Cool. Fair visibility. Temperature 69 to 65 degrees.

....

Headquarters,
57th Division.

E.W.391.

REPORT ON GAS SHELL BOMBARDMENT OF ARMENTIERES, ON NIGHT OF 28/29th JULY, 1917.

1. AREA AFFECTED.

The areas shelled were mainly those occupied for billeting, and of small extent. A very intense bombardment with Gas Shell, and also H.E. commenced at midnight, and continued with intervals until about 3-30 a.m. The number of shells is difficult to estimate, but was probably not less than 6000-7000, as a cloud was formed, which drifted as far as FLEURBAIX.

During the night the BOIS GRENIER Section was also shelled with a small number of Gas Shells.

2. NATURE OF GAS.

From its effects, and from specimens found, the Gas appears to have been chiefly of the type used in the last attack on ARMENTIERES. A small proportion of diphosgene and phosgene was also used.

3. WIND. - N.E. light, about 2 m.p.h.

4. CASUALTIES.

A large number of casualties were probably due to the sudden and intense nature of the bombardment, which took men by surprise, and gave very little time for protection. The Gas penetrated billets and cellars, and hung about for a considerable time, and in some cases masks were taken off before it had been properly cleared out.

The greatest care should be taken to clear unprotected cellars before men remain in or enter them without masks on and fully adjusted. All possible measures to do this, i.e., by fanning and by lighting fires where practicable, should be taken.

(Sgd) ERIC WALKER, Captain,
Gas Officer, 57th Division.

29-7-1917.

-2-

C.R.A.	.. (21)	A.D.M.S.	.. (5)
C.R.E.	.. (4)	D.A.D.V.S.	.. (2)
Signals,	.. (1)	D.M.G.O.	.. (5)
170th Bde.	.. (6)	D.G.O.	.. (1)
171st Bde.	.. (6)	A.P.M.	.. (1)
172nd Bde.	.. (6)	Camp Cdt.	.. (1)
Train.	.. (5)	"Q"	.. (1)

G.92/158/9.

Forwarded for information.

A. Davis, Major for Lieut-Colonel,
General Staff, 57th Division.

D.H.Q.
31st July, 1917.

Volume 1.

WAR DIARY

of

171st Brigade Light Trench Mortar Battery,

for

Month of AUGUST. 1917.

MAP REFERENCES.

(1) FRANCE. Sheet 36 NW. 1/20000 6c.

(2) TRENCH MAP. HOUPLINES 36 N.W. 2 & NE. 1 parts of 1/10,000 7D

(3) BOIS GRENIER 36 NW 4 1/10000 6d.

Instructions regarding War Diaries and Intelligence Summaries are contained in F. S. Regs., Part II. and the Staff Manual respectively. Title pages will be prepared in manuscript.

WAR DIARY or ~~INTELLIGENCE SUMMARY.~~

(Erase heading not required.)

VOLUME 7.

Army Form C. 2118.

Sheet 1

Place	Date 1917	Hour	Summary of Events and Information	Remarks and references to Appendices
ARMENTIÈRES (C25°C 55·45)	AUG. 1st	12.45AM.	3 Guns cooperated in barrage for dummy raid on Enemy trenches INCENSE I11c 30·30 to form a diversion for a very successful raid which was carried out by D Coy of N Battalion 172nd Inf Bde. Identification obtained of 9th Bavarian Infantry Regiment. Prisoners gave order of Battle from NORTH to SOUTH 431 Landwehr Inf. Regt. 101 Reserve Inf. Regiment. 391 Landwehr Inf. Regiment. There was no further L.T.M. activity through the day but the enemy appeared nervous due probably to the effects of the raid. Hostile Artillery fire was normal except for bursts of heavy shelling on various quarters of the town causing some material damage to civilian property. Rain fell heavily through out the day but there is still a lot of gas hanging about the town. Visibility poor with fair intervals.	
"	2nd		No guns in action the day being spent in clearing up the line which is in a very bad condition owing to the recent heavy rain. Enemy was active at intervals on the HOUPLINES ARMENTIÈRES Road causing much trouble to runners & ration parties. Weather Squally, low visibility & continued rain. 2 Other Ranks reported from 1st Army Rest Camp.	
	3rd	2.15AM.	In response to S.O.S. from L'EPINETTE subsector 30 rounds were fired.	
		11.30pm to 1.30 AM	Central part of Armentières was heavily bombarded with H.E. Shrapnel & Gas Shells	

D. D. & L., London, E.C. (A7883) Wt. W809/M1672 350,000 4/17 Sch. 52a Forms/C/2118/14

Army Form C. 2118.

Instructions regarding War Diaries and Intelligence Summaries are contained in F. S. Regs., Part II. and the Staff Manual respectively. Title pages will be prepared in manuscript.

WAR DIARY
or
INTELLIGENCE SUMMARY.
(Erase heading not required.)

Sheet 2

Place	Date	Hour	Summary of Events and Information	Remarks and references to Appendices
ARMENTIÈRES	3rd		Enemy T.M's & pineapples were active on the whole Brigade front no doubt due to the inactivity of the L.T.M's during the last two days. The weather was again wet.	
	4th	10.AM	The 170th L.T.M.B relieved the men of this battery in the HOUPLINES & L'EPINETTE sectors. 1 Officer & 6 O.R. remaining in the line with them. No guns in action. Enemy Artillerie was quieter in ARMENTIÈRES but HOUPLINES Road was again shelled at intervals. 77 mms TM's & pineapples were very active on front line & CT'S. Weather again bad.	
	5th		Day was spent in cleaning up billet in Armentières & preparing to move. No guns in action. 1st Army held service in commemoration of 3rd Anniversary of War.	
		12.15AM.	Enemy put down barrage on Front & Support lines C 23 & 29. ARMENTIÈRES was shelled at the same time. Combined with the above bombardments the enemy attempted to put over a gas cloud which was observed moving towards L'EPINETTE SALIENT. Hostile aeroplanes were flying low as though to drown the sounds of the gas escaping from the cylinders. Weather fine. 1 Officer & 6 other ranks returned from line. 1 other rank reported back from Hospital.	
	6th.	9.30AM	Lieut: Smallpage, St. Leonard & 21 OR left to relieve the 170th L.T.M.B in FLEURBAIX Sector.	
		12.0pm	Relief complete commands pass. 3 OR returned from 1st ARMY School of Mortars.	

D. D. & L., London, E.C.
(A7883) Wt. W809/M1672 350,000 4/17 Sch. 52a Forms/C/2118/14

(1) AUBERS. 36SW1. 1/10000 8a (2) RADINGHEM. 36SW 2 1/10000 6C. (3) France 36NW3 1/10000 6. (4) BOIS GRENIER 36NW4 1/10000 6B.

MAP REFERENCES.

Instructions regarding War Diaries and Intelligence Summaries are contained in F. S. Regs., Part II. and the Staff Manual respectively. Title pages will be prepared in manuscript.

WAR DIARY
or
INTELLIGENCE SUMMARY.
(Erase heading not required.)

Army Form C. 2118.

Sheet 3

Place	Date	Hour	Summary of Events and Information	Remarks and references to Appendices
FLEURBAIX.	6th	9.45 pm	Enemy aeroplane dropped 5 bombs in vicinity of Brigade HQ. doing some material damage	
(H21d 20.70)			There was a rather noticeable increase of T.M. activity in HUDSON BAY, BAY AVENUE area.	
			The Germans seem determined to improve their defences in depth in the area opposite this piece	
			of line. The tramway through 07a TO 1C has been very much used.	
			Visibility was bad in the morning improving in the afternoon.	
"	7th		No guns in action. Work was done clearing up ammunition pits etc & reconnoitring the sector.	
		3pm	Enemy T.M's. again bombarded HUDSON BAY area doing some damage to our trenches.	
			"A" Bn. 4th Brigade C.E.P. relieved 2/7 K.S.R. in BOUTILLERIE subsector.	
			Quiet day with fair visibility.	
"	8th	9.15 PM	2 Guns in action firing on to NEPHEW TRENCH N9D 40.20. with very satisfactory results.	
		10.07 PM	2 Guns in action firing on NEDSWITCH N.11A 30.20 & NECK RESERVE N11B 60.60. Very good shoot.	
			The enemy does not appear to object to T.M. activity in this part of the line & does not retaliate.	
			Visibility was very low but the German air service took advantage of the bright intervals, and	
			enemy aircraft were active. One aeroplane dropped a list of (presumably) all British pilots	
			& observers who have become casualties behind the German lines between APRIL 1st & JULY 25th.	
			38th Landwehr Division are still in this section of the line & have not been relieved for XI months.	

D. D. & L., London, E.C.
(A7883) Wt. W809/M1672 350,000 4/17 Sch. 52a Forms/C/2118/14

Instructions regarding War Diaries and Intelligence Summaries are contained in F. S. Regs., Part II, and the Staff Manual respectively. Title pages will be prepared in manuscript.

WAR DIARY
or
INTELLIGENCE SUMMARY.
(Erase heading not required.)

Army Form C. 2118.

Sheet 4

Place	Date	Hour	Summary of Events and Information	Remarks and references to Appendices
FLEURBAIX (N21d 20.70)	9th	3.0pm	2 Guns in action on to NEBULA support line & CTs N6C 40.10 N6D 55.70 with very good effect	
			A quiet day in the line. Battery position N27B was shelled throughout the morning but with that exception the enemy has not been hostile. The shooting was very remarkable out of several hundred shells only 1 or two fell more than 50 yds from the Battery position.	
			Enemy aeroplanes were active the weather being quite fine. Bombs were dropped in back areas.	
			The unusual TM activity ceased for the day. 3 O.R. were evacuated to Hospital suffering from the effects of the gas 10 days before.	
			2nd Lieut. Sage 6th Glosters attached 2/57th KLR & batman attached to Battery.	
"	10th	9.0AM	Two guns in action on S.L. & CT'S N6C 40.10 good results, Enemy retaliated considerably.	
		3.30pm 5.0pm	Two guns fired on F.L. N6B 60.30 doing considerable damage to enemy trenches.	
			Enemy Artillery was active on the extreme right of the CORBONNERIE subsector apparently registering, otherwise very quiet on this sector. A barrage was opened on our extreme right just before midnight but no Infantry action was reported. German aeroplanes were active during the night & bombed back areas SAILLY & ERQUINGHEM. It was noticed that German balloons were showing steady lights, possibly to assist aeroplanes in navigation.	
	11th	6.0AM	2 guns in action on NECK N4b 25.88 & NEAR O1a 30.70 where Enemy had been reported to be working.	

D. D. & L., London, E.C.
(A7883) Wt. W803/M1672 350,000 4/17 Sch. 52a Forms/C/2118/14

Instructions regarding War Diaries and Intelligence Summaries are contained in F. S. Regs., Part II. and the Staff Manual respectively. Title pages will be prepared in manuscript.

WAR DIARY
or
INTELLIGENCE SUMMARY.
(Erase heading not required.)

Army Form C. 2118.

Sheet 5

Place	Date	Hour	Summary of Events and Information	Remarks and references to Appendices
FLEURBAIX (H21d 30.70)	11th	8.0AM	1 Gun in action on Enemy S.L. N 10 c 30.15 with good results. Enemy Artillery was very quiet in this sector during the day his T.M's were fairly active in replying to our shoots but did no great damage, from observation of his firing it would appear that he has either increased his range for T.M's or has brought them further forward than is his usual practice. During the night of 9th/10th PERENCHIES Church tower a well known landmark in this part of the line disappeared, our Artillery do not claim to have destroyed it. A patrol from 3rd regiment CEP in BOUTILLERIE subsector reported a party of about 50 in enemy in no mans land ????	
"	12th	8.AM	2 Guns in action on Enemy T.T.S.L's O1a 50.75 in conjunction with M.T.M's. Results satisfactory. Enemy Artillery was quiet in this sector. Recently the Germans have been using a number of long range naval guns on railway mountings 15 cm is most frequently employed the maximum range hitherto reported is 18.200 yds. The enemy left a number of copies of the Gazette des Ardennes on our front line parapet. One copy contained an account in English of the Russian disasters & a cartoon of Mr Lloyd George. This is a new departure in Bosche Propaganda. 2 O.R. were transferred to 24 Inf. Base Depot being under 19 years of age.	

D. D. & L., London, E.C.
(A7883) Wt. W803/M1672 350,000 4/17 Sch. 52a Forms/C/2118/14

Instructions regarding War Diaries and Intelligence Summaries are contained in F. S. Regs., Part II. and the Staff Manual respectively. Title pages will be prepared in manuscript.

WAR DIARY
or
INTELLIGENCE SUMMARY.
(Erase heading not required.)

Army Form C. 2118.

Sheet 6

Place	Date	Hour	Summary of Events and Information	Remarks and references to Appendices
FLEURBAIX (H21d 20.70)	13th	3.15PM	2 Guns in action firing onto enemy dugout at N5D/75.10 many direct hits were obtained causing much damage. Retaliation 10 [illegible] to left of guns. One of our aeroplanes dropped bombs at same time.	
		3.30pm	2 Guns fired on suspected day post at N10C/80.50 doing considerable damage. retaliation nil.	
			Hostile Artillery more active especially on right of sector where he appears to be registering.	
			One of our aeroplanes was brought down by direct hit from AA. falling behind Enemy F.L. at N9C.	
		10.15PM	Enemy attacked two posts in Fleurbaix sector N8D/50.95 & N8D/95.95 the raiding parties were driven off one of the enemy being killed no identification was obtained.	
		12.0PM	Enemy again attempted to raid same posts was driven off before reaching our lines.	
			Enemy Aeroplanes were again active. Our aeroplanes carried out night bombing raid on CISNES, CARVIN	
"	14th	5.0AM	Enemy put down a heavy barrage on our F.L.S lines on right of CORDONNERIE salient. The S.O.S. being sent up No1 Gun N9b/60.30 opened up on S.O.S line. At the same time the enemy carried out a big raid which was launched at 6.15Am on the Portugese in the FAUQUISSART sector. The raid was repulsed leaving two prisoners of 6 Bavarian I.R. (normal)	
		2.0pm	2 Guns in action firing onto enemy S.L. at O1C/35.50 with some success. Retaliation Nil.	
		3.30pm	1 Gun fired on enemy front & support lines at N6C/30.25 with good results.	
			A wounded prisoner was brought in from no mans land, he belonged to 107th Reserve I.R. 24th Division	
			Lieut Smallpage proceeded on leave.	

D. D. & L., London, E.C.
(A7883) Wt. W809/M1672 350,000 4/17 Sch. 52a Forms/C/2118/14

Instructions regarding War Diaries and Intelligence Summaries are contained in F. S. Regs., Part II. and the Staff Manual respectively. Title pages will be prepared in manuscript.

WAR DIARY
or
INTELLIGENCE SUMMARY.
(Erase heading not required.)

Army Form C. 2118.

Sheet 7

Place	Date	Hour	Summary of Events and Information	Remarks and references to Appendices
FLEURBAIX (H21d/20/70)	15th	12·30pm	A small German raiding patrol of about 25 men attacked a post in BOUTILLERIE subsector. This is the first time the enemy have shown any enterprise during daylight hours since the Division has been in the line. The object of the raid may have been to confirm suspicions regarding the garrison. German aeroplanes were again active dropping bombs on back areas at night. Enemy artillery were not active but he is using many pineapples in vicinity of TINBARN LANE & ABBOTS LANE. There appears to be fired from saps in front of his F.L. but is not yet confirmed. 2nd Lieut [illegible] & 3 O.R's left for 1st Army Rest Camp Boulogne.	
"	16th	6·45AM	Two shoots were carried out by 5 Gun on Enemy S.L. at N11B/40.90 Observation was bad owing to mist. No 7 Gun fired on new work in front line at N6B 80·45 making a gap in his trench & throwing up considerable woodwork. Retaliation about 20 pineapples which fell short of our parapet.	
		11·20AM	1 Gun fired onto work at N.14B/50·80 doing considerable damage. Retaliation nil. Enemy aircraft were again active dropping bombs on back areas at night. The weather still continued fine with good visibility.	
"	17th	2·30pm	1 Gun fired on to new work on parapet at N6B/80·35 with very good results.	
		3·30pm	2 Guns repeated the dose destroying all the new work & leaving a big gap in his parapet. Retaliation 4 minnies. Hostile artillery was principally active in counter battery work one battery at H31b received 150 rds. The enemy appeared to be registering new positions in H33 a & b. Visibility was good. An enemy patrol was discovered attempting to penetrate our line but withdrew on being bombed this is the 2nd attempt to gain identification in the past week on CORDONNERIE.	

(A7092). Wt. W12839/M1293. 750,000. 1/17. D. D. & L., Ltd. Forms/C.2118/14.

Instructions regarding War Diaries and Intelligence Summaries are contained in F. S. Regs., Part II. and the Staff Manual respectively. Title pages will be prepared in manuscript.

WAR DIARY
or
INTELLIGENCE SUMMARY.
(Erase heading not required.)

Army Form C. 2118.

Sheet 8

Place	Date	Hour	Summary of Events and Information	Remarks and references to Appendices
FLEURBAIX (H21d/20.70)	18th	8.15 AM.	15 Rounds onto C.T. N8d 70.20 with good results. Retaliation nil.	
		3.0pm	2 Guns in action firing onto N11b 70.80 & N11a 60.40 Enemy dugout destroyed.	
			Enemy Artillery were considerable more active Battery position H31b received 150 5.9's.	
		9.0pm	About ten 4.2's fell in Fleurbaix several of them failing to detonate properly.	
			There was more than the usual activity movement in Bosche lines.	
			One of our aeroplanes came down in H18 central	
"	19th		No guns in action work was carried out in preparation for early morning shoot on 20th inst.	
		2.30pm	A successful projector gas attack was carried out on left of BOUTILLERIE Sector 8 tons of gas being discharged. Hostile retaliation was almost negligible.	
			Enemy aircraft was again very active were heavily engaged by our A.A. fire.	
			1 O.R. proceeded on leave & 3 O.R. left for Course at XI Corps School of Mortars.	
	20th	7.30AM	2 Guns in action on N11a 10.70 & N11b 40.90 carried out successful shoot enemy retaliated with pineapples & 77mm's.	
		2.45pm	Shoot was carried out on prominent structure at N8d 80.20 several direct hits being obtained Bosche retaliated with ten 4.2's this being the first time that he has retaliated for T.M. activity in CORDONNERIE Subsector	

(A7092). Wt. W12839/M1293. 750,000. 1/17. D. D. & L., Ltd. Forms/C.2118/14.

Army Form C. 2118.

Sheet 9

WAR DIARY
or
INTELLIGENCE SUMMARY.
(*Erase heading not required.*)

Instructions regarding War Diaries and Intelligence Summaries are contained in F. S. Regs., Part II. and the Staff Manual respectively. Title pages will be prepared in manuscript.

Place	Date	Hour	Summary of Events and Information	Remarks and references to Appendices
FLEURBAIX (H21d/20.70)	20th		The enemy continues to show nervousness bombing his wire and firing flares of all descriptions.	
			Hostile aircraft was again active 5 bombs being dropped at DEAD DOG Dump H 34 C. An aeroplane dropped messages including a casualty list of British Airmen brought down behind German lines & private letters from Officers of R.F.C. who have been made prisoners.	
	21st	6.7AM	Shoot carried out on New Trench at N6C 95.40 drawing heavy retaliation from Minnies & pineapples	
		3.30pm	Shoot on N6B 93.02 with satisfactory results again bringing down heavy retaliation.	
			Enemy succeeded in locating Battalion H.Q. at Foray House & shelled it for several hours about 500 5.9's are estimated to have fallen in this area.	
			About 11.45 AM a Minnie was observed firing from N12a/50.60 a premature explosion occurred at 5th round	
			There was no enemy aircraft activity during the night probably due to the bombing of his aerodromes.	
			Weather was still fair but visibility was indifferent improving in the evening.	
			3 O.R. trained T.M. Gunners reported from 2/4 K.L.R.	
	22nd	9.AM	Shoot carried out on N10C 90.30 Retaliation nil.	
		11.30AM	Shoot on N6C 95.45 & N6B 10.90 with satisfactory results Enemy retaliated with Minnies & pineapples.	
		3.30pm	A small balloon came over from enemy lines with copies of Gazette des Ardennes.	
			There was more hostile aircraft activity during the day 5 machines tried to cross our lines on two occasions but were driven off by AA fire.	
			There was considerable improvement in weather conditions and consequently an increase in Artillery activity on both sides. 1 O.R. reported back from Hospital.	

(A7092). Wt. W12839/M1293. 750,000. 1/17. D. D. & L., Ltd. Forms/C.2118/14.

Instructions regarding War Diaries and Intelligence Summaries are contained in F. S. Regs., Part II. and the Staff Manual respectively. Title pages will be prepared in manuscript.

WAR DIARY
or
INTELLIGENCE SUMMARY.

(Erase heading not required.)

Army Form C. 2118.

Sheet 10

Place	Date	Hour	Summary of Events and Information	Remarks and references to Appendices
FLEURBAIX (H 21d/20.70)	23rd	4.pm	Shot on C.T. at N6B 80.10 drawing fairly heavy retaliation 8 minnies two to 30 Whizbangs	
		7.15pm	35.9's fell near H 21d/20.70 doing some damage to civilian property.	
		12.pm	Gas alarm received from right sector.	
			9 O.Ranks were attached for training purposes.	
	24th	1.0AM.	Enemy put down a heavy barrage of 77's and minnies on N5D N6B with a strong artillery diversion about BRIDOUX SALIENT & BOIS GRENIER Sector. An enemy raiding party of 2 Officers & 20 other ranks entered our lines between posts at N5D/50.85 N5d/50.80 N6B/25/52 The enemy were immediately engaged by rifle fire bombs & were driven out after severe fighting. 1 Officer 3 O.R dead were left in our lines & 3 prisoners were taken none of our men were missing. The prisoners belong to 78th Landwehr Infantry Regiment.	
			Two guns replied to S.O.S. call firing 150 rounds into front of our wire on sector raided.	
		11.30AM	Shot on N5d/50.20 doing considerable damage to trench.	
			Enemy aircraft was less active there being no night flying.	
			There was slight increase in artillery activity for 2 hours in the morning he put over a considerable number of 77's 4.2's & some gas shells	
			Weather was fair with a rising wind Visibility good.	
			1 O.R slightly wounded	

(A7092). Wt. W12839/M1293. 750,000. 1/17. D. D. & L., Ltd. Forms/C.2118/14.

Instructions regarding War Diaries and Intelligence Summaries are contained in F. S. Regs., Part II. and the Staff Manual respectively. Title pages will be prepared in manuscript.

WAR DIARY
or
INTELLIGENCE SUMMARY.
(Erase heading not required.)

Army Form C. 2118.

Sheet 11

Place	Date	Hour	Summary of Events and Information	Remarks and references to Appendices
FLEURBAIX (H21d/20/70)	25th	7.30AM	Shot on trench N6C 93.30 Poor observation owing to bad weather. Retaliation 6 Minnies. Enemy aircraft were not active Observation Balloons were reported in the evening. Hostile Artillery were much quieter but there was considerable T.M. activity. 3 O.R. joined for instruction. Lieut Smallpage returned from leave.	
	26th	11.15AM	10 Rounds onto new work behind screen at N6D/80.20 Screen destroyed & work damaged.	
		4.30pm	30 Rounds onto N6C/50.15 where pineapple gun was observed firing from. Infantry observers report that 12 rounds fell into the emplacement completely destroying it. Hostile aircraft was very active during the morning flying low & well forward over his own lines several attempts were made to cross our lines but were driven off by AA MG & LG fire. Weather continues to be unsettled with high wind.	
	27th	2.15pm	Shot onto enemy front line N9D/80.10 traversing for about 80 yds many direct hits obtained. Enemy artillery were abnormally quiet during the whole day firing only about 30 rounds. Aircraft was reduced to a minimum owing to the high wind & constant rain showers. Lieut Leonard proceeded on leave.	
	28th	5.0AM	40 rounds onto Enemy Support line at N6C/50.12 observation impossible owing to the very bad weather conditions retaliation 8 pineapples. Enemy Artillery very quiet owing to high wind about 80 rounds fell on Brigade sector. 2 O.R. left for 1st Army Rest Camp.	

(A7092). Wt. W12839/M1293 750,000. 1/17. D. D. & L., Ltd. Forms/C.2118/14.

Army Form C. 2118.

WAR DIARY
or
INTELLIGENCE SUMMARY.
(Erase heading not required.)

Instructions regarding War Diaries and Intelligence Summaries are contained in F. S. Regs., Part II. and the Staff Manual respectively. Title pages will be prepared in manuscript.

Sheet 12

Place	Date	Hour	Summary of Events and Information	Remarks and references to Appendices
FLEURBAIX	29th	11.45AM	2 Guns in action firing onto N10C/35.25 & N15C/90.20 enemy C.T. Considerable damage was done to enemy trenches & a footbridge over drain was destroyed.	
		7.30pm	2 Guns fired on O1C/30.60 & N6d 80.80. Enemy retaliated with Pineapples & 77's. There was no enemy activity except in retaliation to our T.M.s. A very quiet day. Owing to heavy rain & strong wind. Visibility was poor & observation difficult. 2nd Lieut. Jardine & 3 O.R. reported back from 1st Army Rest Camp. 1 O.R. returned from Hospital.	
	30th	11.0AM	30 rounds on to NEBULA AVENUE Tramway. Shooting was erratic owing to high wind. 6 pineapples in retaliation. Another very quiet day but slight increase in hostile M. G fire during night.	
	31st	4.30 pm.	Between 4.30pm & 5.30pm 4 guns cooperated in combined T.M. shoot by all T.M.s in division. Targets engaged by us were Tramway & NEGATIVE AVENUE N10D/35.15 NEATLANE N6d NEAR SUPPORTS N6C. The shoot was very successful much damage was done to Enemy trenches. His retaliation was very slight only a few pineapples & medium minnies falling on the Brigade front. Apart from this shoot the day was very quiet. Our aeroplanes were active during the night dropping bombs behind his enemy lines. 3 O.R. left for XI Corps School of Instruction.	

(A7092). Wt. W12839/M1293. 750,000. 1/17. D. D. & L., Ltd. Forms/C.2118/14.

Army Form C. 2118.

Sheet 13.

Instructions regarding War Diaries and Intelligence Summaries are contained in F. S. Regs., Part II. and the Staff Manual respectively. Title pages will be prepared in manuscript.

WAR DIARY
or
INTELLIGENCE SUMMARY.

(Erase heading not required.)

Place	Date	Hour	Summary of Events and Information	Remarks and references to Appendices
	31st		Effective Strength of Battery at end of month 5 Officers & 52 O.R's.	
			Harold R Barrow. Capt Cdg 171st S. T. M. B	

(A7092). Wt. W12839/M1293. 750,000. 1/17. D. D. & L., Ltd. Forms/C.2118/14.

WAR DIARY.

Vol. 8.

SEPTEMBER 1917.

To Headquarters 57th Division

Herewith War Diary (Volume 8) for month of September 1917 please.

Eric Smallpage Lieut.
Cdg 171st L.T.M.B.

MAPS: FRANCE 36 N.W. 1/20000.

Instructions regarding War Diaries and Intelligence Summaries are contained in F. S. Regs., Part II. and the Staff Manual respectively. Title pages will be prepared in manuscript.

WAR DIARY

~~or~~

~~INTELLIGENCE SUMMARY.~~

(Erase heading not required.)

VOLUME 8.

Army Form C. 2118.

Sheet 1.

Place	Date	Hour	Summary of Events and Information	Remarks and references to Appendices
FLEURBAIX. (H 21.d 20.70)	1917 Sept. 1st	–	Trench Strength of Battery – 4 Officers, 43 other ranks.	
	1st	–	During day, 120 rounds fired on various targets with good results – enemy retaliation weak. Enemy T.M's located at O.1.a.17.00 (Heavy) N.6.b.80.99 (Light) O.1.c.10.17 (Medium)	
			Little aerial activity owing to bad weather.	
	2nd	pm 5.45	50 rounds fired on INDEX and support line – both trenches and a trench tramline damaged. Enemy replied with 20 "oilcans" and 20 "pineapples" on communication trench (ABBOTTS LANE. N.6.a)	
	"	pm 5.30	Capt A.E. BARROW (commanding the Battery) was admitted to Field Ambulance, suffering from "ulcerated eye". Sergeant J.D. JARDINE assumed command of battery.	
	3rd	pm 2.45	In conjunction with medium T.M.B. – 70 rounds were fired on NAVAL TR. (N.12.a.45.70) and enemy support line and trench junction at N.12.b.05.15. Considerable damage done to enemy works. Large quantities of revetting and other trench material thrown into the air. Several 4.2s and 6 heavy minenwerfer fired in retaliation to medium [illegible]. Work done on Offensive positions in BOUTILLERIE Sector. Aircraft on both sides more active during the day. Several enemy machines flew over our lines at night; no bombs were observed to drop.	

(A7092). Wt. W12839/M1293. 750,000. 1/17. D. D. & L., Ltd. Forms/C.2118/14.

Instructions regarding War Diaries and Intelligence Summaries are contained in F. S. Regs., Part II. and the Staff Manual respectively. Title pages will be prepared in manuscript.

WAR DIARY
or
INTELLIGENCE SUMMARY.
(Erase heading not required.)

Army Form C. 2118.

Sect 2.

Place	Date 1917	Hour	Summary of Events and Information	Remarks and references to Appendices
FLEURBAIX. (H 21 d 20 70)	Sept 4th	am 7.30	10 rounds on N 5 d 90 20 and [illegible] where working party had been [illegible]. Revetting material and earth thrown up.	
		pm 4.0	35 rounds on NEPAL and TRAMWAY [illegible] on enemy front line at N 8 a 9 1 – Considerable damage done to [illegible]. Caused to enemy [illegible].	
			Aircraft – observation balloons and aeroplanes up all day – several of our machines flew low over enemy lines. Slightly increased hostile artillery fire.	
	5th	am 7.0	20 rounds fired on enemy working party in vicinity of N 11 a 10 35 (NECKLACE TRENCH). Sounds of knocking ceased. Several direct hits on quantity of building material which was scattered.	
		am 8.0	20 rounds in vicinity of N 11 b 20 45. Number of new screens observed in this neighbourhood. Observation of this [illegible] was poor, owing to low lying ground mist.	
		am 8.15	35 rounds in Communication trench in N 16 a and DEVON'S [illegible] (N 17 d [illegible]). Sounds of working party heard – [illegible] it ceased. Enemy replied with a few pineapples doing no damage.	
		noon 12	50 rounds on INDEX and NEAR Trenches with good results. [illegible] with 20 [illegible] on front line and [illegible] AVENUE (C.T.)	
			180 rounds expended during the day.	
			Aircraft – owing to fine weather, very active, causing some delay in our shooting.	

(A7092). Wt. W12839/M1293. 750,000. 1/17. D. D. & L., Ltd. Forms/C.2118/14.

Army Form C. 2118.

WAR DIARY
or
INTELLIGENCE SUMMARY.
(Erase heading not required.)

Instructions regarding War Diaries and Intelligence Summaries are contained in F. S. Regs., Part II. and the Staff Manual respectively. Title pages will be prepared in manuscript.

Sheet 3

Place	Date 1917	Hour	Summary of Events and Information	Remarks and references to Appendices
FLEURBAIX (H.21.d.20.70)	Sep 6	—	Lieut. SHALLPAGE relieved in trenches by 2/Lt. SAGE.	
		3.30 pm	40 rounds on tramway at O.1.a 55.50, with excellent results. Enemy replied with 20/30 whizzbangs and several minnies left of BAY AV.	
		11.0 am	Aircraft: one of our planes reported to have brought down enemy observation balloon - destroyed. During the afternoon another in the vicinity of FOURNES was forced to descend, the occupants coming down in parachutes.	
	7th	—	Information received from DIV. HQ. that Lieut. J.W. PYBUS (second in Command of battery) underwent a medical board in ENGLAND on 21/8/17 - granted 3 weeks leave, 6 weeks light duty, and 4 months unfit for General Service. Struck off strength of battery as from that date (wounded - gas)	
		—	During day 30 rounds fired on NOVEL TR. (N.8.d.80.20) with satisfactory results. Enemy replied with 5 large minenwerfer on our front line between PINNEYS and BROMPTON AV. - Silenced by our artillery. This is the first appearance of heavy "minnie" on this subsector since our return on 6/8/17.	
	8th	7.45 am	30 rounds on enemy supports at N.15.a 67.20 - no retaliation.	
		11.30	45 rounds on N.6.d.05.42, where working parties had been recently heard. Considerable material damage done. 20 pineapples in retaliation. Generally a quiet day.	

(A7092). Wt. W12839/M1293. 750,000. 1/17. D. D. & L., Ltd. Forms/C.2118/14.

Instructions regarding War Diaries and Intelligence Summaries are contained in F. S. Regs., Part II. and the Staff Manual respectively. Title pages will be prepared in manuscript.

WAR DIARY
or
INTELLIGENCE SUMMARY.
(*Erase heading not required.*)

Army Form C. 2118.

Sheet 4.

Place	Date	Hour	Summary of Events and Information	Remarks and references to Appendices
FLEURBAIX (H 21 d 20.70)	1917 Sep. 9th	pm 2.30	52 rounds on [illegible] line at O 1 a 4 5 to which enemy replied with 15 4.2's on front line and BAY AVENUE, also 50 rounds from his light trench gun. Aircraft – three enemy balloons were up in spite of low visibility in the morning, which however improved later in the day.	
	10th	am 4.0	70 rounds fired on to NEAR TR. (N 6 b 85.50) in conjunction with our 18 pounders. Retaliation slight – a few whizzbangs and pineapples on our front line at N 6 5.	
		am 6 & 7.0	Enemy shelled our support line in CORDONNERIE Sector with shells of light calibre which resembled gas shells on explosion – followed with bursts of M.G. fire	
		pm 3.0	Enemy active with minenwerfers on our front line in vicinity of BAY AV. and TIN BARN AV.	
		—	Aircraft – usual activity on both sides. Enemy machines tried several times in the evening to cross our lines but were driven off by our anti aircraft guns.	
	11th	am 9.0	Authority received from G.O.C. 57th Division for Sec Lieut J.D. JARDINE to wear the badges of rank of LIEUT pending the decision of G.H.Q.	
		pm 1.30	30 rounds on enemy support line (N.15 b 63.55) doing usual damage but causing no retaliation	
		8.0	70 rounds on [illegible] Support and NEAR TR. causing satisfactory amount of damage and drawing some retaliation. (15 4.2 on BAY AV. and 20 rounds from light minnies on front line to left of BAY AV. (I 31 [illegible])	

(A7092). Wt. W12839/M1293. 750,000. 1/17. D. D. & L., Ltd. Forms/C.2118/14.

Army Form C. 2118.

Instructions regarding War Diaries and Intelligence Summaries are contained in F. S. Regs., Part II. and the Staff Manual respectively. Title pages will be prepared in manuscript.

WAR DIARY
or
INTELLIGENCE SUMMARY.
(*Erase heading not required.*)

Sheet 5.

Place	Date 1916	Hour	Summary of Events and Information	Remarks and references to Appendices
FLEURBAIX (H.31.d.20.70)	Sept 12th	am 5.30	35 rounds on enemy supports at O.1.a.65.60, where smoke was observed by Infantry. Enemy retaliated vigorously, using gas shells (15 on ABBOTS LANE)	
		am 10.15	30 rounds on N.8.a.33.18 in conjunction with medium T.Ms — doing much damage. Visibility poor owing to ground mist, and observation was therefore difficult.	
		pm 7-0	71st Inf. Bde Order No. 33 (copy No 18) received, regarding relief of 71st Inf. Brigade by 114th Inf Brigade.	
	13th	pm 4-0	36 rounds on to enemy supports at N.6.c.20.20 — to which enemy replied vigorously with 'pineapples'. Aircraft — Enemy machines troublesome during our shoots. Our machines were active all day, flying low over enemy lines.	
		pm 3-0	Enemy plane fired green lights over our lines, upon which Signal 10 with T.Ms opened fire.	
	14th	am 8-0	60 rounds on N.8.a.80.85 — much material damage caused. Enemy replied with a few 4.2's on our right	
		pm 7.15	60 rounds on INDEX TR. and supports, provoking considerable retaliation in the shape of 30 to 40 gas shells, 200 'pineapples' and 4 minnies.	

(A7092). Wt. W12839/M1293. 750,000. 1/17. D. D. & L., Ltd. Forms/C.2118/14.

Map. FRANCE Sheet 36a 1/40000.

Instructions regarding War Diaries and Intelligence Summaries are contained in F. S. Regs., Part II. and the Staff Manual respectively. Title pages will be prepared in manuscript.

WAR DIARY
or
INTELLIGENCE SUMMARY.

(Erase heading not required.)

Sheet 6

Army Form C. 2118.

Place	Date 1917	Hour	Summary of Events and Information	Remarks and references to Appendices
FLEURBAIX 4.21.d.30.70.	Sept. 15th	am 4.30	At about 4.30 am enemy put down a 4.2 & 77 m barrage on our support line in rear of CORDONNERIE Salient line [illegible] minutes later came back on to our front line at this place. Our artillery replied and our [illegible] TM guns answered S.O.S. by firing 100 rounds on their S.O.S. lines. At 5.30 pm all was quiet. No enemy was seen but [illegible] were heard & golden rain rockets were sent up by the Germans. No other firing – preparation made to hand over to 114th Bde Light T.M.B.	
	16th	am 8.00	Loaded motor lorry with stores &c to send to ST HILAIRE area (Frontal). One Officer & 2 other ranks sent on as billeting party to LA GORGUE (L.34.a)	
		9.30	received relieving party of 114th L.T.M.B. who were guided up to	
		pm 1.0	the line ~~and~~ to relieve the 171st L.T.M.B.	
		pm 7.0	Relief of 171st Inf. Bde L.T.M.B. by 114th Inf. Bde L.T.M.B. completed & receipts [illegible] duly handed over.	
		pm 9.45	Battery paraded and moved off to LA GORGUE (L.34.a) to take over billets vacated by 114th L.T.M.B.	
LA GORGUE (L.34.a)		pm 11.15	Arrived complete, no men falling out.	

(A7092). Wt. W12839/M1293. 750,000. 1/17. D. D. & L., Ltd. Forms/C.2118/14.

Map Sheet 36a [illegible] (FRANCE)

Instructions regarding War Diaries and Intelligence Summaries are contained in F. S. Regs., Part II. and the Staff Manual respectively. Title pages will be prepared in manuscript.

WAR DIARY
or
INTELLIGENCE SUMMARY.
(Erase heading not required.)

Army Form C. 2118.

Sheet 1.

Place	Date	Hour	Summary of Events and Information	Remarks and references to Appendices
LA GORGUE.	17	-	Day spent in resting and tidying up &c.	
"			[illegible] Inf Bde Order No 34 received, re move to next Station	
"	18th	am 9.0	Battery left LA GORGUE and marched via COLONNE and ROBECQ to BUSNES (P.26.c) arriving there by 1.30 pm. March discipline good – no men fell out.	
BUSNES. (P.26.C)	"	pm 6.0	[illegible] Inf. Bde Order No 35 received, re move from BUSNES to LESPESSES (T.12.d)	
"	19th	am 9.0	Battery vacated billets at BUSNES and marched via LILLERS & BURBECQ to LESPESSES (T.12.d)	
LESPESSE (T.12.c.85.00)	19th	12.0 noon	Arrived in billets – good march discipline all the way – no men falling out.	
"	20th	am 9.30	Attended conference of Brigade Bombing Officers & Light T.M.B. Commanders at XI Corps School, MERVILLE. The Corps Commander (Lt General HAKING) was present and several points of tactical and technical interest were discussed.	
"		-	During day men cleaned up equipment &c preparatory to training	
"	21st to 28th	}	Training of unit carried out as per training programmes rendered. (reference being made to SS.135 – Training of Divs. for Offensive action; S.S.148 – Intercommunication in battle; S.S.152 – Instructions for training of British Armies in France.)	

(A7092). Wt. W12839/M1293. 750,000. 1/17. D. D. & L., Ltd. Forms/C.2118/14.

Map. FRANCE Sheet 36a 1/40000.

Instructions regarding War Diaries and Intelligence Summaries are contained in F. S. Regs., Part II. and the Staff Manual respectively. Title pages will be prepared in manuscript.

WAR DIARY
or
INTELLIGENCE SUMMARY.
(Erase heading not required.)

Army Form C. 2118.

Sheet 8.

Place	Date	Hour	Summary of Events and Information	Remarks and references to Appendices
LESPESSES (T.12.c.85.00)	1917 Sept 29th	noon 12	Lieut J.D. JARDINE proceeded on leave to ENGLAND. Lieut SMALLPAGE E. assumed Command of Battery.	
	30	9 pm.	306400 Cpl. Wiggins A. admitted to Field Ambulance: P.U.O.	
	30		Total Effective Strength at end of month. 7 Officers, 67 Other Ranks	

E. Smallpage Lieut.
Cdg. 171st L.T.M.B.

(A7092). Wt. W12839/M1293. 750,000. 1/17. D. D. & L., Ltd. Forms/C.2118/14.

171st Bde. Light. T.M.B.

WAR DIARY

Vol. 9.

OCTOBER. 1917.

Maps: HAZEBROUCK 5A 1/100.000 · Edition 2.
FRANCE 36A 1/40000

WAR DIARY
or
~~INTELLIGENCE~~ SUMMARY.
(Erase heading not required.)

Volume 9.

OCTOBER, 1917.

Army Form C. 2118.

Part 1.

Instructions regarding War Diaries and Intelligence Summaries are contained in F. S. Regs., Part II. and the Staff Manual respectively. Title pages will be prepared in manuscript.

Place	Date 1917	Hour	Summary of Events and Information	Remarks and references to Appendices
HQrs at LESPESSES. (T 12 c 85 05)	Oct. 1st to 18th		– This time was spent in the continuation and completion of training in the ST HILAIRE area.	
	3rd	–	CAPT. H E BARROW returned to duty from XI Corps Rest Station and re-assumed command of the Battery.	
	6th	12 noon	The Brigade inspected by Field Marshal Sir DOUGLAS HAIG, KT GCB GCVO KCIE., Commander in Chief British Armies in FRANCE. The Battery marched past – Capt BARROW in command, 4 officers and 60 other ranks on parade.	
	8th	12.30pm	Whilst on Brigade Operations in the BOMY Special manoeuvre area, No. 2668? Corpl KELLY W.T was accidentally wounded in the right wrist, owing to a Stokes 3" Mortar shell falling short.	H.B
	9th	am 10.30	Corpl Kelly admitted to C.C.S. and struck off the strength of the Battery.	
	10th	–	Lieut. SAGE proceeded on leave to England.	
	10th	pm 10.30	Lieut. JARDINE J.D. returned to duty from leave of absence in England.	
	16th	pm 2.30	Receipt of 7th Bde Order No. 32, giving details of move from ST HILAIRE to RENESCURE Area on 19th October.	
	19th	am 8.30	Battery moved off and joined the Brigade in the march to RENESCURE	
RENESCURE (H. E 55.85)	19th	pm 2.15	Arrived at RENESCURE – no men fell out on the march.	

(A7092). Wt. W12839/M1293. 750,000. 1/17. D. D. & L., Ltd. Forms/C.2118/14.

BELGIUM. Sheet 28 N.W. 1/20000. Edition 6A

Instructions regarding War Diaries and Intelligence Summaries are contained in F. S. Regs., Part II. and the Staff Manual respectively. Title pages will be prepared in manuscript.

WAR DIARY
or
~~INTELLIGENCE~~ SUMMARY.
(Erase heading not required.)

Vol. 9.
Sheet 2.

Army Form C. 2118.

Place HQrs at	Date	Hour	Summary of Events and Information	Remarks and references to Appendices
RENESCURE	20th	am. 8.15	The Battery embussed and at 9.0 am proceeded to PROVEN, debussing there and marching to billets in PROVEN AREA No 4. arriving there about 3.0 pm.	
PLUMSTEAD CAMP. (PROVEN AREA North.	24th	am. 11.0	The Battery paraded and marched to PROVEN STATION, entraining there 12.30 pm and proceeded to ELVERDINGHE Station. Detrained and marched to billets in REDAN CAMP (B.22.d.3.8.), arriving there 2.30 pm.	
REDAN CAMP (B.22.d.3.8)	26th	pm. 9.0	The Battery moved up to the CANAL and encamped there - the men in bivouacs, the Officers & HQrs in dug outs in the CANAL BANK at C.19.c.00.80. The Brigade relieved the 70th Infy. Brigade in the line.	A.R.B.
CANAL BANK C19c 00.80	27th		Day spent in erecting bivouac sheets, cookhouse etc. Officers & N.C.O's reconnoitring A, B & LANGERMACK Tracks.	
	28th	10.20AM	Party of 2 NCO's & 15 OR's road making under orders of No 505 Field Coy R.E's.	
"				
"	29th	9.30AM	1 NCO & 15 OR's road making under No 505 Field Coy R.E's.	
"	"	12.30pm	1 Officer 15 OR's Salvage Work.	
"		7.30pm	1 Officer 30 OR's Carrying timber to BOWER HOUSE for gun positions for 172 L.T.M.B.	
"	30th	6.0pm	1 Officer 22 OR's Laying duckboard tracks.	
"	31st	2.15pm	1 Officer 20 OR's Preparing Shells at Dump RED HOUSE.	

(A7092). Wt. W12539/M1293. 750,000. 1/17. D. D. & L., Ltd. Forms/C.2118/14.

Army Form C. 2118.

WAR DIARY
or
INTELLIGENCE SUMMARY.
(Erase heading not required.)

Volume 9.

Sheet 3.

Instructions regarding War Diaries and Intelligence Summaries are contained in F. S. Regs., Part II, and the Staff Manual respectively. Title pages will be prepared in manuscript.

Place	Date	Hour	Summary of Events and Information	Remarks and references to Appendices
CANAL BANK C19c 00.80	31st		Strength of unit at end of month. 7 Officers. 64 O.R's.	

(A7092). Wt. W12839/M1293. 750,000. 1/17. D. D. & L., Ltd. Forms/C.2118/14.

To Headquarters.
57th Division

Herewith War Diary for Nov 1917. (Vol 10) please

171 BRIGADE TRENCH
B14/59
ORDERLY ROOM
30/11/17
MORTAR BATTERIES

K. Sherman [illegible] Lt.
Cdg 171st L.T.M.B.

171st. Bde. Light. T.M.B.

WAR. DIARY.

Vol. 10.

~~Octo~~ NOVEMBER. 1917.

Instructions regarding War Diaries and Intelligence Summaries are contained in F. S. Regs., Part II. and the Staff Manual respectively. Title pages will be prepared in manuscript.

WAR DIARY

~~or~~

~~INTELLIGENCE SUMMARY.~~

(Erase heading not required.)

Army Form C. 2118.

VOLUME 10.

November 1917. Sheet 1

Place	Date	Hour	Summary of Events and Information	Remarks and references to Appendices
CANAL BANK. (C.19.c.00.80)	Nov. 1st.	5 p.m.	1 Officer 15 O.R's, collecting S.A.A. in vicinity of RED HOUSE. 2 O.R. slightly gassed.	
	"	7 p.m.	1 Officer 11 O.R's carrying solidified alcohol to LEWIS FARM.	
	2nd	9 a.m.	1 N.C.O., 15 O.R's collecting salvage under orders of AREA COMMANDANT, CANAL BANK.	
		4 p.m.	The Battery was relieved by 172nd L.T.M.B. & moved to REDAN CAMP (B.22.d.2.8.) arriving there at 5.45 p.m.	
REDAN CAMP (B.22.d.2.8.)	4th	6 p.m.	Lieut. J.D. Jardine reported sick at Main Dressing Station & was evacuated to 63rd C.C.S. 2/Lt. J.C. Bradbury returned from leave. 1 O.R. (Rfn. Slack) returned to his unit (2/5 K.L.R.)	
	5th	3 p.m.	Capt. H.E. Barrow proceeded on leave to England. Lt. E. Smallpage assumed command of Battery. Receipt of 171st Infantry Brigade Order No 46 giving details of move to NORDAUSQUES area 7 p.m.	
	6th	9 p.m.	Battery paraded & marched to INTERNATIONAL CORNER STATION. Arrived at 11.45 p.m. & having loaded Brigade Transport on omnibus train, entrained at	
	7th		3.45 a.m. arriving at ~~[illegible]~~ AUDRUICQ at 11.45 a.m. & marched to AUTINGUES arriving at 3.30 p.m. Stragglers – nil.	

(A7092). Wt. W12839/M1293. 750,000. 1/17. D. D. & L., Ltd. Forms/C.2118/14.

Instructions regarding War Diaries and Intelligence Summaries are contained in F. S. Regs., Part II. and the Staff Manual respectively. Title pages will be prepared in manuscript.

WAR DIARY
or
~~INTELLIGENCE SUMMARY.~~
(Erase heading not required.)

Army Form C. 2118.

Vol 10
Sheet 2

Place	Date Nov.	Hour	Summary of Events and Information	Remarks and references to Appendices
AUTINGUES	9th	5 p.m.	Lt. D. G. Leonard, batman, & 1 N.C.O. (L/Cpl Caves) proceeded to XIV Corps Trench Mortar School.	
	10th		Period of Training commenced.	
	16th	10 a.m.	Lt. H. F. Eames reported from 2/8th K.L.R and was taken on strength of permanent battery.	
		7.30 p.m.	Cpl. Kelly returned from hospital.	
	24th	12 noon	Lt. D. G. Leonard & 2 O.R. returned from XIV Corps T.M. School.	
	27th	11 a.m.	Lt. E. Smallpage proceeded on leave. Lt. D. G. Leonard assumed command of the Battery.	
	"		List No. 956 D.A.G. received noting transfer to ENGLAND of LIEUT. J. D. JARDINE on 17.11.17. after medical board 14 GENERAL HOSPITAL. Struck of strength as from 17.11.17.	
	30th		Strength of unit at end of month. Officers – 7. Other Ranks – 66.	

(A7092). Wt. W12839/M1293. 750,000. 1/17. D. D. & L., Ltd. Forms/C.2118/14.

171st Bde. Light. T.M.B.

WAR. DIARY.

Vol 11.

DECEMBER. 1917.

To Headquarters
57th Division

Herewith War Diary for
December 1917.

171 BRIGADE TRENCH
B16/44
ORDERLY ROOM
9/1/18
MORTAR BATTERIES

[illegible signature]
Cdg 171st L.T.M.B.

Instructions regarding War Diaries and Intelligence Summaries are contained in F. S. Regs., Part II. and the Staff Manual respectively. Title pages will be prepared in manuscript.

WAR DIARY
or
~~INTELLIGENCE SUMMARY.~~
(Erase heading not required.)

Army Form C. 2118.

VOLUME 11

DECEMBER 1917.

Sheet 1

Place	Date	Hour	Summary of Events and Information	Remarks and references to Appendices
AUTINGUES.	DEC. 1st - 6th		Continuation and completion of training in AUTINGUES	
	3rd		Two OR's returned from Course at XIX Corps T.M. School.	
	5th		Brigade attack scheme at Training area GUÉMY, HAZEBROUCK, 5A - 3A. 20.60. The Battery took part in Scheme.	
	7th	7.0 PM	Brigade Order 49, copy no 5 received giving details of move to PROOSDY AREA on 8th Dec.	
	8th	8.0 A.M.	The Battery (4 Off. + 50 OR's) embussed at AUTINGUES & proceeded to PROVEN, debussing there and marching to PICCADILLY CAMP in the PROOSDY AREA, arriving there about 2.30 P.M. The camp was taken over from 50th Bde L T M B. 17th DIV. Stragglers Nil.	
PICCADILLY CAMP 21.05.95.	9th		One OR. (L'Cpl. Jennings) proceeded on a L.T.M. course at 19th Corps TRENCH MORTAR School at BOLLEZEELE.	
	12th	10.30 AM.	G.O.C. 57th Div. inspected the camp.	
	"	2.15 P.M.	1 Off. + 2 OR's proceeded to ELVERDINGHE as an advance party to reconnoitre the line.	
	13th	6.0 P.M.	LIEUT. E. SMALLPAGE returned from leave and resumed command of the battery.	
	14th		Two OR's returned from 5th Army School of Mortars.	
	15th		Received Brigade Order No. 50 re move to line on 16th	
CANAL BANK. 2.K. 20.75.	16th	9.0 AM	Battery paraded and marched to PROVEN, entraining at 10.AM. – Arrived BOESINGHE Station and took up quarters in CANAL BANK CAMP – (HAZEBROUCK 5A.) 2 K. 17.78.	
	17th		Lieut. H.F. EAMES and 15 OR's relieved the 55th L.T.M.B in the line. Relief completed by 6.50 p.m.	
SIGNAL FARM. V.21.c.15.05.	"		Lieut. E. SMALLPAGE, batman + 2 OR's (runners) took up quarters at SIGNAL FME. (H.Q's), leaving remainder of battery under Lt. Leonard at CANAL BANK. 1 O.R. proceeded to England on leave.	
	20th	6 p.m.	Lt. Sage & 14 O.R. relieved Lt. Eames & party in line. No shooting had been carried out.	
	22nd	4.20 p.m.	Heavy enemy barrage put down on whole Brigade Sector. 4 mortars replied to S.O.S. firing 141 rounds. 3 O.R. wounded, & one gun on YPRES - STADEN railway buried before retirement of our posts. Situation normal at 10 p.m.	
	23rd	6 p.m.	2/Lt. Bradbury & 14 O.R. relieved Lt. Sage & party. 1 O.R. returned from 19th Corps T.M. School.	

(A7092). Wt. W12839/M1293. 750,000. 1/17. D. D. & L., Ltd. Forms/C.2118/14

Army Form C. 2118.

Instructions regarding War Diaries and Intelligence Summaries are contained in F. S. Regs., Part II. and the Staff Manual respectively. Title pages will be prepared in manuscript.

WAR DIARY
or
~~INTELLIGENCE~~ SUMMARY.
(Erase heading not required.)

Vol. 11.
Sheet. 2.

Place	Date	Hour	Summary of Events and Information	Remarks and references to Appendices
SIGNAL FARM.	Dec. 25.		Battery relieved by 172nd L.T.M.B. relief being completed by 9.20 p.m. & took up quarters in MARGUERITE FARM CAMP (B.9.a.2.1.). 3 O.R. proceeded to 19th Corps T.M. School. Copy of 57th Divisional Warning Order re relief of 57th Div. by 18th Div. received.	
MARGUERITE FARM. PRAED CAMP F.9.a.4.9.	29	10 a.m.	Battery paraded & marched to PRAED CAMP (CANADA AREA) arriving at 2.45 p.m. Stragglers – Nil. 2nd Lt. Langton proceeded on leave to England.	
GODE AREA.	30.	8.30 a.m.	Battery paraded & marched to GODE area arriving in billets Q.30.d.3.4. at 3 p.m. Lt. Sage, batman, & 1 O.R. proceeded on course at XV Corps T.M. School. Bde. Order No. 57. re relief of 9th Australian Bde. by 171st Bde. received.	
	31.	10 a.m.	Battery marched to STEENWERCKE area arriving at NENEGATE CAMP at 3 p.m.	
			Strength of unit at end of month. 7 Officers 60 O.R.	

[signature illegible] Lieut.
Cdg. 171st L.T.M.B.

(A7092). Wt. W12839/M1293. 750,000. 1/17. D. D. & L., Ltd. Forms/C.2118/14.

171st Bde. Light T. M. B.

WAR DIARY

Vol 12.

JANUARY 1918.

Instructions regarding War Diaries and Intelligence Summaries are contained in F. S. Regs., Part II. and the Staff Manual respectively. Title pages will be prepared in manuscript.

WAR DIARY
~~or~~
~~INTELLIGENCE SUMMARY.~~

(*Erase heading not required.*)

Volume 12.

Army Form C. 2118.

January 1918. Sheet 1

Place	Date Jan^y.	Hour	Summary of Events and Information	Remarks and references to Appendices
MENEGATE CAMP.	1.	3 p.m.	Battery paraded & marched to ARMENTIÈRES relieving 9th Australian L.T.M.B. Headquarters 14 Rue Sadi Carnot. Lt. Eames & 15 O.R. in EPINETTE SUB-SECTOR, 2/Lt. BRADBURY & 15 O.R. in HOUPLINES SUB-SECTOR. Relief completed 11 p.m.	
ARMENTIÈRES (14 Rue Sadi Carnot)	2–12.		Daily shooting in retaliation to "minnies" & "pineapples". Guns laid nightly to cover our front line.	
–	3.	Noon.	13 O.R. attached to Battery from battalions	
	2.		Pte TATTERSALL awarded MILITARY MEDAL for gallantry & devotion to duty on 22.12.17.	
	4.	–	1 O.R. (Cpl. Roberts) returned from leave. 5 O.R. attached to Battery from battalions. 1 O.R. (Cpl. Murphy) admitted to 5th Australian C.C.S. (Injured knee).	
	7	4 p.m.	Lt. Leonard & 15 O.R. relieved Lt. Bradbury & party in HOUPLINES; Sgt. Major Amos & 15 relieved Lt. EAMES & party on EPINETTE.	
	9		1 O.R. attached to Battery from 2/6 K.L.R.	
	10.	2 p.m.	3 O.R. returned from 19 Corps T.M. School. Dug-out & kit of crew of No. 7 gun destroyed by "minnie". No casualties.	
	11.	9.30 a.m.	3 O.R. killed on EPINETTE by a minnie (Pte Tattersall, Cpl. Conley, Pte Webster). L/Cpls. Jennings & Westbrook to be paid Cpls. 2 O.R. (Cpl. Henderson, Pte S. Wallace) admitted to 3/2nd West Lancs. Field Ambulance, sick.	
	13.		Battery relieved by 172nd L.T.M.B. Relief completed 3 p.m. Battery moved to billets in GENEVA CAMP	
		9.45 p.m.	(Sheet 36 A.N.W. 1/20,000 A.23. c. 1.5.)	
GENEVA CAMP.	14.		Lt. SMALLPAGE E. taken on strength of Battery (A.G. 109/92 (O) of 9.1.18). Ptes Riddick, Woodworth, & McCarthy to be acting L/Cpls. (unpaid.)	

(A7092). Wt. W12839/M1293. 750,000. 1/17. D. D. & L., Ltd. Forms/C.2118/14.

Army Form C. 2118.

Instructions regarding War Diaries and Intelligence Summaries are contained in F. S. Regs., Part II. and the Staff Manual respectively. Title pages will be prepared in manuscript.

WAR DIARY
~~or~~
~~INTELLIGENCE~~ SUMMARY.
(*Erase heading not required.*)

Vol. 12.

Jan. 1918 Sheet 2.

Place	Date Jan.	Hour	Summary of Events and Information	Remarks and references to Appendices
Geneva Camp.	15	Noon.	2nd Lt. Longton P. returned from leave. 1 O.R. to 2/2nd Wessex Field Ambulance (Sick)	
	16.	5.30 a.m.	1 Officer 30 O.R. working party on ARMENTIÈRES defences. 1 O.R. to Field Ambulance. (Sick)	
	17.	6.30 a.m.	Two parties of 1 O. & 15 O.R. at work on ARMENTIÈRES defences. Lt. Eames, batman, & 2 O.R. proceeded to XV Corps T.M. school. 1 O.R. on leave to England; 1 O.R. sick to Field Ambulance.	
	18		14 O.R. transferred from attached personnel & taken on strength of battery. 3 O.R. attached from battalions, 2 O.R. returned to units. ~~[illegible]~~	[illegible]
	19.	9 a.m.	Lt. Sage, batman, & 1 O.R. returned from XV Corps T.M. school. 1 O.R. attached from unit; 1 O.R. to Field Ambulance. (sick)	
	20.		~~[illegible]~~ 171st Infantry Brigade Order No. 60 re relief of 172nd Bde. received. 2 O.R. to Field Ambulance. (sick) Working party of 1 N.C.O. & 10 men at BAC-ST. MAUR.	
	21	8 a.m.	Battery paraded & marched to ARMENTIÈRES relieving 172nd L.T.M.B. Headquarters taken up in 14 Rue SADI CARNOT. Lt. Sage & ~~2~~ 14 O.R. on EPINETTE SUB-SECTOR, 2nd Lt. LONGTON & 14 O.R. on HOUPLINES SUB-SECTOR. 1 O.R. to Field Ambulance. (sick). Relief completed by 3 p.m.	
ARMENTIÈRES 14 Rue Sadi Carnot	21–27		A small amount of retaliatory shooting from both sectors. Line in bad condition owing to thaw & floods.	
	22.		1 O.R. returned from hospital.	
	23.	9 p.m.	1 O.R. (Cpl. Henderson) wounded by M.G. 2 O.R. to Field Ambulance. (sick)	
	24		1 O.R. on leave to England. L/Cpl. CROSTON to be paid Corporal	
	25.		CAPT. BARROW H.E. struck off strength as from 24.12.17 in accordance with A.G. 4a. dated 9.1.18.	

(A7092). Wt. W12839/M1293. 750,000. 1/17. D. D. & L., Ltd. Forms/C.2118/14.

Army Form C. 2118.

Instructions regarding War Diaries and Intelligence Summaries are contained in F. S. Regs., Part II. and the Staff Manual respectively. Title pages will be prepared in manuscript.

WAR DIARY
~~or~~
~~INTELLIGENCE SUMMARY.~~
(Erase heading not required.)

Vol. 12.
Jan. 1918. Sheet 3

Place	Date Jany	Hour	Summary of Events and Information	Remarks and references to Appendices
ARMENTIÈRES 14 Rue Sadi Carnot	26	8 p.m.	171st Inf. Bde Order No 12 re relief of Bde by 172nd Inf. Bde received.	
	27.	–	Relief of battery by 172nd L.T.M.B. completed by 6 p.m. Battery paraded & marched to billets at GENEVA CAMP arriving at 7.30 p.m.	
GENEVA CAMP A.23.c.1.5.	28	3 p.m.	1 O.R. on leave to England	
	29.		1 O.R. returned from hospital. 8 O.R. transferred to Battery from attached personnel to complete establishment.	
	30	6 p.m.	10 O.R. attached from battalions for duty with Battery.	
	31.	3 p.m.	1 O.R. on leave to England. 1 O.R. joined from unit.	
			Strength of unit at end of month. 6 Officers. 82 Other Ranks. [illegible signature]	

(A7092). Wt. W12839/M1293. 750,000. 1/17. D. D. & L., Ltd. Forms/C.2118/14.

171st Bde Light T.M.B.

WAR DIARY

VOLUME No 13.

February 1918.

To:- Headquarters
57th Division.

Herewith War Diary for February 1918 Volume No. 13. please

171 BRIGADE TRENCH
B21/8
ORDERLY ROOM
1/3/18
MORTAR BATTERIES

[illegible] Capt.
Cdg. 171st LTMB.

Instructions regarding War Diaries and Intelligence Summaries are contained in F. S. Regs., Part II. and the Staff Manual respectively. Title pages will be prepared in manuscript.

WAR DIARY
~~or~~
~~INTELLIGENCE SUMMARY.~~
(Erase heading not required.)

VOLUME 13.

FEBRUARY 1918 Sheet. 1.

Army Form C. 2118.

Place	Date Feb.	Hour	Summary of Events and Information	Remarks and references to Appendices
GENEVA CAMP A.23.c.1.5.	1	Noon.	Receipt of 171st Infantry Brigade Order No. 63 re relief of 172nd Infantry Brigade. 2.O.R. proceeded on leave to England, 1 O.R. evacuated to hospital (sick.)	
	2.	9a.m.	Battery paraded & marched to ARMENTIÈRES. Headquarters relieved 172nd L.T.M.B. in 14 Rue Sadi Carnot – Lt. Leonard & 14 O.R. in EPINETTE Subsector, Lt. Bradbury & 14 O.R. in HOUPLINES Subsector. Relief completed 4p.m.	
ARMENTIÈRES 14 Rue Sadi Carnot.			1 O.R. returned from hospital.	
	3.		Receipt of 171st Infantry Brigade Order No. 64. re Special Operation to be carried out. A small shoot of 25 rounds	
		2.30p.m.	destroyed enemy ammn. dump in INCENSE TRENCH.	
	4		3 O.R. returned from hospital. Men out of line engaged in preparing & carrying ammn. for Special Operation. Receipt of 171st Infantry Brigade Order No. 65 ref. reorganisation of Divisional Front.	
	5		Lt. LEONARD & party relieved in EPINETTE sub-sector by 172nd L.T.M.B. Headquarters also relieved by 172nd L.T.M.B. & moved to 130 BOULEVARD FAIDHERBE. Relief completed 2.30p.m. 4 Mortars from EPINETTE transferred to HOUPLINES. 30 O.R. from infantry & all men out of line engaged shell-carrying. 1 O.R. returned from leave. LT. EAMES & 3 O.R. returned from XV Corps T.M. school. Receipt of 171st Infantry Brigade Provisional Defence Scheme.	
130 BOULEVARDE FAIDHERBE				

(A7092). Wt. W12839/M1293 750,000. 1/17. D. D. & L., Ltd. Forms/C.2118/14.

Army Form C. 2118.

WAR DIARY

~~or~~

~~INTELLIGENCE SUMMARY.~~

(Erase heading not required.)

Instructions regarding War Diaries and Intelligence Summaries are contained in F. S. Regs., Part II. and the Staff Manual respectively. Title pages will be prepared in manuscript.

Vol. 13

Feb. 1918 Sheet 2.

Place	Date	Hour	Summary of Events and Information	Remarks and references to Appendices
ARMENTIÈRES 130 BOULEVARDE FAIDHERBE.	Feb. 6	8.30 a.m.	Receipt of Zero hour & day for Special Operation. Day spent in final preparations & in registration.	
		8.30 p.m.	6 guns under Lt. EAMES fired from area between CAMBRIDGE & EDMEADS Avs. from 8.27 until 8.50. ~~[illegible]~~ as diversion on CELT SYSTEM. 2 guns at head of LONDON ROAD fired 350 rounds in barrage on C.29.c.4.9. from 8.30 p.m. to 8.53. Casualties to battery — 1 O.R. (Cpl. [illegible]) slightly wounded by shell, but remained at duty.	
	7	3 p.m.	2Lt. BRADBURY & party relieved by Lt. SAGE & 14 O.R. Ammunition in dumps & in line checked. L.T.M.B. defence scheme submitted to Brigade H.Q. 1 O.R. to hospital, sick. Pte. [illegible] to be acting unpd. L/Cpl.	
	9		1 O.R. returned from hospital.	
	10		1 O.R. returned from hospital, 1 O.R. joined from unit.	
	11		Receipt of 171st Infantry Brigade Warning Order re relief by 114 Inf. Bde. 2 O.R. on leave to England.	
	12		Receipt of 171st Inf. Bde. Order No. 68 re relief & of defence scheme for HOUPLINES SECTOR. Lt. SMALLPAGE E. to be acting Capt. while O.C. battery. Dated 25.12.17. 1 O.R. to hospital sick.	
	13		1 O.R. returned from leave. Authority received for posting of Lt. LEONARD D.G. to battery as from 6.2.18.	
		2 p.m.	Lt. SAGE & party relieved by 1 Officer & 18 O.R. of 114th L.T.M.B.	
	14	1.30 p.m.	Relief of battery by 114 L.T.M.B. completed. Battery proceeded to billets at ROUSSEL FARM (4H.24.00.)	
ROUSSEL FARM.	15		Period of training commences.	

(A7092). Wt. W12839/M1293. 750,000. 1/17. D. D. & L., Ltd. Forms/C.2118/14.

Army Form C. 2118.

WAR DIARY

or

~~INTELLIGENCE SUMMARY.~~

(Erase heading not required.)

Instructions regarding War Diaries and Intelligence Summaries are contained in F. S. Regs., Part II. and the Staff Manual respectively. Title pages will be prepared in manuscript.

Vol. 13

Feb. 1918. Sheet 3.

Place	Date	Hour	Summary of Events and Information	Remarks and references to Appendices
ROUSSEL FARM. 4H.24.00.	Feb. 16	–	Authority received for posting of 2/Lt. LONGTON P. to battery as from 9.2.18. 1 O.R. returned from leave. Sections re-organised & brought to equal strength.	
	18	–	1 O.R. to hospital, sick.	
	19	Noon.	1 Officer (Lt. LEONARD D.G.) & 2 O.R. proceeded on leave to England. 3 O.R. returned from leave.	
	20	–	2 O.R. (attached from 2/6 R.I.R.) returned to unit. Replaced by 2 O.R. from 2/6 R.I.R.	
	23		171st Infantry Brigade Warning Order re move to ST. HILAIRE area received. 2/Lt. BRADBURY, batman, & 6 O.R. proceeded to XV Corps T.M. School. 1 O.R. evacuated to 54 C.C.S. sick.	
	24		L/Cpl. Woodworth to XV Corps Gas-school. 1 O.R. to 51 C.C.S. sick.	
	25.		Receipt of 171st Infantry Bde Order re move to ST HILAIRE. 1 O.R. proceeded on leave to England. 1 O.R. returned from hospital. Receipt of 171st Bde Emergency Orders & entraining scheme.	
	26		1 O.R. to hospital, sick. Receipt of 171st Infantry Brigade Administrative Instructions	
	27		1 O.R. to hospital, sick. Receipt of 171st Inf. Bde Order No. 69 with march table re move.	
	28	1 p.m.	1 O.R. proceeded on leave to England	
			Strength Of Unit At End Of Month. 6 Officers 77 O.R.	[signature] Capt. 171st L.T.M.B.

(A7092). Wt. W12839/M1293. 750,000. 1/17. D. D. & L., Ltd. Forms/C.2118/14.

171st Bde. Light T.M.B.

WAR DIARY.

Vol. 14.

MARCH. 1918.

To Headquarters.
57th Division.

Herewith War Diary (Vol 14) for March 1918, please.

171 BRIGADE TRENCH
B23/49
ORDERLY ROOM
1/4/18
MORTAR BATTERIES

[illegible] Capt
Cdg 171st L.T.M.B.

Army Form C. 2118.

Instructions regarding War Diaries and Intelligence Summaries are contained in F. S. Regs., Part II. and the Staff Manual respectively. Title pages will be prepared in manuscript.

WAR DIARY
~~or~~
~~INTELLIGENCE SUMMARY.~~

(*Erase heading not required.*)

Volume 14 — March 1918 — Sheet 1.

Place	Date March	Hour	Summary of Events and Information	Remarks and references to Appendices
Roussel Farm.	1	7.15 a.m.	Battery paraded & marched to RELY (T.1.d.20.95.) arriving in billets at 2.45 p.m. 1 O.R. proceeded on leave to England. Period of training commences.	
Rely. (T.1.d.20.95)	2		1 O.R. returned to duty from XV Corps Gas-School.	
	4	–	1 O.R. returned to duty from hospital.	
	5	–	Receipt of 171st Infy. Bde. orders for Emergency Action. Lt Eames & batman proceeded on course with No. 4 Squadron R.F.C. 2 O.R. returned from leave, ~~[illegible]~~. 1 O.R. proceeded on leave to England, 1 O.R. admitted to hospital.	
	6	–	Lt Sage on leave to England. 1 O.R. returned from hospital.	
	7	9.15 a.m.	2/Lt. Longton & 40 O.R. paraded for Guard duty at FLECHINELLES aerodrome. 1 O.R. to hospital.	
	8		1 O.R. proceeded on leave to England. 2/Lt. Longton & party returned from guard (1 p.m.)	
	9	11 p.m.	Summer-time came into force. Lt. Leonard & 2 O.R. returned from leave. 2 O.R. detailed for farm-work	
	10	12.50 a.m.	Receipt of B.M./792 warning order. 4 p.m. receipt of 171st Infy. Bde. Order 70 re move to MERVILLE.	
		6.15 a.m.	Battery paraded & marched to NORRENT FONTES embussing at 8 a.m. Arrived in billets ROUSSEL FARM @ 1.30 p.m. Stragglers, Nil. Lt. Eames & batman returned to duty from R.F.C.	
	11	–	2 O.R. on leave to England.	

(A7092). Wt. W12839/M1293. 750,000. 1/17. D. D. & L., Ltd. Forms/C.2118/14.

Army Form C. 2118.

Instructions regarding War Diaries and Intelligence Summaries are contained in F. S. Regs., Part II. and the Staff Manual respectively. Title pages will be prepared in manuscript.

WAR DIARY
or
INTELLIGENCE SUMMARY.

(Erase heading not required.)

Vol 14

March 1918. Sheet 11

Place	Date	Hour	Summary of Events and Information	Remarks and references to Appendices
ROUSSEL FARM.	March. 12.	–	1 O.R. evacuated to 51 C.C.S. (sick.)	
	13	10 a.m.	2/Lt. BRADBURY & 7 O.R. returned to duty from XV Corps T.M. School. 1 O.R. to hospital (sick.)	
	14.	–	2 O.R. on leave to England. 1 O.R. to hospital (sick).	
	16	–	1 O.R. returned to duty from hospital.	
	17.	–	1 O.R. returned from leave.	
	18	5 p.m.	Receipt of 171st Infy. Bde. warning order re move on 21st.	
	19		2 O.R. returned from leave, 1 O.R. from hospital. 2/Lt. BRADBURY & 3 O.R. proceeded on leave to England.	
	20	7-30 a.m.	Receipt of 171st Infy. Bde. Order No. 71. 1 O.R. returned from hospital.	
	21.	8 a.m.	Battery paraded & relieved 36th L.T.M.B. in reserve at SAILLY, arriving 11.45 a.m.	
SAILLY. (G.22.a.5.3)	22	–	Lt. SAGE returned from leave. 2 O.R. on leave. 1 O.R. to hospital (sick). 2 officers & 30 O.R. at work on emergency gun pits.	
	23	8 a.m.	2 Officers 46 O.R. working party under R.E. orders. Receipt of 171st Infy. Bde. Warning Order re relief of 170 Bde. 2 O.R. proceeded on leave to England.	
	24.	–	2 O.R. returned from Railhead Camp, leave having been cancelled. 2/Lt. LONGSTON & batman returned from XV Corps T.M. school.	
	25	–	2 Officers & 50 O.R. on working party under R.E. 1 O.R. to hospital (sick). 2 O.R. returned to duty from leave, owing to cancellation of leave. Receipt of 171st Inf. Bde. Order No. 72 re relief of 170 Inf. Bde. 1 O.R. returned from hospital.	

(A7092). Wt. W12839/M1293. 750,000. 1/17. D. D. & L., Ltd. Forms/C.2118/14.

Instructions regarding War Diaries and Intelligence Summaries are contained in F. S. Regs., Part II. and the Staff Manual respectively. Title pages will be prepared in manuscript.

WAR DIARY
or
INTELLIGENCE SUMMARY.
(Erase heading not required.)

Army Form C. 2118.

March 1918 Vol. 14 Sheet 3.

Place	Date	Hour	Summary of Events and Information	Remarks and references to Appendices
SAILLY (G.?a.5.3)	March 26.	12N'n	Battery relieved 170 L.T.M.B. in BOIS GRENIER sector. LT. EAMES & 10 O.R. on right, LT. SAGE & 10 O.R. on left Bn sector. 6 guns in line. H.Q. in FLEURBAIX H.21.a.4.4. 1 O.R. to hospital (sick) 1 O.R. returned from leave. Programme of daily retaliation commenced with.	
FLEURBAIX H.21.a.4.4	27.		1 O.R. to hospital (sick). 1 O.R. retd. from hospital, 1 O.R. from leave. New S.O.S. posn established in HUDSON BAY.	
	28		1 O.R. taken on permanent strength from 8th K.L.R. 1 O.R. returned to unit.	
	29		2 O.R. returned from leave. 1 O.R. taken on strength of permanent battery. S.O.S. posn selected off COLLEGE GREEN.	
	31.	4 p.m.	Receipt of 171st Bde order No. 75 re relief by 121st Inf. Bde.	
			Strength of unit at end of month: 6 Officers 69 O.R.	[signature]

(A7092). Wt. W12839/M1293. 750,000. 1/17. D. D. & L., Ltd. Forms/C.2118/14.

57th Division.
171st Infantry Brigade

WAR
DIARY

171st LIGHT TRENCH MORTARS.

APRIL 1 9 1 8

171st Bde L.T.M.B

WAR DIARY

Vol. 15

APRIL 1918

Army Form C. 2118.

Instructions regarding War Diaries and Intelligence Summaries are contained in F. S. Regs., Part II. and the Staff Manual respectively. Title pages will be prepared in manuscript.

WAR DIARY
~~or~~
~~INTELLIGENCE SUMMARY.~~
(Erase heading not required.)

VOLUME 15
April. 1918. Sheet. 1.

Place	Date April.	Hour	Summary of Events and Information	Remarks and references to Appendices
FLEURBAIX.	1.	9 p.m.	Battery relieved in line & at H.Q. by 121st. I.T.M.B. & marched to billets in ESTAIRES arriving 4.30 a.m. (2nd). 1 O.R. retd. from course.	No men fell out on any of above marches.
ESTAIRES.	2.	4.30 p.m.	Battery paraded & marched to MERVILLE & entrained at about 7 p.m.	
DOULLENS.	3.	4.30 a.m.	Battery detrained & proceeded by route march to IVERGNY (4.E.68.83.) arriving in billets at 11.30 a.m.	
IVERGNY.	4.		1 O.R. (Pte. McGuire) retd. to unit. 1 O.R. (Pte. Jackson) taken on strength of battery.	
		7 p.m.	Battery paraded & marched to billets in MONDICOURT arriving at 12 midnight.	
MONDICOURT	7.		2Lt. BRADBURY & 5 O.R. returned from base.	
	8.	1.30 p.m.	Battery paraded & marched to BEUVAL, arriving in billets at 5.30 p.m.	
BEUVAL.	9.		1 O.R. attached from 2/7th. H.L.R. & 1 O.R. retd. to unit	
	12.	3 p.m.	Battery paraded & marched to GRENAS, arriving in huts at 7.30 p.m.	
GRENAS	13.	3.30 p.m.	Battery paraded & marched to AUTHIE arriving 7.15 p.m. Bivouaced in open.	
AUTHIE.	14.	—	Tents received & erected. Brigade Scheme "A" (Emergency Action) received	
	15	8 a.m.	Receipt of Brigade Scheme "B" (Emergency Action). 1 O.R. to Field Ambulance. (Sprained ankle)	
	16	9.45 a.m.	Battery paraded & marched to PAS. arriving under canvas at 12.45 p.m.	
PAS.	17	-	Receipt of Brigade Order No. 83 in substitution of Scheme "B".	

(A7092). Wt. W12839/M1293. 750,000. 1/17. D. D. & L., Ltd. Forms/C.2118/14.

WAR DIARY
or
~~INTELLIGENCE SUMMARY.~~
(Erase heading not required.)

Army Form C. 2118.

Vol. 15

APRIL. 1918. Sheet 2.

Instructions regarding War Diaries and Intelligence Summaries are contained in F. S. Regs., Part II. and the Staff Manual respectively. Title pages will be prepared in manuscript.

Place	Date APRIL.	Hour	Summary of Events and Information	Remarks and references to Appendices
PAS	19	8a.m.	2 Officers & 30 O.R. employed constructing T.M. pos^ns. on REDLINE.	
	20	"	2 " & 29 O.R. – do – do.	
	21	"	2 & 14 O.R carried T.M. ammn. to pos^ns. constructed on previous days & fixed it.	
	23.	12 noon.	Approaches to REDLINE reconnoitred by Officers & senior N.C.O.'s. Cpl. CUTHBERT appointed acting Lance Corporal (unpaid). 1 O.R. to D.R.S. 1 O.R transferred from Reserve to Perm^t. Battery, & 1 O.R. vice versa.	
	24	9a.m.	25 O.R. employed on construction of Bayonet-fighting course. 14 O.R. on T.M. positions	
	25	"	25 O.R. ——— do ——— do ——— do. 7 O.R. — do —	
	26.	—	1 O.R. to C.C.S. (sick) 1 O.R. to Field Amb^ce. (sick) 1 O.R. to D.R.S.	
	27	8a.m.	1 Officer & 50 O.R. working party on Div^l. Rifle Range (daily). 1 O.R. retd. from hospital.	
	28	—	1 O.R. to hospital (sick)!	
	29	—	Working party of 1 Officer & 50 O.R. continued on Rifle Range.	
	30	—		
			Strength of Battery at end of Month. 6 Officers 74 Other Ranks.	
			[signature] Capt. Cdg.	

(A7092). Wt. W12839/M1293. 750,000. 1/17. D. D. & L., Ltd. Forms/C.2118/14.

171st Brigade Light T.M.B.

WAR DIARY.

Vol 16.

MAY. 1918

Instructions regarding War Diaries and Intelligence Summaries are contained in F. S. Regs., Part II. and the Staff Manual respectively. Title pages will be prepared in manuscript.

WAR DIARY
or
~~INTELLIGENCE SUMMARY.~~
(*Erase heading not required.*)

Army Form C. 2118.

Vol. 16.

May 1918. Sheet 1

Place	Date May	Hour	Summary of Events and Information	Remarks and references to Appendices
PAS.	1.	9 a.m.	2Lt. BRADBURY & 1 O.R. proceeded to reconnoitre position in neighbourhood of GOMMECOURT. Daily working parties continued with.	
	3.		Pte (acting Lance Corporal) CAVES to be paid Corporal. Pte PROGER to be acting unpaid Lance-Corporal.	
	6.	2 p.m.	Lt. SAGE & 20 O.R. proceeded to Divisional Wing at MARIEUX. Battery relieved 125th L.T.M.B., relief being completed by 5.15 p.m. H.Q. at E.28.d.4.7. (GOMMECOURT) with advanced section H.Q. at K.6.d.78.10. & rear H.Q. at COIGNEUX. 4 S.O.S. guns trained on ROSSIGNOL WOOD, 2 reserve guns at SALMON POINT (K.6.a.3.3.), & 2 in vicinity of Battery Headquarters, one being mounted for A.A. purposes. Programme of desultory harassing fire on ROSSIGNOL WOOD initiated & continued with throughout tour in line. Low-flying hostile aircraft engaged. 2Lt. BRADBURY & 12 O.R. on forward person.	
GOMMECOURT.	9	3 p.m.	2Lt. LONGTON & 12 O.R. relieved 2Lt. BRADBURY & party.	
	11	–	2 O.R. proceeded to IIIrd Army Rest Camp. FONQUEVILLERS & adjacent roads & trenches shelled with gas from 7 p.m. to 2.30 a.m.	
	13.	–	1 O.R. to hospital (Gassed on night of 11th). 1 O.R. to C.C.S. (sick).	
		12.15 p.m.	Battery relieved by 170 L.T.M.B. & moved to billets in BAYENCOURT. Lt. EAMES & 11 O.R. with 4 guns in BEER TRENCH. (F'VILLERS)	
BAYENCOURT	14	4 p.m.	Lt. LEONARD & 24 O.R. working party on deep dugout. Returned 12 midnight.	

(A7092). Wt. W12839/M1293. 750,000. 1/17. D. D. & L., Ltd. Forms/C.2118/14.

Instructions regarding War Diaries and Intelligence Summaries are contained in F. S. Regs., Part II. and the Staff Manual respectively. Title pages will be prepared in manuscript.

WAR DIARY or INTELLIGENCE SUMMARY.

(Erase heading not required.) MAY 1918

Army Form C. 2118.

Vol. 16.

Sheet 2.

Place	Date MAY	Hour	Summary of Events and Information	Remarks and references to Appendices
BAYENCOURT	14.		1. O.R. (BAKER) to hospital sick – from 57th Divl. Wing	
	15.		2. O.R. transferred from Reserve to Permanent Batty to fill vacancies.	
	16.		4. O.R. to hospital sick from 57th Divl. Wing	
	17.		2. O.R. attached for duty to Town Major BAYENCOURT	
	19.		Working party of 1 officer & 15 O.R. on approach to new Bde. H.Qrs. Receipt of warning order re relief of 172nd L.T.M.B in the line	
	20.		Working party of 1 officer & 15 O.R. on new Bde. H.Qrs. Receipt of Bde. order No. 92.	
GOMMECOURT.	21.	4.30pm.	Rear H.Qrs taken over from 172nd L.T.M.B at COIGNEUX J.9.a.30.70	
		5.15.pm.	~~Relief~~ Battery relieved 172nd L.T.M.B. in line (GOMMECOURT RIGHT SECTOR). 2nd Lieut. BRADBURY & 13. O.R. forward. Batty H.Qrs at K.4.b.30.70. 4 guns forward & 4 at Batty. H.Qrs. Programme of nightly harassing fire adopted, principal targets being ROSSIGNAL WOOD & CRUCIFIX in K.11.b.	
	23.	12 midnight	100 shells carried to posns. in K.11a.40.60. Quiet. 2nd Lieut. Longton i/c party	
	24.	12 midnight	100 " " " " " " " ". Enemy Artillery Active. Lieut. Leonard i/c party.	
	25.	3pm.	2nd Lieut. Longton & 13. O.R. relieved 2nd Lieut. Bradbury & party	
	26.		108 Rounds carried to posns. in BIEZ SWITCH. 3 O.R. reported to Divnl Wing from hospital & taken on the strength.	
	27.	6.30–7.pm.	156 rounds fired in barrage on CRUCIFIX area in conjtn with patrol enterprise. Cpl. KELLY proceeded on a L.T.M. course at G.H.Q. School	
	28.		Dugouts gas proofed by R.Es.	

(A7092). Wt. W12839/M1293. 750,000. 1/17. D. D. & L., Ltd. Forms/C.2118.14.

Army Form C. 2118.

Instructions regarding War Diaries and Intelligence Summaries are contained in F. S. Regs., Part II. and the Staff Manual respectively. Title pages will be prepared in manuscript.

WAR DIARY
or
INTELLIGENCE SUMMARY.
(Erase heading not required.)

VOL. 16

MAY. 1918 SHEET 3.

Place	Date	Hour	Summary of Events and Information	Remarks and references to Appendices
GOMMECOURT.	29.	11.30 am.	Direct hit on Res. posn.t in GOMMECOURT by 5.9. ditto on Batty. H.Qrs.	
		12 noon.	Rfn PROCTOR to to field Amb. (sick)	
			~~[illegible]~~ Inter sectional relief carried out (Lieut. Leonard & 2 Lieut. Longton)	
			Pte. BAKER reported to 57th Divnl. Wing from hospital & retaken on strength	
	30.		Owing to shelling of ~~[illegible]~~ COIGNEUX Rear H.Qrs. removed to open ground at J.2 b.65.20.	
	31		Cpl. CROSTON to hospital sick	
			Strength of Battery at end of month 4 Officers & 69. O.R	
			H. F. Eames Lieut for. O.C. 171st L.T.M.B	

D. D. & L., London, E.C.
(A8004) Wt. W1771/M2-31 750,000 5/17 Sch. 52 Forms/C2118/14

171st Bde. Light T.M.B.

WAR DIARY.

Vol. 17.

JUNE 1918.

To
Headquarters
57th Division.

Herewith War Diary (Vol 17)
for June 1918, please.

[illegible]
Capt.
Cmdg 171st L.T.M.B.

171 BRIGADE TRENCH MORTAR BATTERIES
ORDERLY ROOM
B25/26
1/7/18

Army Form C. 2118.

Instructions regarding War Diaries and Intelligence Summaries are contained in F. S. Regs., Part II. and the Staff Manual respectively. Title pages will be prepared in manuscript.

WAR DIARY
or
~~INTELLIGENCE SUMMARY.~~
(Erase heading not required.)

Vol. 17.

JUNE. 1918. SHEET. No 1.

Place	Date	Hour	Summary of Events and Information	Remarks and references to Appendices
GOMMECOURT.	June 1st		2 OR^s (Cpl. Roberts + Rfn. Read) went to Hospital – Sick.	
	2		1 O.R. (Pte. Howard) to Hospital wounded (Shell).	
	"		2 OR^s (Pte. Eccles + Pte McCarthy) to hospital – Sick.	
	4		1 OR (Pte. Scholes) " " (N.Y.D. – Gas)	
	6		Lt. Sage + batman returned to unit (2/6th Kings L'pool Regt)	
BAYENCOURT	7		14 OR^s being 33% personnel rejoined Battery from 57th Div. Wing MARIEUX.	
	"		170th L.T.M.B. relieved the battery in GOMMECOURT. (Right Sector) The 171st L.T.M.B going into reserve at BEER TRENCH (2 sections) and BAYENCOURT. – Lt. Longton + 10 OR^s in BEER TRENCH	
			REAR HQ^s at BAYENCOURT. (Sheet 57D – J.4.d.40.00)	
	8		2 OR^s (Sgt. Morris + Pte. Shackleton) proceeded to 3rd Army Rest Camp. 1 OR. (Pte. Scholes returned from D.R.S.	
	"		1 OR (Pte. Wallace) rejoined from hospital.	
			Capt. Smallpage went to hospital – Sick –. Lt. Leonard took over command of battery pro tem.	
	"		1 O.R. (Pte Scholes) to C.C.S.	
	10.		Cpl. Murphy rejoined from 57th Div. Wing.	
			1 OR. (Pte. Robinson) rejoined from Unit	
	11		Working party of 1 Off. + 22 OR^s constructing L.T.M.B. HQ^s (rear) at COUIN.	
	"		1 OR (L/Cpl. Cuthbert) proceeded to 3rd Army Cookery School	
	"		1 OR (Pte. Russell) to hospital – Sick –.	
	12		Working party of 1 Off. + 22 OR^s at Rear L.T.M.B. H.Q^s.	
	13		Working party of 1 Off. + 22 OR^s at rear L.T.M.B. HQ^s.	

D. D. & L., London, E.C. (A8004) Wt. W1771/512 31 750,000 3/17 Sch. 52 Forms/C2118/14

Instructions regarding War Diaries and Intelligence Summaries are contained in F. S. Regs., Part II. and the Staff Manual respectively. Title pages will be prepared in manuscript.

WAR DIARY
or
~~INTELLIGENCE SUMMARY.~~
(Erase heading not required.)

Vol. 17

June 1918. Sheet 2.

Army Form C. 2118.

Place	Date	Hour	Summary of Events and Information	Remarks and references to Appendices
	June.			
BAYENCOURT.	13.	-	Cpl. Kelly retd. from G.H.Q. L.T.M. school.	
	14.	-	Gnr. Church to be acting Lance Corporal (unpaid).	
GOMMECOURT		6.30pm.	Battery relieved 172nd L.T.M.B in GOMMECOURT (Left Sector). Headquarters at E.28.d.3.8. Lt. EAMES & 17 O.R. on forward guns. General harassing policy carried out on ROSSIGNOL WOOD & approaches.	
	15.	-	Advice received that Sgt. Morris was admitted to Hpltl. from 3rd Army Rest Camp on 12/6/18.	
		9a.m.	Pte. Hughes killed & Gnr. Jones wounded by shell.	
	17.	-	1 O.R. on leave to England.	
	18	3pm.	2/Lt. LONGTON & 14 O.R. relieved Lt. EAMES & party in forward positions	
	19	–	Following targets registered. K.12.b.10.27; K.12.b.05.52; K.12.b.00.55; K.12.a.98.60. Code H.16 came into force.	
	20.	-	1 O.R. on leave to England. 4 O.R. transferred to Battery from attached personnel.	
		11.30pm	In support of raid by 2/6 K.L.R. 370 rounds fired on previously registered targets. 8 guns used in operation conducted by Lt. LEONARD & 2/Lt. LONGTON.	
	21.	-	Sgt. (acting B.S.M.) AMOS to England for commission. Sgt. Morris retd. to Rest Camp from Hpltl.	

D. D. & L., London, E.C.
(A8004) Wt. W1771/M2 31 750,000 5/17 Sch. 52 Forms/C2118/14

Instructions regarding War Diaries and Intelligence Summaries are contained in F. S. Regs., Part II. and the Staff Manual respectively. Title pages will be prepared in manuscript.

WAR DIARY
or
~~INTELLIGENCE SUMMARY.~~

(Erase heading not required.)

Vol. 17

June 1918. Sheet 3

Army Form C. 2118.

Place	Date June	Hour	Summary of Events and Information	Remarks and references to Appendices
GOMMECOURT	22.	-	2 O.R. to 3rd Army Rest Camp.	
	-	3 p.m.	Lt. EAMES & 17 O.R. relieved 2Lt. LONGTON & party on forward posn.	
	-	-	New L.T.M. dump of 90 rds. formed at K.6.a.52.80.	
	23.		New dump increased to 180 rds. 1 O.R. retd. to duty from hospital.	
	24.	6 p.m.	Capt. SMALLPAGE retd. from Hptl. & resumed command of battery. 2 O.R. retd. from 3rd Army Rest Camp.	
			Sgt. Morris appointed acting B.S.M. (unpaid) as from 21/6/18 & Cpl. Wiggins promoted Sergt. as from 21/6/18.	
	25	noon.	Capt. SMALLPAGE to forward H.Q. with 2 O.R.	
			L.T.M. dump in E.29.c. hit & 47 rounds destroyed.	
	29	3.30 p.m.	Battery relieved by 170 L.T.M.B. Lt. LEONARD & 9 O.R. in BEER TRENCH. Battery H.Q. J.7.a.2.2.	
	30	-	3 O.R. to Hptl. (sick)	

Strength at end of month. Officers 4. O.R. 55

[illegible] Capt.
O.C. 171 L.T.M.B.

D. D. & L., London, E.C.
(A8004) Wt. W1771/M2 31 750,000 5/17 Sch. 52 Forms/C2118/14

171st Bde. L.T.M.B.

WAR. DIARY.

Vol. 18.

July. 1918.

Army Form C. 2118.

WAR DIARY
or
~~INTELLIGENCE SUMMARY.~~
(Erase heading not required.)

Instructions regarding War Diaries and Intelligence Summaries are contained in F. S. Regs., Part II. and the Staff Manual respectively. Title pages will be prepared in manuscript.

VOL. 18. JULY 1918 SHEET No. 1.

Place	Date	Hour	Summary of Events and Information	Remarks and references to Appendices
COUIN	July 1st.		1 officer + 9 ORs in reserve at BEER TRENCH. Remainder of Battery at Rear HQrs COUIN – Sheet 57D 1/40000 J.7a 40.20.	
	"		1 OR (Rfn. Gregory) joined Perm. battery from unit (2/6th K.L.R.)	
LOUVENCOURT	2nd	9.00am	Battery paraded & marched to LOUVENCOURT (to Corps Reserve) The camp at COUIN was handed over to 2nd N Z Bde HQrs. Arrived at billets LOUVENCOURT at 10.45am. HQrs at billet No. 103 I34b 40.20. 1 officer + 9 ORs arrived from BEER TRENCH at 5.30pm. Incoming T.M.B. did not take over at BEER TRENCH but remained at HAYENCOURT.	
	"		Capt Smallpage & batman proceeded to L.T.M. Course (G.H.Q. School) Lieut. LEONARD assumed command of battery.	
	"	Noon	1 OR (Pte. Shackleton) from hospital.	
	"	7.30pm	1 OR (" Baxter) returned to unit.	
	3.		1 OR (" Foster) proceeded on leave to England.	
	"		Receipt of 191st Bde Defence Scheme (Provisional) with appendices I to IV & tracings.	
	"		Cpl. Kelly W.J. appointed acting L/c/Sergt. (unpaid)	
	"		Battery cleaning up & resting.	
	4.		Battery still resting – cleaning up.	
	"		Pte Pennington W. appointed acting L/c/Cpl. (unpaid)	
	"		" Murphy T.J. transferred from Res. to perm. battery.	
	5	7.30am	Received "Test Precautions" by wire. Blankets, packs etc stacked outside HQrs, battery did not move.	
	6		Daily training according to programme submitted to Bde HQrs.	

D. D. & L., London, E.C. (A8004) Wt. W1771/M2031 750,000 5/17 Sch. 52 Forms/C2118/14

Instructions regarding War Diaries and Intelligence Summaries are contained in F. S. Regs., Part II. and the Staff Manual respectively. Title pages will be prepared in manuscript.

WAR DIARY
or
~~INTELLIGENCE SUMMARY.~~
(Erase heading not required.)

Army Form C. 2118.

VOL. 18
JULY 1918 SHEET. No 2.

Place	Date	Hour	Summary of Events and Information	Remarks and references to Appendices
LOUVENCOURT	July 6th		1 OR (Pte ROBINSON) proceeded on leave to England.	
	"		1 OR (" Bradley) " to Third Army Rest Camp.	
	8.		1 OR. returned to duty from Cookery Course	
			1 OR " " " " leave	
			2 ORs " " " " Rest Camp.	
	9.		1 OR " " " leave.	
	10.		Lt. EAMES & 1 O.R. on leave to England.	
	12.		1 O.R. (Cpl. Gordon) returned from hospital & re-taken on strength.	
HENU	15	11 a.m.	Battery paraded & marched to billets in HENU (D.19.a.9.7) arriving at 1.30 p.m. Headquarters at Billet 136. Provisional Bde Defence Scheme received. Training continued in accordance with programme.	
	16		1 O.R. on leave to England.	
	19		1 O.R. on leave to England.	
	20		1 O.R. to 3rd Army Rest Camp. CAPT. SMALLPAGE (& batman) returned from L.T.M. course at G.H.Q. School & resumed command. 1 O.R. retd. from hospital. Cpl. [illegible] appointed acting Lance-Sergt (unpaid) as from 3/7/18.	

D. D. & L., London, E.C.
(A6004) Wt. W1771/M2031 750,000 5/17 Sch. 52 Forms/C2118/14

Army Form C. 2118.

Instructions regarding War Diaries and Intelligence Summaries are contained in F. S. Regs., Part II. and the Staff Manual respectively. Title pages will be prepared in manuscript.

WAR DIARY
or
~~INTELLIGENCE SUMMARY.~~
(Erase heading not required.)

VOL. 18.

JULY 1918. Sheet. iii

Place	Date	Hour	Summary of Events and Information	Remarks and references to Appendices
HENU.	JULY. 21		1 O.R. retd. from leave. 3 O.R. transferred from attached personnel to complete establishment. Acting L/Cpl. (unpaid) [illegible] to be paid Corporal.	
	22		1 O.R. returned to duty from Rest Camp.	
	23.		2 O.R. retd. to unit (2/6 (Rifles) K.L.R.) & replaced by battalion.	
	24.		Receipt of 171st Inf. Bde. Defence Scheme. Reconnaissance of area by O.C. & Sergt. Major. 1 O.R. retd. to duty from leave	
	25.		Emplacements constructed in accordance with Defence Scheme "E".	
	26.		1 O.R. on leave to England. 1 O.R. to IV Corps. L.T.M. School. 1 O.R. to hospital (dental)	
	28		Lieut. Eames & 1 OR returned from leave.	
SUS-ST-LEGER.	29		Received Bde. Order No. 153 re move to SUS-St. LEGER. Battery paraded 6.30 am. and marched to SUS-St. LEGER - arrived at 11.0 am. billeting there for the night.	
ARRAS	31		Battery paraded 3.30 pm. and marched to ARRAS arriving at 5 pm. Location G 22 d. 2.62. and billeted for the night.	
LOUEZ	30.		Battery paraded at 9.30 am & marched to LOUEZ arriving 4.45 pm. and billeted for the night.	

STRENGTH OF BATTERY at end of Month 4 officers 58 OR

D. D. & L., London, E.C.
(A8004) Wt. W1771/M2 31 750,000 5/17 Sch. 52 Forms/C2118/14

Instructions regarding War Diaries and Intelligence Summaries are contained in F. S. Regs., Part II. and the Staff Manual respectively. Title pages will be prepared in manuscript.

WAR DIARY
or
~~INTELLIGENCE SUMMARY.~~
(Erase heading not required.)

Vol. 19. August 1918. Sheet 1.

Army Form C. 2118.

Place	Date	Hour	Summary of Events and Information	Remarks and references to Appendices
ARRAS (FAMPOUX Sector)	Aug. 1st.		The Battery relieved the 12th Canadian L.T.M.B. on the FAMPOUX Sector – Lt. EAMES + 12 ORs went into line. Forward HQrs established at H.13 d.5.5 and Rear HQrs at ARRAS – G.22 d.12.62. Relief carried out without incident. Lt. LEONARD O.C. REAR HQrs.	
	3rd		General reconnaissance of line. Sighting of gun positions. No firing. 1 OR proceeded on leave to PARIS (Cpl. Jennings). 1 OR returned from leave + 1 OR from hospital. 1 OR transferred to permanent Battery to complete establishment.	
	4th		60 rounds TMC carried to forward positions from CAM Valley. No. 3 S.O.S. position deepened and line altered.	
	5th		4 ORs proceeded on leave to England. 15 rounds fired on enemy post at H.17 d.55.90 (between 10 pm + midnight) 60 rounds carried from dump in ATHIES to CAM Valley emplacement.	
	6th		120 rounds carried from dump in ATHIES to No. 5 gun emplacement. 10 rounds fired on movement at cross roads at H.17 d.60.85 and along road to N for 50 yds. 1 OR returned to duty from leave.	
	7th		Rear HQrs moved from ARRAS to transport lines at ANZIN – G.1 d.9.5. 1 OR proceeded on leave to England. 1 OR returned from Third Army Rest Camp.	
	"		Work done on reserve gun emplacements + ammunition carried up.	
	"		2/Lieut. LONGTON + 14 ORs relieved LIEUT. EAMES + 12 ORs in the line. Preliminary Defence Scheme Copy No. 4 received.	
	8th		No. 4 Defensive Gun position completed + occupied. Work continued on No. 5 position	

D. D. & L., London, E.C. (A8004) Wt. W1771/M031 750,000 5/17 Sch. 52 Forms/C2118/14

WAR DIARY

~~or~~

~~INTELLIGENCE SUMMARY.~~ AUGUST 1918

(Erase heading not required.)

Vol. 19.

Sheet 2.

Army Form C. 2118.

Instructions regarding War Diaries and Intelligence Summaries are contained in F. S. Regs., Part II. and the Staff Manual respectively. Title pages will be prepared in manuscript.

Place	Date	Hour	Summary of Events and Information	Remarks and references to Appendices
FAMPOUX SECTOR	Aug. 8th		11 rounds fired during night.	
	9th		Work continued on No. 5 gun emplacement. 120 rounds T.M.C. prepared & fused.	
	10th		Improved gun position in CAM AVENUE. Work commenced on No. 7 Reserve gun emplacement	
	11th		No. 5 Reserve gun emplacement completed. Work continued on No. 7.	
	12th		Commenced new emplacement for No. 3 gun. Work continued on No. 7	
	"		Received BDE. ORDER No 109 Copy No. 4.	
	13th		2 ORs proceeded on leave to England. Work continued on Nos 3 & 7 gun emplacements.	
			No firing owing to Infantry wiring parties.	
	14th		Work continued on No. 3 gun emplacement. 1 OR returned from leave.	
	15th		Inter-sectional relief carried out. 3 ORS proceeded on leave to England	
	"		Capt. Smallpage proceeded on leave to England.	
	16th		201 rounds T.M.C. drawn from Brigade dump. Ammunition shelters built for Nos 7 & 8 guns.	
			1 OR. (Cpl. Church) proceeded on Light T.M. course. 1 OR. returned from Paris leave.	
	17th		1 OR returned to duty from IV Corps L.T.M. course.	
	18th		The Battery were relieved by the 152nd L.T.M.B. in FAMPOUX Sector. Relief complete – 11 opm.	
MONCHY-BRETON.	19th		Battery paraded at 5.30 am and marched to ARTILLERY CORNER, entraining at 6.15 am and arrived at MONCHY-BRETON at 9.50 am. HQs at Billet No. 13.	
	20th		Training carried out during morning.	
	21st		Battery paraded at 11.10 pm. and marched to ~~[illegible]~~ GIVENCHY LE NOBLE, arriving there at 3.40 am	

D. D. & L., London, E.C.
(A8001) Wt. W1771/M231 750,000 5/17 Sch. 52 Forms/C2118/14

Army Form C. 2118.

WAR DIARY
or
~~INTELLIGENCE SUMMARY.~~
(*Erase heading not required.*)

Vol 19.

Aug. 1918. Sheet 3.

Instructions regarding War Diaries and Intelligence Summaries are contained in F. S. Regs., Part II. and the Staff Manual respectively. Title pages will be prepared in manuscript.

Place	Date	Hour	Summary of Events and Information	Remarks and references to Appendices
GIVENCHY LE NOBLE	Aug 22	9.15 pm	Battery paraded & marched to IVERGNY arriving 1.40 a.m. Stragglers - 2 O.R.	
IVERGNY	23	–	2 O.R. proceeded on leave to England, 3 O.R. retd from leave.	
	25	3.30 pm	Battery paraded & marched to GOUY-en-Artois arriving 7.45 p.m. 2 O.R. retd. from leave.	
GOUY	26	11 p.m.	" " " FICHEUX arrived 3.45 a.m. & bivouacked for the night. 1 N.C.O. & 2 men left in charge of stores at GOUY.	
FICHEUX	27.		1 N.C.O. & 10 working at Divl H.Q. 1 N.C.O. & 3 left i/c stores in quarry. Battery marched at MERCATEL, arriving 7.15 p.m. in bivouac. 1 N.C.O. & 6 as guard at Bde H.Q. Lt. LEONARD as liaison officer with 170 Inf. Bde H.Q.	
MERCATEL	28.	10.30 am	Bty paraded & marched to HENINEL	
HENINEL	29	1.30 pm	" " " HINDENBURG LINE. (N.35.c.30.25)	
HINDENBURG LINE	30.	–	2 O.R. wounded on guard at dump at FONTAINE. Replaced by 2 O.R.	
	31.	–	180 rds. T.M.C. prepared & ground reconnoitred for attack on HENDECOURT.	
			Strength at end of month 4 officers 56 other ranks.	

[illegible] Capt.

D. D. & L., London, E.C.
(A8004) Wt. W1771/M2-31 750,000 5/17 Sch. 52 Forms/C2118/14

To Headquarters 57 Division

Herewith War Diary (Vol 20) for September 1918, please

[illegible] Capt
Cdg 171st L.T.M.B.

171 BRIGADE TRENCH MORTAR BATTERIES
ORDERLY ROOM
B33/57
1/10/18

Instructions regarding War Diaries and Intelligence Summaries are contained in F. S. Regs., Part II. and the Staff Manual respectively. Title pages will be prepared in manuscript.

WAR DIARY

or

~~INTELLIGENCE SUMMARY.~~

(*Erase heading not required.*)

Army Form C. 2118.

Vol. 20.

Sept. 1918.

Sheet 1.

Place	Date	Hour	Summary of Events and Information	Remarks and references to Appendices
HINDENBURG LINE.	Sept. 1	4.50 am	2 guns in action in attack on HENDECOURT-LEZ-CAGNICOURT. 1 gun advanced under 2/Lt. LONGTON into HENDECOURT: (in conjunction with 2/7 K.L.R.) Pte. WALLACE who was carrying barrel was hit (shell) & detachment failed to get into action. 2 gun (Cpl. Caves) worked with 8th K.L.R. & fired 21 rounds in barrage but did not advance.	
		12 noon	Capt. SMALLPAGE returned from leave & re-assumed command of battery.	
	3	–	2 O.R. returned from leave.	
	5	–	3 O.R. on leave to England.	
	6	–	3 O.R. (Ammn. Guard) withdrawn from dump at FONTAINE-LEZ-CROISILLES. 4 O.R & stores brought up from dump at FICHEUX. 1 O.R. on leave. 1 O.R. retd. from leave. 3 O.R. (attached) transferred to Battery to complete establishment.	
	7	10 a.m.	Battery paraded & marched to V.21.c. (Sheet 51B) where rear H.Q. were established. Battery relieved 190 L.T.M.B. in the line, headquarters at V.28.d.0.0. Lt. LEONARD & 10 O.R with 2/7 K.L.R.; Lt. EAMES & 10 O.R. with 8th K.L.R. No S.O.S. posns. or ammn. taken over. Relief completed 11.45 p.m.	
V.28.d.0.0.	8	–	Rear H.Q. moved to V.6.b.7.5. Reconnaissance of sector & work on S.O.S. pits.	
	9	"	1 O.R. on leave. 1 O.R. retd. from course. 3 O.R. & stores arr. from GOUY. 300 rds. T.M.C. got up.	
	10	"	2 O.R. from leave. 5 rds. ranging on Boche posts.	

D. D. & L., London, E.C.
(A8004) Wt. W1771/M2 31 750,000 5/17 Sch. 52 Forms/C2118/14

Instructions regarding War Diaries and Intelligence Summaries are contained in F. S. Regs., Part II. and the Staff Manual respectively. Title pages will be prepared in manuscript.

WAR DIARY
or
~~INTELLIGENCE SUMMARY.~~
(*Erase heading not required.*)

Army Form C. 2118.

Vol. 20.

Sept. 1918. Sheet ii

Place	Date Sept.	Hour	Summary of Events and Information	Remarks and references to Appendices
V.28.d.0.0.	11	5 a.m.	Direct hit by shell on S.O.S. pit. E.1.b.4.4. Cpl. CAVES killed. Cpl. JENNINGS, Ptes THOMSON & BUCKLEY wounded.	
		6.15 p.m.	Three guns cooperated in attack on enemy line west of CANAL DU NORD. 50 rounds fired on MŒUVRES CEMETERY, 50 on canal crossings. One gun detailed to advance along HOBART STREET held up by M.G's & fired 20 rds. 2 O.R. wounded	
	12.	8.30 p.m.	Battery relieved by 172nd L.T.M.B. & moved to V.26.d.9.8.	
V.26.d.9.8.	13	–	1 O.R. on leave to England. [illegible] to England.	
	14	–	3 O.R. transferred to Battery from attached list.	
	16.	5.30 p.m.	Battery relieved in Divl. Reserve by 156 L.T.M.B. & marched to camp T.30.a. S.E. of CROISILLES. 2/Lt. LONGTON on leave to England.	
T.30.a.	17	1.30 p.m.	Battery paraded & marched to BOYELLES entraining 4 p.m. & arriving at SAULTY 5.30 p.m. marched to billets at BARLY arriving P.15.a.8.7. at 7.20 p.m.	
BARLY	18-25	–	Reorganisation & training.	

D. D. & L., London, E.C.
(A8004) Wt. W1771/M2931 750,000 5/17 Sch. 52 Forms/C2118/14

Instructions regarding War Diaries and Intelligence Summaries are contained in F. S. Regs., Part II. and the Staff Manual respectively. Title pages will be prepared in manuscript.

WAR DIARY
or
~~INTELLIGENCE SUMMARY.~~
(*Erase heading not required.*)

Army Form C. 2118.

Vol. 20

Sept. 1918.

Sheet 111

Place	Date	Hour	Summary of Events and Information	Remarks and references to Appendices
BARLY	Sept 19	–	Pte Patrick (?) Robinson to be acting unpd. L/Cpl.	
	23	–	2 O.R. rejd from leave, 1 from hospital. Pte (acting unpd L/Cpl) Progers (?) to be paid Corporal	
	24	–	1 O.R. rejd from leave. 2 O.R. on leave. L/Sgt. Perry (?) to England to Officer Cadet Unit	
	25	6.30 AM	Battery paraded & marched to SAULTY, entraining 9.40 a.m. Detrained at VAULX VRAUCOURT & marched to D.13.b.10.80. & bivouaced for night 5.15 p.m. 1 O.R rejd from leave.	
QUEANT.	26	–	351 rds. T.M.C. drawn & prepared. 2 guns & ammn. placed on limbers supplied by Bns. 1 from each unit.	
	27	5.20 AM	Brigade took part in XVII Corps attack. Lieut. LEONARD, 1 O.R. & limber with 2 guns & ammn. with 2/7 K.L.R. & Lieut. EAMES with equal strength with 8th K.L.R. Reserve section (equal strength under B/Sgt. Major Morris M.S.M.) & headquarters rendezvoused at ANNEUX FACTORY at 7 p.m. No guns came into action during the day. 3 O.R. on leave. 2 on XVII Corps T.M. course. 1 O.R. rejd. from leave	
ANNEUX	28	5 p.m.	Touch obtained with detached sections, & battery concentrated at F.20.a.05.45. Rear H.Q. moved from QUEANT to E.27.b.	
	29	3 p.m.	Lt EAMES & section moved off to assist 8th K.L.R. in F.17 & 23. Remainder of battery moved off at 5.15 p.m. to F.22.b.9.1. where detached section rejoined, not having come into action. Rear H.Q. at F.19.c.6.1.	

D. D. & L., London, E.C.
(A8004) Wt. W1771/M2 31 750,000 5/17 Sch. 52 Forms/C2118/14

Army Form C. 2118.

Vol. 20

WAR DIARY
or
~~INTELLIGENCE SUMMARY.~~
(*Erase heading not required.*)

Sept. 1918 Sheet IV.

Instructions regarding War Diaries and Intelligence Summaries are contained in F. S. Regs., Part II. and the Staff Manual respectively. Title pages will be prepared in manuscript.

Place	Date	Hour	Summary of Events and Information	Remarks and references to Appendices
F.22.b.9.1	Sept. 30.	11 a.m.	One gun brought into action from A.13.d. against M.G.'s in A.14c. (PROVILLE TRENCH). Lieut EAMES wounded (shell) while getting into position. 17 rounds fired at 11 a.m. & 20 at 1 p.m.	
		3 p.m.	Battery relieved by 170 L.T.M.B. & proceeded to rear H.Q. in ANNEUX	
			Strength of Battery at end of month. 3 Officers 49 Other Ranks	

[illegible] Capt. Cdg.
171 L.T.M.B.

D. D. & L., London, E.C.
(A8004) Wt. W1771/M2-31 750,000 5/17 Sch. 52 Forms/C2118/14

171st Bde Light T.M.B.

WAR DIARY.

Vol. 21.

OCTOBER. 1918.

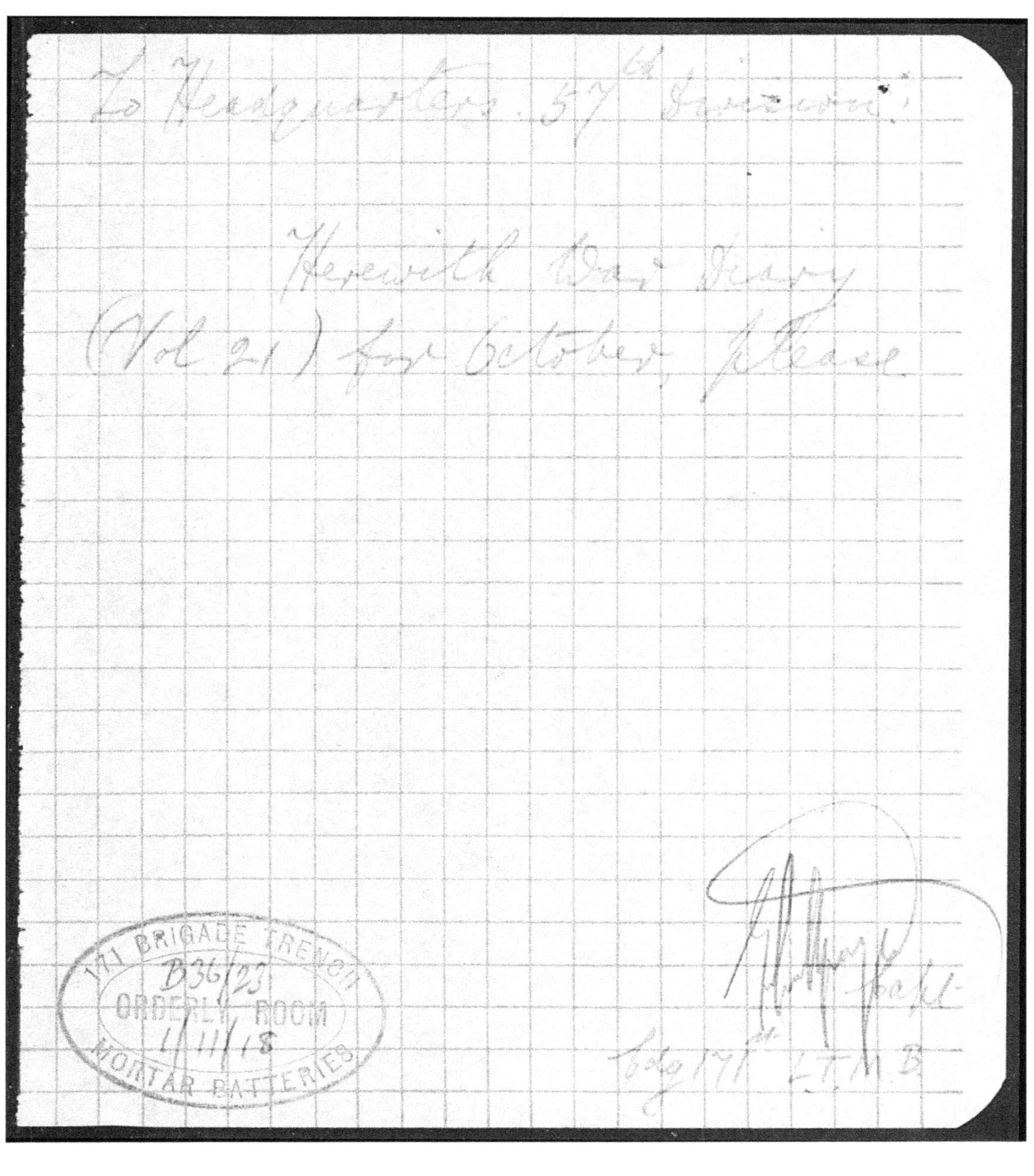
To Headquarters. 57th Division:
Herewith War Diary
(Vol 21) for October please
171 BRIGADE TRENCH
B36/23
ORDERLY ROOM
1/11/18
MORTAR BATTERIES
Capt.
Cdg 171st L.T.M.B

Instructions regarding War Diaries and Intelligence Summaries are contained in F. S. Regs., Part II. and the Staff Manual respectively. Title pages will be prepared in manuscript.

WAR DIARY

or

~~INTELLIGENCE SUMMARY.~~

(*Erase heading not required.*)

Army Form C. 2118.

Vol. 21.

October 1918. Sheet i.

Place	Date	Hour	Summary of Events and Information	Remarks and references to Appendices
	October.			
ANNEUX.	1	–	1 O.R. to hospital (accidental injury.)	
	2	–	Pte (a/l/cpl.) Pennington to be paid Corporal as from 24/9/18.	
	4	–	1 O.R. returned from leave to England. 2 O.R. proceeded on leave to England. Battery marched to FONTAINE-NOTRE DAME, relieving 170th L.T.M.B. in the line. Relief completed 1700 hrs. H.Qrs at F.16.c.8.2. Two guns attached to 8th K.L.R. under Lt. Leonard. Rear H.Q. at F.25.a.0.3.	
FONTAINE-N.D.	5	2045.	1 limber of T.M.C. hit by 5.9. Blew up causing much material destruction but no loss of personnel. 2 guns under Lt. [illegible] relieved 172nd L.T.M.B. in PROVILLE – relief completed 0130. hrs.	
	6.	1200.	240 rds. T.M.C. carried to posn in PROVILLE.	
	7.	–	2 mortars complete handed over to 170 L.T.M.B. for active operation in accordance with Bde. Instructions.	
	8	–	2 " " received from D.A.D.O.S. to replace those lost on 5th.	
	9	–	1 O.R. to hospital sick. Battery concentrated on H.Q. at 1700 hrs.	
	10	–	1 O.R. to hospital, sick. Battery paraded at 0800 & marched to D.23.c. arriving 1315. Bivouaced for the night. 2 O.R. transferred to Battery from attached personnel.	
D.23.c.	12	0900.	Battery paraded & marched to FREMICOURT entraining there at 1240. Detrained at FOUQUIÉRES 2330. & marched to BARLIN (1.H.25.55)	
BARLIN.	13	0320.	Arrived at BARLIN in huts. 2 O.R. retd. from leave.	
	14	–	1 O.R. on leave.	
	15	–	1 O.R. on leave. Battery embussed at 0900 & proceeded to PONT DU HEM, debussing & marching to LAVENTIE, arriving in billets at 1345. 1 O.R. returned from leave.	
LAVENTIE.				

D. D. & L., London, E.C.
(A8004) Wt. W1771/M2 31 750,000 5/17 Sch. 52 Forms/C2118/14

Army Form C. 2118.

Instructions regarding War Diaries and Intelligence Summaries are contained in F. S. Regs., Part II. and the Staff Manual respectively. Title pages will be prepared in manuscript.

WAR DIARY
~~or~~
~~INTELLIGENCE SUMMARY.~~

(Erase heading not required.)

Vol. 21.

October 1918. Sheet ii

Place	Date	Hour	Summary of Events and Information	Remarks and references to Appendices
LAVENTIE.	October 16	0845.	Battery paraded & marched to LE MAISNIL O. 13. a. 85. arriving 11.40. Billeted in huts. 2Lt. LONGTON retd. from leave.	
LE MAISNIL.	17.	0930.	Brigade passed through 142 Inf. Bde. 1 Section L.T.M.B. with each battalion. Battery concentrated 1700 hrs. at LE MARAIS.	
LE MARAIS.	18	1400.	Battery paraded & marched to billets in HELLEMMES, arriving 1615. 2 O.R. transferred to Battery from attached men.	
HELLEMMES.	19	1400.	Battery paraded & marched to billets in WILLEMS. Lt. LEONARD proceeded on leave to England.	
WILLEMS.	20.	1000.	Battery paraded & marched to BLANDAIN. Operating in conjunction with 8th K.L.R. H.Q. established N.16.b.9.7. 1 O.R. wounded (shell.)	
BLANDAIN.	21	–	Lt. LONGTON & section advanced with "B" Coy. 2/6 K.L.R. towards ESCAUT. Battery H.Q. established at N.12.a.8.4. with rear H.Q. in same location as previously. 1 O.R. retd. from leave, 1 O.R. from course. 8 rounds fired on M.G. post.	
FROYENNES.	22	1300.	Battery H.Q. advanced to FROYENNES – O.14.b.9.9. 1 O.R. on special leave to England. 1 O.R. from leave. 1 O.R. from course.	
	23	1530.	18 rds. fired (direct observation) on Boche post on TOURNAI – FROYENNES road. 1 O.R. retd. from leave.	
	24	1630.	Battery relieved in line by 172 L.T.M.B. & marched into Divisional Reserve in billets at WILLEMS. 1 O.R. on leave to England.	
WILLEMS.	25	–	1 O.R. transferred to Battery from attached personnel.	
	26	–	1 O.R. from leave. 1 O.R. retd. to unit.	

D. D. & L., London, E.C.
(A8004) Wt. W1771/M2 31 750,000 5/17 Sch. 52 Forms/C2118/14

Instructions regarding War Diaries and Intelligence Summaries are contained in F. S. Regs., Part II. and the Staff Manual respectively. Title pages will be prepared in manuscript.

WAR DIARY

~~or~~

~~INTELLIGENCE SUMMARY.~~

(Erase heading not required.)

Army Form C. 2118.

Vol. 21.

October 1918. Sheet iii

Place	Date	Hour	Summary of Events and Information	Remarks and references to Appendices
WILLEMS.	29	1200.	Battery inspected by B.G.C.	
	30	0840.	Battery relieved by 141 L.T.M.B. & proceeded by march route to Corps Reserve in HELLEMMES. Billets at Q.5.c.4.6. occupied at 12.10.	
HELLEMMES.	31.	1900.	3 O.R. joined from 2/7 K.L.R.	

Strength of Battery at end of month: 3 Officers 47 Other Ranks.

[illegible] Capt.
Cdg. 171 L.T.M.B.

D. D. & L., London, E.C.
(A8004) Wt. W1771/M2 31 750,000 5/17 Sch. 52 Forms/C2118/14

171st Bde Light T.M.B.

WAR DIARY

Vol. 22.

NOVEMBER. 1918.

To Headquarters 57th Division

Herewith War Diary (Vol 22) for November 1918.

171 BRIGADE TRENCH
R39/44
ORDERLY ROOM
1/12/18
MORTAR BATTERIES

[illegible] Capt
Cdg 171st T.M.B.

Army Form C. 2118.

Instructions regarding War Diaries and Intelligence Summaries are contained in F. S. Regs., Part II. and the Staff Manual respectively. Title pages will be prepared in manuscript.

WAR DIARY

or

~~INTELLIGENCE SUMMARY.~~

(Erase heading not required.)

VOL. 22.

Nov. 1918. Sheet 1.

Place	Date	Hour	Summary of Events and Information	Remarks and references to Appendices
HELLEMMES.	Nov. 1.	0900	6 men attached from Bn for training.	
	2	–	2 O.R. returned from leave: 1 O.R. to hospital.	
	3	–	1 O.R. to hospital.	
	4	–	1 O.R. from hospital.	
	7	–	1 O.R. retd. from leave. 2 O.R. returned to units, 2 O.R. attached from units.	
	8	–	1 O.R. to hospital.	
	9	1030.	Inspection of Brigade by B.G.C. Battery parade strength 2 Officers 43 O.R.	
	10	–	1 O.R. on leave. 1 O.R. on Paris leave. Stores brought up from BAVINCOURT.	
	11	1020.	Notification received of CESSATION OF HOSTILITIES at 11 a.m.	
	12	1030	Inspection by Major General Barnes, Divl. Commander. 1 O.R. from leave.	
	14	–	2Lt. NICHOLAS & batman attached from 8th K.L.R. 2 O.R. on leave. 2 O.R. transferred from attached personnel.	2Lt. NICHOLAS taken on strength as from 13/11/18
	15	–	1 O.R. to C.C.S.	
	16	–	1 O.R. attached from 2/7 K.L.R.	
	17	–	Cpl. CULSHAW on L.T.M. course in England.	
	18	–	LT. LEONARD retd. from leave.	

D. D. & L., London, E.C. (A8004) Wt. W1771/M2-31 750,000 5/17 Sch. 52 Forms/C2118/14

Army Form C. 2118.

Instructions regarding War Diaries and Intelligence Summaries are contained in F. S. Regs., Part II. and the Staff Manual respectively. Title pages will be prepared in manuscript.

WAR DIARY

~~or~~

~~INTELLIGENCE SUMMARY.~~

(*Erase heading not required.*)

Vol. 22.

Nov. 1918. Sheet ii

Place	Date	Hour	Summary of Events and Information	Remarks and references to Appendices
	Nov.			
HELLENNES.	19	–	1 O.R. retd. from hospital.	
	21	–	1 O.R. taken on strength from attached personnel.	
	22	–	1 O.R. from hospital.	
	23	–	1 O.R. to C.C.S. (accidental injury) 1 O.R. from leave.	
	24	–	2Lt. NICHOLAS on leave to England.	
	28	–	1 O.R. from leave.	
	29	–	1 O.R. to hospital, sick.	
	30	8 a.m.	Receipt of B.O. 150 re move.	
			Strength at end of month. 4 Officers 53 O.R.	

[illegible] Capt.
Cmdg. 171 L.T.M.B.

D. D. & L., London, E.C.
(A8004) Wt. W1771/M2 31 750,000 5/17 Sch. 52 Forms/C2118/14

171st Bde. Light T.M.B.

WAR DIARY.

Vol. 23

DECEMBER. 1918.

Army Form C. 2118.

Vol. 23.

Instructions regarding War Diaries and Intelligence Summaries are contained in F. S. Regs., Part II. and the Staff Manual respectively. Title pages will be prepared in manuscript.

WAR DIARY
~~or~~
~~INTELLIGENCE SUMMARY.~~
(*Erase heading not required.*)

Dec. 1918. Sheet i

Place	Date	Hour	Summary of Events and Information	Remarks and references to Appendices
HELLEMMES	Dec. 2	0800	Battery paraded & marched via SECLIN to CARVIN arriving in huts 1.L.95.80. (LENS 11) at 1340. Stragglers – nil.	
CARVIN	3	0715.	Battery paraded & marched via LENS to ARRAS. Midday halt of 1 hour South of LENS. Arrived in billet 4 Rue St. Claire at 1530. Stragglers – nil.	
ARRAS (4 Rue St. Claire)	6	–	2 O.R. retd. from leave.	
	8	0930.	1 officer & 6 O.R. proceeded to WANQUETIN to improve billets.	
	9	–	Educational training commenced.	
	10	–	1 O.R. from hospital, 1 O.R. to unit for demobilisation (coalminer).	
	11	–	1 O.R. on leave to England.	
	13	–	2 O.R. retd. from hospital.	
	14	–	2 OR retd. from Paris (leave)	
	15	–	Receipt of Bde Order No. 151.	
	16	–	Battery paraded – marched to WANQUETIN (Sheet 51 C, K 32 b 50.20) arriving at billets at 12.15 hrs.	
WANQUETIN		–	1 Or. proceeded on 'Horse Management' Course.	
	17	–	2/Lt. Nicholas returned from leave.	
	19	–	1 OR to hospital – sick.	

D. D. & L., London, E.C.
(A8004) Wt. W1771/M2-31 750,000 5/17 Sch. 52 Forms/C2118/14

Army Form C. 2118.

Instructions regarding War Diaries and Intelligence Summaries are contained in F. S. Regs., Part II. and the Staff Manual respectively. Title pages will be prepared in manuscript.

WAR DIARY
or
INTELLIGENCE SUMMARY.

(*Erase heading not required.*)

Vol. 23
Sheet II
1 December 1918

Place	Date	Hour	Summary of Events and Information	Remarks and references to Appendices
WANQUETIN.	Dec. 21	–	1 O.R. proceeded on leave to Paris.	
	23	–	1 O.R. " to hospital – sick.	
	"	–	1 O.R. rejoined from hospital.	
	"	–	1 O.R. " " leave	
	"	–	1 O.R. " " Course.	
	26	–	2nd Lt Langton proceeded on leave to Paris.	
	27	–	2 O.Rs " on Courses of carpentry & horse management.	
	"	–	1 O.R. " to hospital	
	28	–	1 O.R. " "	
	30	–	Advance party – 1 off + 6 O.Rs proceeded to Dainville. 1 O.R. to hospital (sick).	
	31	–	Battery paraded & marched to DAINVILLE. L.28.d.3.1. arriving 1315	
			Strength of battery at end of month. 4 Officers 51 Other Ranks.	
			[signature] Capt. [illegible] 171 L.T.M.B.	

D. D. & L., London, E.C.
(A8004) Wt. W1771/M2 31 750,000 5/17 Sch. 52 Forms/C2118/14

171st Bde L.T.M.B.

WAR DIARY

Vol. 24

JANUARY 1919

Instructions regarding War Diaries and Intelligence Summaries are contained in F. S. Regs., Part II. and the Staff Manual respectively. Title pages will be prepared in manuscript.

WAR DIARY
or
INTELLIGENCE SUMMARY.
(Erase heading not required.)

Army Form C. 2118.

Vol. 24

Sheet I. JANUARY 1919.

Place	Date	Hour	Summary of Events and Information	Remarks and references to Appendices
DAINVILLE	Jan. 1		Battery in charge of HORSESHOE DUMP DAINVILLE, sorting and evacuating contents and engaged on general salvage.	
	2		1 OR returned from hospital	
	"		1 " " " leave.	
	4		1 Off. + 1 OR " " Paris leave.	
	"		2 ORs " " hospital	
	"		1 OR attached for duty to Town Commdt. ARRAS.	
	6		L/Sgt. Kelly proceeded on Kings leave to England.	
			1 OR returned from course	
			1 " proceeded on "	
	9		1 " "	
	"		No. 266531 Pte Russell H. appointed acting (unpaid) Lce/Cpl.	
	11		1 OR returned to unit for demobilization	
	13		" " " "	
	14		" " " "	
	15		1 OR returned from hospital	
	17		1 " " Course	
	18		1 " to unit for demobilization	
	23		1 " proceeded on leave to England	
	25		1 " " to England for demobilization	
	27		Capt. E. Smallpage proceeded to England for demobilization.	
	"		Lieut. D G LEONARD assumed Command of Battery	

D. D. & L., London, E.C.
(A8004) Wt. W1771/M2 31 750,000 5/17 Sch. 52 Forms/C2118/14

Instructions regarding War Diaries and Intelligence Summaries are contained in F. S. Regs., Part II. and the Staff Manual respectively. Title pages will be prepared in manuscript.

WAR DIARY
or
INTELLIGENCE SUMMARY.
(Erase heading not required.)

Army Form C. 2118.

VOL. 24.
Sheet II January 1919.

Place	Date	Hour	Summary of Events and Information	Remarks and references to Appendices
DAINVILLE	JAN. 27.		1 OR. proceeded to ENGLAND for demobilization.	
	"		1 OR. returned from course.	
	28		Cpl. Church appointed a/Q.M.S. (unpaid) as from 26/1/19.	
	"		Cpl. Murphy " acting paid Sergt. as from 28/1/19.	
	"		1 OR. proceeded to ENGLAND for demobilization.	
	30.		Acting (unpaid) L/Cpl. Robinson promoted acting paid Corporal as from 29/1/19.	
	"		1 OR. returned from Course.	
			STRENGTH OF BATTERY at END OF MONTH. –	
			3 OFFICERS and 45 OTHER RANKS.	
			[signature] Lieut.	
			Commanding 141st L.T.M.B.	

D. D. & L., London, E.C.
(A8004) Wt. W1771/M2-31 750,000 5/17 Sch. 52 Forms/C2118/14

171st Bde. L.T.M.B.

WAR DIARY.

Vol. 25

FEBRUARY. 1919.

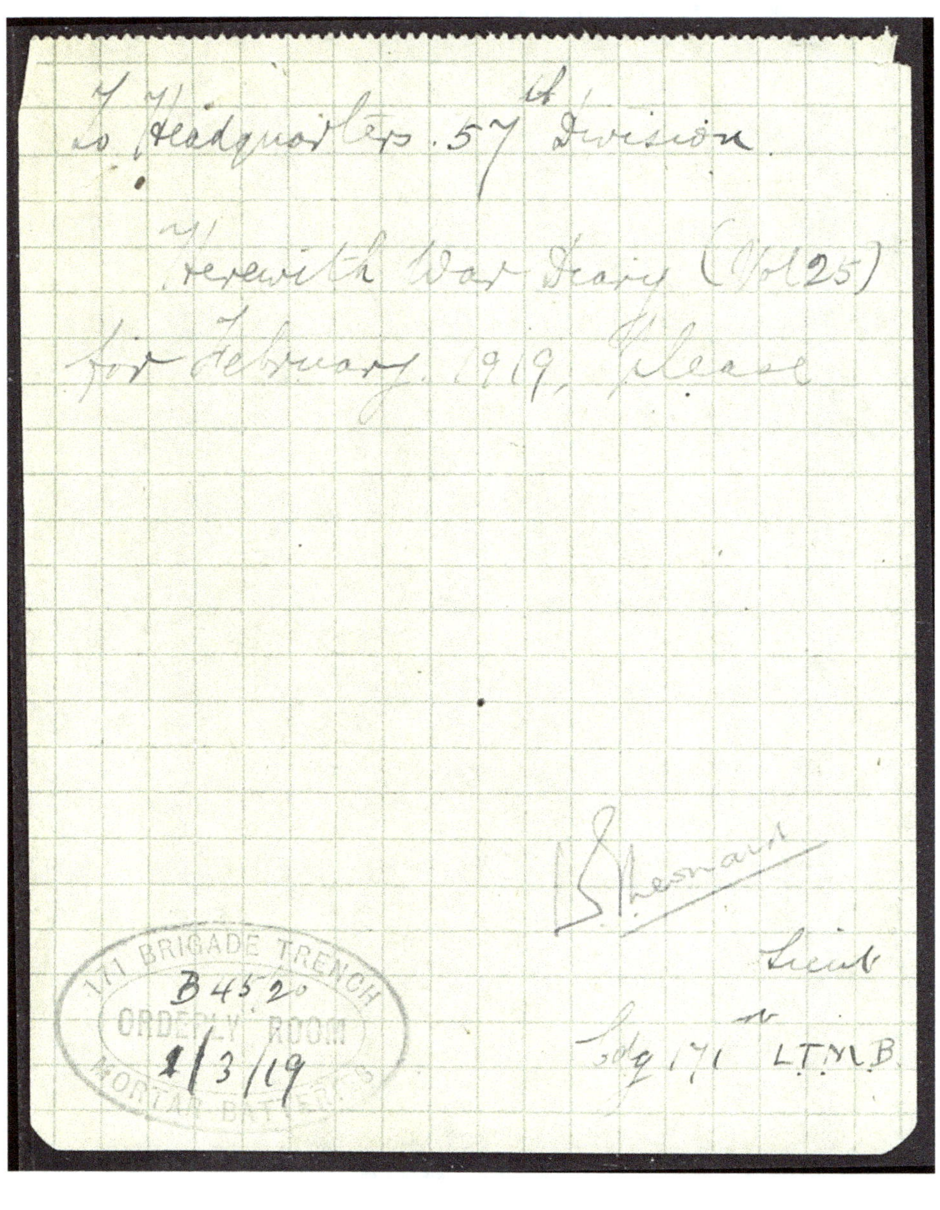

To Headquarters 57th Division

Herewith War Diary (Vol 25) for February 1919, please

[illegible]
Lieut
Cdg 171st L.T.M.B.

171 BRIGADE TRENCH MORTAR BATTERIES
ORDERLY ROOM
B 45 20
1/3/19

Army Form C. 2118.

Instructions regarding War Diaries and Intelligence Summaries are contained in F. S. Regs., Part II. and the Staff Manual respectively. Title pages will be prepared in manuscript.

WAR DIARY
or
INTELLIGENCE SUMMARY.

(*Erase heading not required.*)

VOL 25 Sheet I

February 1919.

Place	Date	Hour	Summary of Events and Information	Remarks and references to Appendices
DAINVILLE	Feb. 1st		Battery continued salvage work and guard duties at HORSESHOE DUMP DAINVILLE.	
	"		1 OR proceeded to ETAPLES for duty as clerk.	
	"		6 OR transferred from Reserve to permanent battery.	
	2nd		3 OR proceeded to ENGLAND for demobilisation.	
	"		1 OR returned to unit " "	
	3rd		1 OR proceeded to ENGLAND on leave.	
	5th		1 OR " " " "	
			1 OR attached for duty to 171st Inf Bde H.Q.	
	8th		1 OR returned to unit for demobilisation.	
	9th		1 OR proceeded to hospital - sick.	
	12th		1 OR returned to unit for demobilisation	
	13th		1 OR proceeded to ENGLAND on leave.	
	14th		1 OR returned from leave.	
	"		LIEUT. P. LONGTON proceeded to ENGLAND for demobilisation.	
	15th		8 ORs recalled to unit (2/6th R.W.R.) as being retainable for ARMY of Occupation. [illegible]	
	16th		1 OR attached for duty to 171st Inf Bde H.Q.	
	"		1 OR returned from hospital.	
	18th		2 ORs recalled to unit (2/6th R.W.R.) as being retainable for Army of Occupation	
	21st		1 OR returned from leave.	
	"		1 OR returned to unit for demobilisation.	
	22nd		1 OR proceeded to ENGLAND on leave	
	23rd		1 OR " " " for demobilisation.	

D. D. & L., London, E.C.
(A8004) Wt. W1771/M2·31 750,000 5/17 Sch. 52 Forms/C2118/14

Army Form C. 2118.

Instructions regarding War Diaries and Intelligence Summaries are contained in F. S. Regs., Part II. and the Staff Manual respectively. Title pages will be prepared in manuscript.

WAR DIARY
or
~~INTELLIGENCE SUMMARY.~~

(Erase heading not required.)

VOL 25. SHEET II.
FEBRUARY 1919

Place	Date	Hour	Summary of Events and Information	Remarks and references to Appendices
DAINVILLE	FEBY. 24th	-	1 OR returned from leave.	
	25th	-	1 Officer (2 LIEUT NICHOLAS C.E) and 8 ORS. returned to unit (8th K.L.R) for inclusion in draft for 25th K.L.R.	
	"		2 ORS returned to unit for demobilisation.	
	26th		2 ORS returned to unit for inclusion in draft to 59th Division.	
	"		7 ORS " " " demobilisation.	
	27th		No. 241370 Cpl. Church A.E.V. promoted acting paid Sergeant as from 25/1/19 vice Sergeant Wiggans - demobilised.	
	28th		1 OR returned to unit for demobilisation	
			STRENGTH of BATTERY at end of month 1 Officer 6 O.Rs. (7 ORS attached from battalions for temporary duty)	
			K. Lessnaw Lieut	

D. D. & L., London, E.C.
(A8004) Wt. W1771/M2 31 750,000 5/17 Sch. 52 Forms/C2118/14

171st L.T.M.B.

WAR DIARY

Vol. 26.

MARCH. 1919

www.ingramcontent.com/pod-product-compliance
Lightning Source LLC
Chambersburg PA
CBHW082012220426
43670CB00014B/2605

* 9 7 8 1 4 7 4 5 3 0 6 5 1 *

Army Form C. 2118.

Instructions regarding War Diaries and Intelligence Summaries are contained in F. S. Regs., Part II. and the Staff Manual respectively. Title pages will be prepared in manuscript.

WAR DIARY
or
INTELLIGENCE SUMMARY.
(Erase heading not required.)

VOL. 26.
MARCH 1919
SHEET I

Place	Date	Hour	Summary of Events and Information	Remarks and references to Appendices
DAINVILLE	1st		Battery in charge of HORSESHOE DUMP DAINVILLE	
	2nd		1 OR returned from leave	
	6th		Cpl. WESTBROOK promoted to paid acting Sergt as from 26/2/19 to fill a vacancy	
	10th		1 OR returned from leave	
			Pte. JACKSON promoted to paid acting Corporal as from 25/2/19 to fill a vacancy	
	12th		Battery H Qrs moved to WARLUS and attached to 171st INF Bde H Qrs for rations	
	14th		1 OR returned to unit for demobilization	
MAROEIL	15th		Battery H Qrs removed to MAROEIL	
	20th		HORSESHOE DUMP and contents handed over to No. 248 Employment Coy.	
	21		2 ORs returned to unit	
	22		LIEUT LEONARD posted to Chinese Labour Corps NOYELLES	
			Strength of Battery to date - 1 OR. (Cadre)	
			22/3/19.	
			[signature] Lieut	
			171st LTMB	

D. D. & L., London, E.C.
(A8004) Wt. W1771/M2 31 750,000 5/17 Sch. 52 Forms/C2118/14

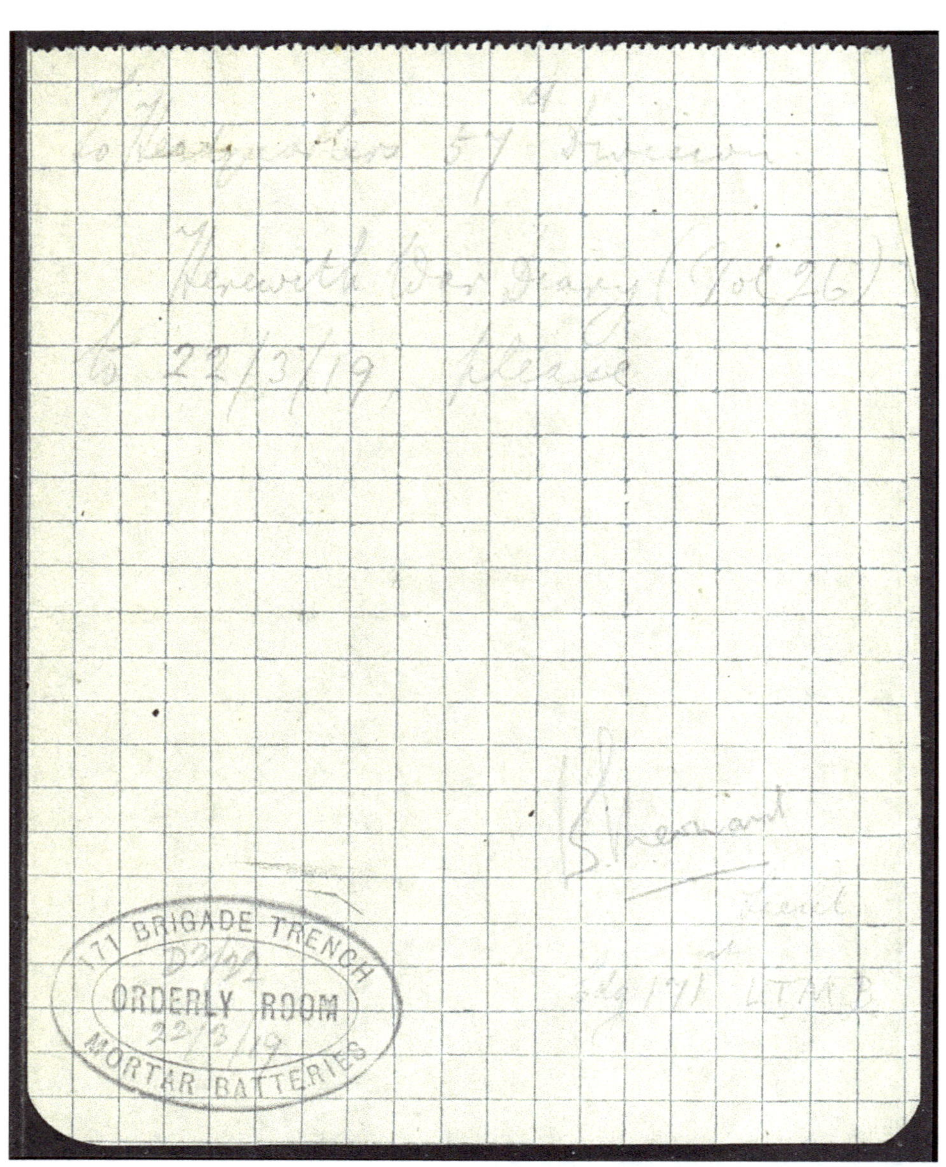

To Headquarters 57 Division

Herewith War Diary (Vol 26) to 22/3/19, please

171 BRIGADE TRENCH MORTAR BATTERIES
ORDERLY ROOM
D2/22
22/3/19

[illegible signature]
Lieut
Adjt 171 LTMB